The Great Recession and the Distribution of Household Income

Reports for the Fondazione Rodolfo DeBenedetti

The Great Recession and the Distribution of Household Income

Edited by
Stephen P. Jenkins
Andrea Brandolini
John Micklewright
Brian Nolan

OXFORD
UNIVERSITY PRESS

Great Clarendon Street, Oxford, OX2 6DP,
United Kingdom

Oxford University Press is a department of the University of Oxford.
It furthers the University's objective of excellence in research, scholarship,
and education by publishing worldwide. Oxford is a registered trade mark of
Oxford University Press in the UK and in certain other countries

© Fondazione Rodolfo Debenedetti 2013

The moral rights of the authors have been asserted

First Edition published in 2013
Impression: 1

British Library Cataloguing in Publication Data
Data available

ISBN 978–0–19–967102–1

Printed in Great Britain by
MPG Books Group, Bodmin and King's Lynn

Links to third party websites are provided by Oxford in good faith and
for information only. Oxford disclaims any responsibility for the materials
contained in any third party website referenced in this work.

Preface

This book is a substantially revised version of a report commissioned by the Fondazione Rodolfo Debenedetti (Milan) in 2010, and presented at its 13th European Conference in Palermo in September 2011. How to analyse important socioeconomic phenomena when suitable data are not yet fully available is a critical issue, and especially relevant to the topics addressed in this book. Throughout the book we indicate what the most recent data available to us were, particularly in Chapter 2 which draws on a large variety of sources in its cross-national analysis. In short, the latest data update refers to no later than mid-February 2012.

The editors would like to thank the Fondazione Rodolfo Debenedetti for their support, especially its research director Professor Tito Boeri who has encouraged us from the outset of the project. Jenkins also acknowledges support from the UK Economic and Social Research Council via the Research Centre on Micro-Social Change (award RES-518-285-001). Micklewright acknowledges the hospitality of the Melbourne Institute of Applied Economic and Social Research during his tenure of the 2012 R. I. Downing Fellowship.

Gaetano Basso (Fondazione Rodolfo Debenedetti) provided excellent research assistance for Chapter 2. We are grateful to the authors of the country case studies for their contributions.

We especially wish to thank our two conference discussants, Tony Atkinson (University of Oxford) and John Martin (OECD), whose oral remarks and written comments strongly influenced our revision of the manuscript. For other comments and suggestions at various stages of our work, we are grateful to Tito Boeri, Robert Joyce, Luke Sibieta, and Lucinda Platt, and participants at the Palermo conference and at seminars at which we have presented our work, at the European Central Bank, Institute of Education (University of London), London School of Economics, Nuffield College Oxford, the Universities of Cambridge and Sussex, the Productivity Commission (Melbourne, Australia), and the annual conference of Fondazione Roberto Franceschi at the Università Bocconi, Milan. The research was also the subject of Micklewright's Downing Lecture at the University of Melbourne.

It is with great sadness that we note the death in December 2011 of Joachim Frick, co-author of Chapter 3. Joachim was a wonderful friend, researcher, and all-round team-player, who will be sorely missed by many people from all round the world in addition to us. Readers will begin to understand why we write such things about Joachim if they read his obituary (in English), available from the DIW Berlin website (at http://tinyurl.com/83rulur).

Stephen P. Jenkins
Andrea Brandolini
John Micklewright
Brian Nolan

March 2012

Table of Contents

List of Figures

List of Figures

List of Figures

List of Tables

Notes on Editors and Contributors

Stephen P. Jenkins is Professor of Economic and Social Policy at the London School of Economics, and a former director of the Institute for Social and Economic Research at the University of Essex where he is now Visiting Professor. He has served as Chair of the Council of the International Association for Research on Income and Wealth, and as President of the European Society for Population Economics. He is a research professor at DIW Berlin, and a research fellow of IZA Bonn, and was a member of the UK's National Equality Panel that reported in 2010. His research interests are in topics related to the distribution of income, the labour market, and the tax-benefit system. He is the author of *Changing Fortunes: Income Mobility and Poverty Dynamics in Britain* (OUP, 2011) and co-edited *Inequality and Poverty Re-Examined* (OUP, 2007, with John Micklewright), and *The Dynamics of Child Poverty in Industrialised Countries* (Cambridge University Press, 2001, with Bruce Bradbury and John Micklewright).

Andrea Brandolini is an economist in the Department for Structural Economic Analysis of the Bank of Italy. He has served as Chair of the Council of the International Association for Research on Income and Wealth. He was a member of the executive committee of the Luxembourg Income Study. He chaired the Italian statistical office's commission for the revision of absolute poverty measurement, and was a member of the poverty commissions established by Italian governments from 1994 to 2007. He is Associate Editor of the *Journal of Economic Inequality*. His research interests are income and wealth distribution, poverty and social exclusion, measurement of economic well-being, labour economics. He co-edited *Povertà e benessere* (Il Mulino, 2007, with Chiara Saraceno) and *Dimensioni della disuguaglianza in Italia. Povertà, salute, abitazione* (Il Mulino, 2009, with Chiara Saraceno and Antonio Schizzerotto).

John Micklewright is Professor of Economics and Social Statistics at the Institute of Education, University of London. He was previously Professor of Social Statistics at the University of Southampton, Professor of Economics at Queen Mary, University of London, and at the European University Institute, Florence, and Head of Research at the UNICEF Innocenti Research Centre. He is a research fellow of IZA, Bonn, and CEPR, London. His research addresses various issues relating to the distribution of income, the labour market, child outcomes, educational achievement, charitable giving, and survey methods. He co-authored *Economic Transformation in Eastern Europe and the Distribution of Income* (Cambridge University Press, 1992, with Tony Atkinson) and co-edited *The Dynamics of Child Poverty in Industrialised Countries* (Cambridge

University Press, 2001, with Bruce Bradbury and Stephen Jenkins) and *Inequality and Poverty Re-Examined* (OUP, 2007, with Stephen Jenkins).

Brian Nolan has been Professor of Public Policy in UCD's School of Applied Social Science since 2007, and Principal of UCD's College of Human Sciences since September 2011. He was previously at the Economic and Social Research Institute and the Central Bank of Ireland. He has a BA in economics and history from UCD, an MA in economics from McMaster University (Ontario), and a doctorate in economics from the London School of Economics and Political Science. His main areas of research are poverty, income inequality, the economics of social policy, and health economics. Recent publications include studies on social inclusion in the EU, top income shares, child poverty, deprivation and multiple disadvantage, tax and welfare reform, and the distributional impact of the economic crisis. He co-edited *The Oxford Handbook of Economic Inequality* (OUP, 2009), and co-authored *Poverty and Deprivation in Europe* (OUP, 2011, with Christopher T. Whelan).

Gaetano Basso is a PhD student in economics at the University of California Davis and an affiliate of the Fondazione Rodolfo Debenedetti. His research interests are in the fields of labour and public economics. He has contributed several articles on the Italian labour market and the liberalization of professional services to Italian economic watchdog websites. Before starting his PhD, he worked at Fondazione Rodolfo Debenedetti (2009–11). He graduated cum laude from Università Bocconi in 2009.

Anders Björklund is currently the Director of the Swedish Institute for Social Research (SOFI) at Stockholm University, where he has been Professor of Economics since 1990. His PhD (Stockholm School of Economics, 1981) was concerned with unemployment dynamics. His research continued with evaluations of labour market policy and later with income and earnings inequality and intergenerational mobility. He has also written several public policy reports on these topics in Swedish, often published by the Centre for Business and Policy Studies (SNS). His most frequently-cited academic papers have examined the gender wage gap (*Journal of Labor Economics*, 2003, with James Albrecht and Susan Vroman), treatment effects of labour market policy (*Review of Economics and Statistics*, 1987, with Robert Moffitt), and intergenerational income mobility (*American Economic Review*, 1997, with Markus Jäntti).

Tim Callan is a research professor at the Economic and Social Research Institute, Dublin. His research focuses on income tax and welfare policy, the labour market, pension policy and poverty and income distribution, with a particular interest in the design and use of microsimulation models. He has published widely in national and international journals, and has participated in many international comparative research projects including EUROMOD, the tax-benefit model for Europe.

Francesco D'Amuri is an economist at the Department for Structural Economic Analysis of the Bank of Italy and an IZA Research Affiliate. He studied economics at Università Bocconi and the University of Essex. He was a visiting scholar at the Federal Reserve Bank of San Francisco and at the University of California Davis. His research focuses on policy evaluation, migration, and industrial relations.

Ivan Faiella is a senior economist at the Bank of Italy. He graduated in international economics and holds an MSc in environmental economics and law (Siena University and LUISS) and an MSc in environmental and energy economics (ENI Corporate University). From 1998 to 2008 he worked at the Sample Survey division of the Bank of Italy's Research Department (from 2002 in charge of the Survey on Households Income and Wealth). In 2009, he moved to the Economic Structure and Labour Market Division where he follows environmental and energy issues. His other research interests are survey sampling methods, microeconometrics and income and wealth distribution analysis.

Joachim R. Frick († 16 December 2011) was Senior Research Manager at DIW Berlin and Deputy Director of the German Socio-Economic Panel Study (SOEP), *Privatdozent* at the Technical University Berlin, and Research Fellow at IZA Bonn. He studied at the University of Trier, where he was awarded an MA in Economics (*Diplom-Volkswirt*). In 1996, he received a PhD in Social Science (Dr. rer. soc.) from the Ruhr University Bochum. In 2006, he was awarded his habilitation (*venia legendi*) in empirical economic research at the Technical University in Berlin, where he served as Acting Professor of Empirical Economics, 2008–9. His research interests centred on social and welfare policy, immigration, personal income distribution, housing, spatial mobility, and subjective well-being. He published in journals such as *Ageing & Society*, *Economica*, *International Migration Review*, *Journal of Comparative Economics*, *Journal of European Social Policy*, *Journal of Population Economics*, *Oxford Economic Papers*, *Population Research and Policy Review*, and *Review of Income and Wealth*.

Markus M. Grabka is a senior researcher at the German Institute for Economic Research (DIW) in Berlin. He studied sociology and informatics at the Technical University of Berlin. In 2004, he received his PhD in public health in a research training group of the German Science Foundation. He has worked in the department of longitudinal data and microanalysis—the German Socio-Economic Panel Study (SOEP), DIW Berlin—since 1999. His research interests are in topics related to the distribution of income and wealth, and health economics. He was involved in all three reports on poverty and wealth of the German federal government. He has advised the German council of economic experts with regard to income and wealth inequality in Germany and acted as advisor to the OECD about income inequality in Germany. He has published in journals such as the *European Economic Review*, *Journal of Income Distribution*, *Journal of Economic Inequality*, and *Oxford Economic Papers*.

Markus Jäntti is Professor of Economics at the Swedish Institute for Social Research (SOFI) at Stockholm University, and Research Director at the Luxembourg Income Study. He was previously Professor of Economics at Åbo Akademi University and at the University of Tampere, Visiting Associate Professor of Economics at the University of Michigan, and Scientific Director at Statistics Finland. His research addresses inequality, poverty, and mobility, often in a comparative perspective. He is Co-editor of *Persistence, Privilege, and Parenting: The Comparative Study of Intergenerational Mobility* (Russell Sage Foundation, 2011, with Robert Erikson and Timothy Smeeding), and *From Parents to Children: The Intergenerational Transmission of Advantage* (Russell Sage Foundation, 2011, with John Ermisch and Timothy Smeeding).

Robert Joyce is a research economist in the Direct Tax and Welfare Sector at the Institute for Fiscal Studies (IFS) in London. He studied economics at the University of Oxford and University College London. His main research interests are in the distribution of income and the design of the tax and benefit system. He has been involved in several projects using micro-simulation techniques to project the future distribution of income, and co-authored the last two editions of the IFS's annual commentary on poverty and inequality in the UK.

Luke Sibieta is a senior research economist in the Education Sector at the Institute for Fiscal Studies (IFS) in London. He has previously studied economics at the London School of Economics and University College London. He has led much of the IFS's recent work on poverty, inequality, and living standards. This has included research on the effects of previous recessions on the income distribution, trends in top incomes, and the relationship between income and other measures of living standards. His research interests also include school finance and public sector labour markets.

Bertrand Maître is Research Officer at the Economic and Social Research Institute, Dublin. He is a graduate in economics from the University of La Sorbonne Paris I. He carries out analysis of microdata across a range of Irish and European projects. His current research focuses on poverty and inequality, social exclusion and income distribution.

Timothy M. Smeeding is the Arts and Sciences Distinguished Professor of Public Affairs and Economics at the University of Wisconsin-Madison, and Director of the Institute for Research on Poverty (IRP). His recent books include *Persistence, Privilege and Parenting: The Comparative Study of Intergenerational Mobility* (Russell Sage Foundation, 2011, co-edited with Robert Erikson and Markus Jäntti), *From Parents to Children: The Intergenerational Transmission of Advantage* (Russell Sage Foundation, 2011, co-edited with John Ermisch and Markus Jäntti), *The Oxford Handbook of Economic Inequality* (OUP, 2009, co-edited with Brian Nolan and Weimer Salverda), and *The American Welfare State: Laggard or Leader?* (OUP, 2010, co-authored with Irving Garfinkel and Lee Rainwater). His recent research has been on mobility across generations, and inequality, wealth, and poverty, in both national and cross-national contexts.

Jeffrey Thompson is Assistant Research Professor at the Political Economy Research Institute. He has a PhD in economics from Syracuse University and an MA in economics from the New School for Social Research. His research has been published in *Research in Labor Economics*, the *Industrial and Labor Relations Review*, *State Tax Notes*, and the *National Tax Journal*, which awarded him the 2010 Musgrave Prize for the best article published each year in the journal. His research focuses on income and wealth inequality, as well as domestic economic policy, and state and local government finance in the USA.

1

Scope, review of approaches, and evidence from the past

Stephen P. Jenkins, Andrea Brandolini, John Micklewright, and Brian Nolan

The Great Recession that followed the financial crisis of 2007–8 was the first contraction in the global economy since the Second World War (Keeley and Love 2010: 11). The economy of the OECD area as a whole reduced in size by 5% between the first quarter of 2008 and second quarter of 2009. This contraction is smaller and briefer than occurred in many of the same countries during the Great Depression of the 1930s: between 1929 and 1932, total GDP in Western Europe, the USA, Canada, Australia, and New Zealand fell by about 17%, driven by the exceptionally large fall for the USA (Crafts and Fearon 2010: table 1, drawing on work by Angus Madison). None the less, the recession in most OECD countries following 2007 was the worst macroeconomic downturn since the 1930s.

The Great Depression had wide-ranging and long-lasting impacts on household incomes that are embedded in the popular consciousness. One might therefore expect the Great Recession to be associated with impacts on poverty and income inequality on a scale not seen for almost 80 years. However, the role of governments and the extent of welfare states have developed enormously since the Great Depression, and partly in response to it. Rich nations now have social safety nets that ameliorate the impact of economic and financial crisis on the poorest and social insurance programmes to offset the effects of risks such as unemployment. The instruments of economic and social policy that have been developed since the 1930s mean that we are better equipped to deal with a deep downturn. What then are the effects on the distribution of household incomes of the Great Recession (GR)? Answering this question is the central concern of this book. For a range of countries, we describe the nature of changes in household incomes on average and in total, in household income inequality, and in poverty, that have been measured so far and speculate about subsequent changes.

Three core features characterize our book. The first is the focus on the distribution of household income. Our interest is in measures of economic well-being that are more comprehensive than employment status or labour earnings. Most individuals derive income from other sources besides the labour market, including social security benefits and retirement pensions from the government, and interest on savings and other financial assets such as private pensions. How well off people are also depends on the fortunes of the people with whom they live: income sharing and household composition are relevant to individuals' economic well-being. Second, and related, we examine the distribution of income for the whole population, not simply for (say) employees, or households headed by a person of working age.

The third core feature of our book is its cross-national perspective. The origins of the financial crisis preceding the GR were in the USA (and the 'Great Recession' label was coined there), and there has been much research about the recession in that country. (See *inter alia* the book edited by Grusky, Western, and Wimer 2011.) One of the themes of our book is the diversity of the GR across rich nations; the USA's experience has not been universally shared. Even among countries where there have been similarities in macroeconomic change, there are variations in distributional impact reflecting differences in socioeconomic institutions, social programmes, and policy responses.

When considering the impact of the GR on household incomes, it is tempting to say that it's too early to tell. The GR may be over in a number of countries in the sense that positive GDP growth has returned. But at the time of writing, it appears than another downturn is possible—a 'double-dip' recession—and there is a more widespread concern about the persistence of low growth rates for the foreseeable future. More generally, the consequences of the GR for household incomes are likely to remain for many years. For these reasons, it is important to distinguish between the immediate and longer-term impacts of the GR on the distribution of income. Long-term effects are outside the remit of this book. But some medium-term effects require our attention. In particular, not only do we consider the short-run distributional impact of increased government expenditure during 2008–9, but also we reflect on the likely impact of subsequent fiscal consolidation.

Timeliness of data availability is an issue even when considering the period between 2007 and 2011. Although a country's statistical office may produce first estimates of national income within a few weeks of the end of each calendar quarter, estimates of the distribution of household incomes and of poverty derived from household surveys or administrative record data appear with far longer lags—typically years. Analysis of the topics addressed by this book is constrained by a lack of up-to-date information. Nonetheless, and as we show in later chapters, there are sufficient data for many countries to describe many aspects of the changes in the distribution of household incomes between 2007 and 2009 and we can draw on other data sources and approaches to describe some of the subsequent changes.

1.1 The Scope of the Book

Our aim is to measure the effects of the GR on the level and distribution of household incomes in rich industrialized countries. In this section, we explain the three components of that statement in more detail.

First, how are the effects of the GR to be assessed? A common method of assessing effects is to compare observed outcomes with what would have happened were the change of interest not to have occurred. What is the counterfactual for assessing the impacts of the GR? One answer would be the distribution that would have prevailed if neither the boom nor the bust had happened, so 'potential GDP' had been on and had remained on a sustainable path. This and other possible counterfactuals are difficult to estimate with confidence. Hence we are left with the less satisfactory but feasible alternative of measuring changes relative to a baseline distribution for around 2007, while also looking at earlier years to consider outcomes for that year in the context of the previous trends.

The second component refers to the distribution of household income. Economic downturns generally reduce real incomes, and hence poverty rates are likely to increase when the low-income threshold is fixed in real income terms. An economic downturn may also change the dispersion of household incomes. So, we consider changes in real income levels, income inequality, and poverty rates. We are concerned with all income groups: the top, the bottom, and the middle.

How well off people are is measured throughout the book in terms of household income rather than using other indicators such as household consumption expenditure, material deprivation, happiness, or other measures of personal well-being. Income is not the only concept of interest, but it is commonly used and data are collected in a reasonably consistent manner across countries. As mentioned earlier, we consider all forms of money income and the household income total derived by aggregating income sources over all the individuals within each household. This focus distinguishes us from a narrower analysis, for example, of the impact of the GR on the distribution of earnings of employees. We are interested in the household circumstances of each worker, as well as the young, the old, and anyone else with no labour market earnings, and in all sources of income: investment income, social security benefits and other forms of non-labour income, as well as earnings.

The book is about changes in the distribution of household income, not the distributions of household wealth or debt, though we discuss aspects relating to financial assets at several points.

The leading option for the definition of household income is the one conventionally used in many countries' official income statistics, namely total household income including cash benefits received from the state and after the deduction of payments of direct taxes. This concept of 'net' or 'disposable' income is used in much of this book. The definition excludes realized capital gains and losses unless otherwise stated because data about them are not generally available.

There are arguments for using a wider definition of income, one that also includes the value of non-cash social benefits, as advocated by the Canberra Group (Expert Group on Household Income Statistics 2001) and, at the aggregate level, by the Commission on the Measurement of Economic Performance and Social Progress with its concept of 'adjusted household disposable income' (Stiglitz, Sen, and Fitoussi 2009). This non-cash income refers to 'goods and services such as education, housing, cultural and recreational services [that] may be provided [by governments] either free or at greatly reduced cost at the point of use' (Expert Group on Household Income Statistics 2001: 23). A wider definition of income could also take account of indirect taxes paid by households in addition to direct taxes. The relevance of these components of income is underlined by the reductions in a range of public services and increases in indirect taxation as part of governments' fiscal consolidation in a number of countries as an aftermath of the GR. Although the distributional impacts of these changes are potentially important, measures based on the wider definition of income are not available in our data sources.

Some economists have argued that household consumption expenditure is a better measure of living standards than is household income, at least in principle. There is evidence that consumption expenditure inequality tends to be lower than inequality of household income (Goodman and Oldfield 2004; Johnson, Smeeding, and Boyle Torrey 2005) and, moreover, that it has not changed as much as income inequality in the course of past recessions (Krueger et al. 2010). The standard explanation is that households' spending depends on their permanent income and to the extent that income changes in economic downturns (e.g. due to unemployment) are transitory rather than permanent, many households can smooth their consumption by borrowing, drawing on savings, or postponing durable purchases (Blundell, Pistaferri, and Preston 2008; Krueger et al. 2010). Establishing whether this also describes the case of the GR must await the availability of suitable data. Some preliminary calculations are provided for working-age households in the USA by Heathcote et al. (2010). A more extensive study using data for the UK through to the end of 2009 by Crossley, Low, and O'Dea (2011) demonstrates that, relative to previous recessions, there has been a greater prevalence of cuts in households' non-durable expenditure than their durable expenditure.

The third component of our statement refers to rich countries. The countries we consider are all members of the Organisation for Economic Co-operation and Development (OECD). We provide a broad overview for 21 OECD countries and consider the experience of six of them in depth. We do not analyse the experience of emerging economies or countries from the developing world, nations that have had a very different experience. China, Brazil, and India 'weathered the economic storm relatively well', while GDP fell in only six African countries in 2009 (Keeley and Love 2010: 38–9). (The nature of the crisis around the world is summarized by Lane and Milesi-Ferretti 2011. See also UN Department of Economic and Social Affairs 2011.) OECD economies contracted significantly in the GR but, as we show, there is a diversity of experience among the countries we consider.

Our focus on the GR's distributional impact means that we do not consider the question of whether earlier changes in the distribution of income helped cause the GR, for example whether the boom was unsustainable in part because of what had happened to the distribution of incomes during that period. As noted by Atkinson and Morelli (2010) in their extensive review of inequality and banking crises over the last hundred years, this is a possibility that has been suggested by a number of commentators including former Chief Economists of the World Bank and the International Monetary Fund. Investigation of the topic is outside the remit of our book: see Atkinson and Morelli (2011) for further discussion.

1.2 Outline of the Book

This section outlines the content of the remainder of this chapter and of the rest of the book. In Section 1.3 we discuss the potential routes by which changes in the macroeconomy, including severe recessions, affect the distribution of household income. We summarize various frameworks for analysing the relationship between changes in macroeconomic variables and changes in household incomes. We review what empirical research about past recessions tells us about this relationship in Section 1.4. In Section 1.5, we consider whether economies have been changing in ways such that the impact on household incomes of the GR is likely to differ from the impact of previous recessions. In the final section of this chapter (1.6), we draw the elements of our discussion together and highlight the complexity of the relationship between the macroeconomy and the income distribution.

Chapter 2 reviews the experience of 21 OECD countries: Australia, Austria, Belgium, Canada, Denmark, Germany, Greece, Finland, France, Ireland, Italy,

Japan, the Netherlands, New Zealand, Norway, Portugal, Spain, Sweden, Switzerland, the UK, and the USA. Thus, no country is included from Africa, Asia (other than Japan), Central Europe, Eastern Europe, or Latin America. Our focus is therefore on rich countries.

The chapter first describes the nature of the macroeconomic changes that characterize the GR in these countries, and how these have worked through to household incomes. The discussion highlights how the characteristics of the GR have varied across countries. In some, there have been major declines in economic activity and sharply rising unemployment; in others, there have been more modest changes in output and employment. Furthermore, the financial aspects of the crisis have played out very differently in different countries. In some there has been a banking sector crisis and the bursting of a real estate price bubble, but others have escaped these events. For the purposes of this book, the diverse nature of the GR gives rise to different expectations about its distributional consequences in different countries. Second, we report the evidence available to date about how the GR has affected household incomes on average and in total, household income inequality, and poverty across the 21 OECD countries. This evidence is limited because the GR began in late 2007 and household survey or administrative record data about the distribution of household incomes emerges with a significant lag, but the initial effects through to 2009, and in some cases into 2010, are observed. The chapter finishes by considering the distributional consequences of governments' current efforts to consolidate their finances.

In Chapters 3 to 8, we focus on six countries in depth: Germany, Ireland, Italy, Sweden, the UK, and the USA. Through this case study approach, macroeconomic change, channels of transmission, and distributional outcomes can be analysed in more detail. The six countries experienced a wide range of macroeconomic changes in 2007–9, with some marked differences in the nature of the initial shock in particular. The fact that this set of countries draws attention to this variation is sufficient justification for their selection. We have the country that is the largest economy in the world and the origin of the financial crisis that became the GR (the USA). We also have three of the largest economies and most populous countries in Europe (Germany, Italy, and the UK). There are five EU members, of which three participate in the monetary union (Germany, Ireland, and Italy) and two do not (Sweden and the UK). The countries belong to different welfare state regimes (Esping-Andersen 1990; Ferrera 1996): Liberal (Ireland, UK, and the USA), Corporatist (Germany), Scandinavian (Sweden), Southern (Italy). And, as we show in Chapter 2, income distributions differed across these six countries at the time of the onset of the GR, ranging from Sweden—with a comparatively equal household income distribution and low relative poverty rates—through to the USA with the highest degree of inequality and poverty.

In the final chapter, Chapter 9, we summarize what these case studies, together with the evidence from the 21 OECD countries, suggest about the distributional impact of the GR, insofar as it can be ascertained at this stage. We draw tentative conclusions about the factors associated with having a relatively 'soft landing' in terms of the distributional outcomes. We end the book with consideration of the lessons that arise for policy-makers.

1.3 Macroeconomic Change and the Distribution of Income—Frameworks and Tools

The opening paragraphs of this chapter raised the question of what one would expect the distributional impact of the GR to be, and contrasted expectations of large changes (by reference to the Great Depression) with the possibility of their amelioration by contemporary institutions and policy instruments. That brief discussion suggested that the distributional impact of a major recession is not straightforwardly predictable. There is also the complication that distributional impacts may vary depending on which dimension one considers, whether average living standards, poverty, or inequality. The source of many ambiguities in predictions is our interest in a measure of economic well-being that combines multiple income sources and multiple income recipients (going from individual receipt to a household total).

In this section, we review the distributional impacts of recessions that are suggested by existing analytical frameworks. (We do not consider the long-term relationship between economic growth and the income distribution about which see e.g. the pioneering analysis by Kuznets 1955.) The review underscores the point that clear cut conclusions about the GR's likely impact rarely drop out and, hence, empirical analysis of the kind offered in the rest of the book is required. A second purpose of this section is to motivate and justify the approaches that are employed in the later chapters. The discussion that follows highlights a number of key elements and it is these that are tracked in the subsequent empirical analysis.

First we consider the insights offered by formal economic models and second we discuss two descriptive frameworks based on decompositions— breakdowns by type of person ('population subgroup') and by type of income received ('income source'). Finally we consider the potential of tax-benefit microsimulation models.

1.3.1 *Formal Models*

Stochastic neoclassical growth models and their close cousins, dynamic stochastic general equilibrium (DSGE) models, are now widely used to summarize macroeconomic trends and to assess the consequences of macroeconomic policy. They increasingly incorporate distributional features. For recent examples of the former, see Castañeda, Díaz-Giménez, and Ríos-Rull (1998), Maliar, Maliar, and Mora (2005), and Heer (2007); on the latter, see Smets and Wouters (2003) and Schorfheide (2011). At the heart of these models are utility-maximizing households that choose current and future consumption and work, with income derived from the labour market, dividends and returns on capital, and forward-looking profit-maximizing firms producing goods and hiring labour. The models have the advantage from the analytical point of view that implications about the macroeconomy are related to microfoundations in a consistent manner. Nonetheless, many demographic complexities are suppressed: although the models refer to the household as the unit, they model the behaviour of individuals devoid of household context. The population typically refers to people of working age, and model calibrations are often based on data for men only. More generally, Peseran and Smith argue that the DSGE approach 'has been at the expense of adequately representing the data and of being relevant to central policy issues' (2011:2). Others have criticized the degree of knowledge and foresight that the models attribute to economic agents and the way in which 'shocks' and uncertainty are modelled: see for example Caballero (2010) and Quiggin (2010). This is particularly relevant since, arguably, the GR is more of a structural break than a standard shock. For a more sympathetic perspective on neoclassical models, and a discussion of how the GR is incorporated in them, see Ohanian (2010).

Neoclassical models proposed by authors such as Castañeda, Díaz-Giménez, and Ríos-Rull (1998) are concerned with cyclical variation rather than major recessions like the GR. The aim of the models is to highlight the economic mechanisms that explain observed covariations between changes in the income distribution over time and the business cycle. For instance, Castañeda, Díaz-Giménez, and Ríos-Rull (1998) emphasize the role of differences in labour market attachment, arguing that a five-fold partition of the population along this dimension accounts for most aspects of the distributional dynamics observed in the USA. By contrast, they argue that cyclical variation in factor income shares, including income from capital, plays a minor role. It is not the aim of these models to explain the nature of the impact of an economic downturn on the income distribution, which is the goal of our book.

An illustrative microeconomic model is that of Atkinson and Brandolini (2006). This was developed as a framework for thinking about the distributional impact of 'globalization' (in relation to the movement of low wage production to developing countries) and of skill-biased technological change but also illustrates the complexities involved in assessing the impact of recessions. At first the authors consider people of working age only, distinguishing between unskilled and skilled workers (the focus is on individuals and labour earnings). More layers of complexity are then incorporated incrementally: a third class (unemployed workers) is added and then, finally, the 'welfare state' (benefits and taxes, which must be financed). Thus workers are classified into four groups (insured and uninsured unemployed workers, and skilled and unskilled employed workers).

At the heart of Atkinson and Brandolini's (2006) framework is a relationship between inequality (the Gini coefficient) and model parameters such as the skilled wage premium, the proportions of unemployed workers and of unskilled workers among the unemployed, the benefits–earnings replacement rate, and the tax rate on earnings. The distributional impact of the GR can be considered in terms of the way in which it affects these parameters. No implications are derived for poverty rates; the analytics are in terms of the Lorenz curve and Gini coefficient.

Unsurprisingly, 'even for the very simplified distribution sketched here, the Gini indices turn out to be a rather intricate function of the macroeconomic variables...and the institutional parameters' (Atkinson and Brandolini 2006: 56). In other words, even in this relatively simple characterization of the economy, the relationship between change in unemployment and changes in income distribution is not clear cut. It depends on how much welfare states replace the income of unemployed workers, the tax rates required to finance this, and the extent to which the recession hits skilled rather than unskilled workers. Another of Atkinson and Brandolini's conclusions is that '...one needs to have clearly in mind the inequality of "what". The distribution of wages among workers has to be distinguished from the distribution of market incomes among the whole population (including the unemployed), which in turn must be distinguished from the distribution of disposable incomes' (2006: 57). Although made in the context of assessing the distributional impact of globalization, the conclusion also applies to analysis of the GR. In particular, trends in household income for the population as a whole do not necessarily track trends in wages for employees.

The complexity of the relationship between recessions and inequality is also highlighted by the model of individual earnings developed by Barlevy and Tsiddon (2006). They allow cyclical and trend inequality to be related, and show that this implies that the impact of a recession depends on the trend in inequality: recessions are more disequalizing when longer-run inequality is increasing and more equalizing when it is decreasing. The authors refer to historical evidence for the USA to support their theoretical arguments. The general lesson is that one must be cautious about inferring from the past to the present without considering contextual trends. We return to this issue in Section 1.5.

1.3.2 Decomposition Analysis: By Population Subgroup
or by Income Source

The idea underpinning decomposition analysis is that the overall income distribution can be described in terms of a relatively small number of constituent elements, and hence changes in the overall distribution can be analysed in terms of changes in those elements. One can either classify the total population into groups according to individuals' and households' characteristics and then examine the distributions within and between groups, or one can break down total income into its sources and look at the distributions of each type of income and the relationships between them. Although the two approaches are conceptually distinct, they yield similar conclusions about recessions if individuals are classified into groups according to the principal income source of their household (as is done in the Atkinson–Brandolini model).

The idea that different sources of income can be associated with different groups of individuals within the population is used by Muriel and Sibieta (2009) in their analysis of the distributional impact of UK recessions. For example, they state that 'the economic literature gives a reasonably clear answer as to which groups' living standards are likely to be most cyclical, and hence worst affected by recessions—we expect to see strong effects of recessions on the incomes of working-age individuals, but weaker effects on individuals who are retired or who are not strongly attached to the labour force' (2009: 14).

To elaborate, suppose that individuals can be classified into one of three groups according to their household's main income source: (a) 'rentier households' whose main income is from financial assets (including self-employed professionals; rich individuals living off income from the stock market; rich pensioners living off occupational and private pensions); (b) working households whose income is from employment income; and (c) non-working households whose income is largely from the state (unemployed working-age people; pensioners with income only from a state retirement pension). There is an income distribution for each class with mean income highest for rentier households and lowest for non-working households; the density functions for the classes—summarizing the concentration of persons at each point along the income range—are $f_a(y)$, $f_b(y)$, and $f_c(y)$. The density function for the incomes of the population overall, $f(y)$, is a weighted average of the subgroup distributions:

$$f(y) = p_a f_a(y) + p_b f_b(y) + p_c f_c(y)$$

where p_j is the fraction of the population in group j, and $p_a + p_b + p_c = 1$.

It follows that recessions have impacts on the overall distribution through several channels. There may be changes in the population shares of each group: a rise in unemployment corresponds to an increase in p_c and a fall in p_b. Other things being equal, this change shifts the income distribution for the population as a whole to the left: average living standards decline and absolute poverty increases. The impact on overall inequality is unclear because the net effect also depends on the location and shape of the distribution for each subgroup (summarized by its density function).

Recessions induce changes in the location and shape of the income distribution for each group. For example, there may be a shift to the left in the rentier households' distribution associated with declines in stock prices and interest rates on financial assets. There may also be a shift to the left in the income distribution among working households combined with a greater dispersion associated with reductions in work hours or pay cuts among employees in some occupations and little change in other occupations. How the income distribution among non-employed households is affected depends on the nature of changes to benefits and state retirement pensions (and the taxes that finance them). If benefits are not uprated at the same rate as earnings increase (e.g. because of fiscal consolidation measures introduced as a consequence of a recession), the growing gap between the incomes of unemployed and working households increases inequality (between-group inequality is greater).

There are further complications. The discussion has conflated distributions among individuals with distributions among households (our interest). The distributional impact of a general rise in the unemployment rate depends on the extent to which job loss is correlated within multi-adult households—is there a rise in the share of households with no work at all or simply a change in the shares of single- and dual-earner households? The discussion has also ignored behavioural responses to the first-round changes, but they may also play important roles.

Income loss as a consequence of the recession may lead people to alter their living arrangements, for instance. Greater unemployment may lead more young people to return to live with their parents, and unrelated adults may be more likely to share accommodation to benefit from economies of scale. Formerly retired workers may return to the labour market to offset the impact of lower interest rates on their income from assets. The decomposition framework implicitly assumes that the total population is fixed in number, but a recession may also induce more people to leave a country and fewer to enter—though one would expect the distributional impact to be small for most countries since the numbers of people moving is relatively small.

If one employs the subgroup decomposition approach to analyse the impact of recessions, the key elements that are tracked over time are the sizes of the various subgroups, the distributions within each subgroup, and the income gaps between the subgroups. By contrast, the income source decomposition approach characterizes the channels by which a recession has effects on income inequality in terms of changes in three sets of elements: the share of each type of income in total income, the inequality of each income type, and the correlations between the income sources. (Explicit formulae are provided in Chapter 2, drawing on the work of Shorrocks 1982a, b.) If one describes the shapes of the distributions of the income sources using parametric functional forms, one can also derive expressions relating the overall poverty rate to the level of the poverty line and the parameters summarizing distributional shape. (See e.g. Gottschalk and Danziger 1985 who use displaced lognormal distributions.)

The distribution of household income is typically much more equal than the inequality of any one of its constituent sources: see for example Jenkins (1995: table 6) for UK examples. For instance, although income from investments and savings is very unequally distributed in most countries, its share in total income is relatively small, hence moderating the disequalizing contribution of this source. Income taxes are broadly progressive in relation to employment income and this has an equalizing effect. However, when looking at the impact of macroeconomic downturn, it is the relative size of the changes in the decomposition elements that is of particular relevance.

Most decomposition analyses show that employment income typically makes a larger contribution to household income inequality than does every other source (Chapter 2 below confirms this). This suggests that the distributional impact of a recession is largely driven by what happens to the contribution of income from the labour market, but this is not the only relevant channel. On the one hand, the share of labour income typically falls in macroeconomic downturns, because of greater unemployment. This may have an equalizing impact because less weight is given to an income source that comprises a relatively large share of total household income. But, on the other hand, the combined share of all other income sources must rise, which increases inequality if sources with increased shares are those that are more unequally distributed than employment income (e.g. income from investments and savings). The net effect on overall household income inequality depends on the precise nature of the recession, and the policy responses to it (which may change the cash transfers received and taxes paid). For example, does the share of investment income fall or rise, and how much does the share of income from cash transfers increase? The inequalities of each income source may also change: for example, if there are reductions in work hours for middle- and lower-paid workers but no changes for the higher-paid salariat, the inequality of employment income will increase, and this has a disequalizing impact on the household income distribution.

Formal analysis of the distributional impact of recessions using inequality decomposition formulae (by group or income source) is rare, largely because few countries have income data for a sufficiently long period of time to enable analysts to isolate the impact of downturns separately from other factors affecting inequality trends. One exception is the study by Aaberge et al. (2000) of the distributional impact of the early-1990s recession in Sweden—this is discussed in Section 1.4. More common is informal description. For example, Krueger et al. (2010) usefully review the association between inequality among working-age households and the business cycle for a number of countries. They observe that 'in all countries earnings inequality at the bottom increases during recessions' (2010: 8), but '[t]he general pattern is that, in all countries and in all recessions, inequality in disposable income during the recession rises less than inequality in earnings, reflecting the significant role played by automatic stabilizers. Quantitatively this role appears to be larger in some countries (i.e. Canada, Sweden, Germany) and smaller in others (US, Italy)' (2010: 9).

In sum, analysis of the distributional impact of recessions using decomposition approaches (whether by population subgroup or income source) shows that it is possible for a macroeconomic downturn to lead to either a decrease or an increase in overall income inequality. There are multiple elements that may change in offsetting directions, so the net effect is unclear in principle. There is some descriptive evidence that, in practice, recessions are associated with greater inequality, but that evidence mainly refers to working-age households rather than the whole population, and what happens to other groups in the population can affect the distributional outcome for the population as a whole.

In Chapter 2, we draw on the decomposition by income source framework to guide our analysis. In the rest of this chapter, we consider other approaches and tools, and review empirical work about the distributional impacts of recessions.

1.3.3 *Tax-Benefit Microsimulation Models*

Tax-benefit microsimulation models are not analytical frameworks in the same sense as the approaches discussed so far. A model for a particular country uses detailed survey data about the market incomes and other characteristics of households which, when combined with a set of tax and benefit rules, produce estimates of the distribution of household income. By comparing estimates derived using the prevailing system's rules with estimates derived using the rules implied by a tax-benefit reform proposal, one can investigate what the distributional impact of the reform is likely to be. While this has been the most common way in which microsimulation models have been used, they also allow investigation of issues directly relevant to this book.

Indeed, tax-benefit models can be used to consider the distributional impact of changing household characteristics—in particular to assess the implications of changes to the labour force attachment of household members or cuts in pay for employed workers. (These applications are sometimes described as a 'stress tests' of the tax-benefit system.) The key challenge for any application of tax-benefit models in this way concerns the nature of the assumptions that are used to describe a recession's onset for households and individuals of different types—the extent to which it is possible to characterize in an informed and detailed way who becomes unemployed, whose work hours and wages change and by how much, etc. Studies of the GR include Callan et al. (2011); Callan, Nolan, and Walsh (2011); Dolls, Fuest and Peichl (2011; 2012); Figari, Salvatori, and Sutherland (2011); and Matsaganis and Leventi (2011). We refer to these studies in our review of evidence in the next section.

We view microsimulation models as potentially valuable tools for predicting the distributional impact of recessions, especially when up-to-date household survey or administrative record data are not yet available. They are employed in several of the country case studies reported later in the book (for Ireland, Italy, and the UK). For many of the countries we consider, especially the 21 country pan-OECD analysis of Chapter 2, such models are either not available on a comparable basis, or it has been infeasible to employ them within the time constraints of this project. Therefore, much of the analysis in this book is framed in terms of description of changes in the components identified by decomposition analyses.

1.4 Evidence About the Distributional Impact of Macroeconomic Change

In this section, we review the empirical evidence about the distributional impacts of macroeconomic change, and especially recessions. The evidence is diverse, ranging from econometric analysis of the relationship between summary measures of inequality (and poverty) and macroeconomic aggregates, to studies relating changes in the macroeconomy in general with changes in the fortunes of the richest or the poorest individuals within a nation. Much of this research is based on a single country and that country is typically the USA. We also summarize some non-US case studies of distributional impacts, referring specifically to the Nordic crisis at the beginning of the 1990s, three recessions in the UK since the 1970s, and the New Zealand recession of the late 1980s. The latter is contrasted with the Irish boom from the mid-1990s to emphasize the important contribution of changes in median income to changes in relative poverty rates in times of macroeconomic change. (We do not include coverage of the Asian crisis of the 1990s as that involved countries at a different level of economic development to those that we consider in this book.) We end by reviewing the findings of some recent studies based on tax-benefit microsimulation modelling.

1.4.1 Econometric Studies of the Link Between Income Distribution and the Macroeconomy

There is a long history of studying the relationship between unemployment (and inflation) and income inequality and poverty in the USA. An early set of papers addressed the topic by fitting parametric models of the income distribution year by year and relating changes in model parameters to macroeconomic factors (see e.g. Metcalf 1969 and Thurow 1970). However, the most imitated studies have been regression analyses that relate time series data about income shares (or quantiles) to macroeconomic variables including unemployment rates: see for example Beach (1977) and Blinder and Esaki (1978). Blinder and Esaki state that 'the one unequivocal message seems to be that the incidence of unemployment is quite regressive. We estimate that each one percentage point rise in the unemployment rate takes away about 0.26%–0.30% of the national income from the lowest 40% of the income distribution and gives it to the richest 20%' (1978: 607). Beach refers to a 'definite pattern of cyclical sensitivity that is particularly strong at the bottom end of the income distribution' (1977: 64). Other studies, also reporting a regressive impact of greater unemployment, include McWatters and Beach (1990) for Canada; Björklund (1991) for Sweden; and Nolan (1988–9) for the UK. For a review, see Parker (1998–9).

Such definitive conclusions have disappeared from more recent analysis. Two related sources of fragility are the nature of the data—the time series used are relatively short (typically annual data for less than 30 years) making reliable identification of relationships difficult—and the nature of the econometric methods used. Recent time series econometric research argues that one needs to test for (co)integrated relationships and modify estimators accordingly: see Parker (2000) for more discussion. The problems are illustrated by Jäntti and Jenkins (2010) who extend Nolan's data series for the UK from 1961–76 to 1961–99, but find no robust evidence of any relationship between the income distribution and macroeconomic variables such as unemployment according to several different econometric approaches. A more general issue is that the GR might be viewed as a structural break in a series, likely to change the relationship between the inequality and the macroeconomy itself, so models fitted to past data may no longer be a reliable guide.

Whatever the early popularity of the regression approach, it is now little used and this stream of work is not cited in two recent comprehensive reviews of income distribution analysis (Atkinson and Bourguignon 2000; Salverda, Nolan, and Smeeding 2009). New approaches are being developed, however. For example, Farré and Vella (2008) examine the link between changes in macroeconomic conditions and changes in income distribution in Spain between 1989 and 1994 by estimating counterfactual densities conditional on different macroeconomic scenarios. By contrast with the Blinder–Esaki approach, they use information about individual incomes rather than modelling distributional summary statistics directly. A semi-parametric regression model is used to relate incomes to both individual characteristics and to macro variables such as the unemployment rate and GDP and, from the fitted model parameters, distributional summary statistics can be derived under different scenarios. In particular, Farré and Vella argue that the high unemployment rates of the early 1990s in Spain were partly responsible for the greater income inequality at that time (but there was no statistically significant association with inflation).

1.4.2 Changes in Incomes at the Top of the Distribution

The burgeoning literature deriving and analysing long term series of data about top incomes is potentially informative about the impact of recessions and other macroeconomic phenomena. The modern literature on the topic, stimulated by Piketty (2001) and Piketty and Saez (2003) in particular, is reviewed by Atkinson, Piketty, and Saez (2011). For many countries around the world, developed and less-developed nations, there are now historical series going back a century or more, with information about the shares of total pre-tax income for tax units (rather than individuals or households) held by the richest 10% and richest 1% (and so on) derived from administrative record data on income taxes (see Atkinson and Piketty 2007). One might worry that top income shares are not indicative of inequality across the whole distribution, although Leigh (2007) argues from country panel regression evidence that there is an association between trends in top income shares and more comprehensive inequality measures such as the Gini coefficient.

Atkinson, Piketty, and Saez (2011) usefully summarize the distributional consequences of the Great Depression that are suggested by the top income studies. They report that:

> Among the thirteen countries for which we have data, the period 1928–31(2) saw a rise in top shares in Canada (top 1 per cent), India, Indonesia, and Ireland, and no change in Finland and Germany. The remaining seven all saw top shares reduced. The top 0.1 per cent lost a fifth or more of their income share in Australia, France, the Netherlands, New Zealand, the UK, and the USA. In many countries, therefore, the depression reduced inequality at the top. (2011: 64)

All in all, the effects on inequality over this period appear to differ across countries. Where there is a reduction in inequality, it is primarily driven by the shock to capital rather than labour income. Looking at the data for individual countries, Atkinson, Piketty, and Saez (2011) cite decreases in top income shares around the Great Depression in the USA, the UK, the Netherlands, and Sweden, but they point to a much smaller decline in Japan.

The leading econometric study of the long-term determinants of trends in top income shares is by Roine, Vlachos, and Waldenström (2009) who use top income share data for 16 countries observed annually over the twentieth century. Their raw data series (2009: figure 1) illustrate the diversity of trends around the period of the Great Depression that Atkinson, Piketty, and Saez refer to. According to multivariate regression estimates, 'periods of high economic growth disproportionately increase the top percentile income share at the expense of the rest of the top decile' (2009: 974); by implication, a reduction in economic growth (as in a recession) is associated with a decline in the share for the richest 1%. The authors also find that financial development is pro-rich and the onset of banking crises reduces the income share of the rich.

In summary, recessions appear to have been associated with decreases in income shares for the richest groups on average, but there is heterogeneity in the experience around that average none the less.

1.4.3 *Changes in Incomes at the Bottom of the Distribution*

By its very nature, the top income literature can say little about how the fortunes of the poorest individuals in a society vary with the business cycle. There is a literature that reverses this emphasis, mostly about the USA, which considers whether the benefits of economic growth are shared by all groups including the disadvantaged—whether a rising tide lifts all boats and, conversely, what happens when the tide ebbs.

Several authors observed that the previously strong association in the USA between aggregate economic growth and poverty reduction became much weaker in the 1980s. See for example Blank and Blinder (1986) and Cutler and Katz (1991). Cutler and Katz's principal explanation of the changed association is that 'while the disadvantaged are greatly affected by the state of the macroeconomy, economic growth is not the only factor affecting the economic outcomes of the disadvantaged' (1991: 3). And, although acknowledging that 'the experience of the 1990–1 recession reinforces the perception that the poor bear a disproportionate share of the losses from a recession', Cutler and Katz draw attention to factors other than the aggregate macroeconomy that are particularly relevant. In particular, they argue that:

[c]hanges in relative labor demand against the less skilled offset the effects of improved aggregate employment opportunities during the expansion of 1983 to 1989. In an environment of persistent and severe shifts in relative labor demand

against the less skilled, a buoyant macroeconomy alone may not be sufficient to improve the absolute and relative living conditions of those from disadvantaged backgrounds. (1991: 4)

The strength of the macroeconomy remains important nonetheless, as emphasized by Blank (2000) a decade later in her review of the situation. Asking what lessons can be drawn for anti-poverty policy from the 1990s, her 'Lesson 1' is 'A strong macroeconomy matters more than anything else' (2000: 6).

Recent research suggests that the relationship between poverty rates and the macroeconomy has continued to evolve in the USA. Bitler and Hoynes (2010) consider whether the impact of the business cycle on disadvantaged families changed with the mid-1980s welfare reforms. Among their findings is the fact that the poverty rate, which varies counter-cyclically (higher when unemployment rates are higher) became 'significantly more responsive across economic cycles after welfare reform' (2010: 71).

In sum, there is clear evidence for the USA that the poor do badly in recessions but the extent to which an ebb tide raises poverty rates varies over time, being contingent on other prevailing factors such as the nature of the labour market and social safety nets (which also change). This suggests that the extent to which poverty rises during a recession will vary significantly across countries reflecting their different labour markets and socioeconomic institutions.

In Europe, there is concern about 'disappointing poverty trends' as well (this is the title of a recent study of the issue by Vandenbroucke and Vleminckx 2011). Poverty did not fall as fast as hoped during the years of economic growth prior to the GR even though average incomes and employment increased: see the EU's 2004 mid-term review of the 2000 Lisbon Strategy and proposals for change by the 2005 Council, culminating in the new EU 2020 Agenda which has an explicit poverty reduction target. For further discussion, see also Cantillon, Marx, and Van Den Bosch (2003), Atkinson (2010); de Beer (2007) and Cantillon (2011). Cantillon's diagnosis is that 'rising employment has benefited workless households only partially; income protection for the working-age population out of work has become less adequate; social policies and, more generally, social redistribution have become less pro-poor' (2011: 432). These explanations are similar to those provided for the weakening relationship between poverty reduction and economic growth in the USA.

It appears that US and European social protection systems face similar problems in not helping people sufficiently during economic upturns, and so the question arises of whether they are also similarly inadequate in insulating their citizens from poverty in the face of macroeconomic downturns. However, there are comparability issues. The USA uses a poverty line—the official standard—that is fixed in real terms rather than a relative standard (defined as a fraction of average income) that is common in Europe and incorporated in EU official statistical monitoring. The relevance of which type of poverty line is used is underlined further by the case studies of New Zealand and Ireland below.

1.4.4 Case Study 1: The Great Depression in the USA

Our first case study is the Great Depression in the USA. This deserves attention because the GR is widely viewed as the largest macroeconomic downturn since the Great Depression. The experience of the Great Depression places an upper bound on the magnitude of the distributional impacts effects that are likely to be found today.

We have already summarized what the literature on top incomes has said about the impact of the Great Depression—in general top income shares fell. Much of the US evidence on changes in the income distribution as a whole has been carefully reviewed by Atkinson and Morelli (2010, 2011). The evidence is sparse. As in other countries, the 1930s were a time before the introduction of regular sample surveys collecting information on household incomes. Atkinson and Morelli note that available estimates of the overall US income distribution for the interwar period are 'hedged with qualifications' (2010: 25). They are able to compare the year of the crash, 1929, with 1935–6, concluding that the Gini coefficient fell (by around 3 percentage points according to their Figure US2), although they are careful to warn that this comparison could 'mask a rise in inequality followed by an immediate fall' (2010: 26).

Some evidence of higher inequality in the USA in the years immediately after 1929 comes from another source. Mendershausen (1946) set out to assess the impact of the crash in 33 large and middle-sized cities from across the country. Some 240,000 families were surveyed in 1934 and asked to recall their incomes in 1929 and 1933, years when unemployment rose from 5% to its peak of 25%. The data do not provide a national level estimate and in several respects the information is not ideal, for example income is measured using respondent recall over a substantial interval of time.

Mendershausen estimated that the Gini coefficient rose across the two years in all 33 cities and by an average of 5 percentage points (1946: table 7). This is a substantial change and occurred while income levels fell in absolute terms throughout the distribution. The increases in inequality were attributed to a growth in inequality within the lower part of the distribution (the lower 50% to 70%) and also within the top of the distribution, combined within a growing gap between the average incomes of the bottom and top groups. Mendershausen's summary of the likely explanations for this pattern refers to a fall in unearned income, impacting most at the top of the distribution, and a rise in unemployment hitting in particular the low-skilled at the bottom of the distribution.

Poverty must have risen sharply when judged in absolute terms given the changes at the bottom of the distribution and the drop in real incomes generally. (Between 1929 and 1933, nominal incomes fell by 37% (Mendershausen 1946: 11) while prices in urban areas fell by around a quarter (Bureau of Labor Statistics 2011*b*).) A lack of data severely limits any national estimates of poverty rates. Atkinson and Morelli (2010: 25) note that the national estimates for the Great Depression period that are reported by Plotnick et al. (1998) are based on backward projections from the post-war period. Atkinson and Morelli also report estimates for 1929 and 1935–6 of a relative poverty measure which are quite similar in these two years.

Evidence about the impact of more recent recessions in the USA is provided by the US Census Bureau using data from the annual Current Population Survey (DeNavas-Walt, Proctor, and Smith 2011: in particular, tables 2 and 5). Their charts and tables refer to seven recessions between 1970 and 2008–9 (the GR), as determined by the National Bureau of Economic Research in its chronology of the US business cycle. During each of these, real median household income fell, though in most cases the decline began before the recession and continued after it officially ended. The declines in real income were experienced across the income range from poorest to richest groups, though in absolute dollar terms the declines were greatest at the top and small at the bottom. Falling real incomes during recessions translate directly into a rise in poverty rates during each of the recessions considered though, as for the changes in the median, these trends occur within longer-run rises in poverty. Indeed, the prolonged negative effects of the last three US recessions are shown by the further fall of median income and rise of poverty rates in the first calendar year following the end of the recessions. The decline in real incomes and rise in poverty associated with the onset of the GR in the USA is taken up in greater detail in Chapter 8.

1.4.5 *Case Study 2: New Zealand at the End of the 1980s and Ireland from the Mid-1990s*

The New Zealand case is of interest not only because it provides further evidence about the distributional impact of a recession but also because it highlights how different definitions of the poverty line can provide substantially different pictures about changes in low income prevalence at a time of major macroeconomic change. The Irish case, a boom rather than a bust, underlines this point.

New Zealand's economy stagnated in macroeconomic terms over the 1970s and 1980s: growth rates slowed and unemployment rates rose. Major structural changes were introduced by the incoming government in 1984 aiming to liberalize the economy (Evans et al. 1996). The macroeconomy did not recover and a significant downturn began in the mid- to late-1980s. 'By 1992, the economy had been in its most prolonged recession since World War II' (Statistics New Zealand 1999: 11). Macroeconomic recovery only began thereafter.

The extent of the recession is illustrated by the more than doubling of the unemployment rate from 4% in 1986 to around 10% in 1991, with annual real GDP growth between about 1% and –1% per annum during the period (much less than the historical trend). As a result, median real equivalized household income fell by almost 4% between 1986 and 1991 (Statistics New Zealand 1999: figure 5.1). This means that the real income value of a 'relative' poverty line defined as a fraction of median income also fell.

The change in the value of the poverty line helps explain why, despite the major recession, the proportion of persons with an income below 60% of the contemporary median was the same in both 1986 and 1991: 14% (Statistics New Zealand 1999: figure 6.9). The picture of low-income prevalence is rather different if a threshold that is fixed in real terms is used. For example, with a cut-off equal to the real value of the 20th percentile in 1996, the poverty rate rose from around 15% in 1986 to 20% by 1991 (Statistics New Zealand 1999: 78).

These different pictures reflect differences in income growth in different parts of the income distribution. Between 1986 and 1991, average income fell for the bottom six decile groups and increased for the top four groups, especially the richest one for which the increase in the average was around 15%. It is hardly surprising that overall inequality rose substantially, with the Gini coefficient rising by around one-fifth, from 0.25 in 1986 to 0.31 in 1991 (Statistics New Zealand 1999: figures 5.4, 5.5).

That absolute and relative poverty measures may provide different impressions about trends in low income prevalence during rapid macroeconomic change is also illustrated by the case of Ireland during the Celtic Tiger boom of the 1990s.

Layte, Nolan, and Whelan (2004) report that between 1994 and 2001, median household income increased by more than 97% and yet, over the same period, the proportion of persons counted as poor using a 60-per-cent-of-median threshold increased from 16% to 22% (2004: 4, 5), an increase of 38%. If the poverty line is instead anchored at its 1994 value in real terms, then the proportion of persons counted as poor fell by 55% between 1994 and 2000 (Nolan, Munzi, and Smeeding 2005). As in the New Zealand case, the explanation for the divergent trends using different poverty measures is differential income growth across the distribution. Although everybody's real income grew, incomes grew more for recipients of labour and capital income (concentrated towards the top) than for recipients of state support such as pensioners (concentrated towards the bottom).

The general lesson from both countries' experience is that in times of rapid macroeconomic change (such as the GR), it is important not to rely on a single poverty measure and, if possible, to track the changes in real income throughout the income distribution. Supplementary indicators, about trends in material deprivation for example, may also be useful. For more on this, see the case study of Ireland in Chapter 4.

1.4.6 *Case Study 3: The Nordic Countries at the end of the 1980s*

Our third case study is the Nordic crisis of the late 1980s and early 1990s. As with the GR, this crisis was initially a financial crisis (following rapid economic growth and financial market liberalization) which turned quickly into a more general and major recession in Denmark, Finland, Norway, and Sweden. Unemployment rates increased substantially from relatively low levels to rates that had not occurred since the 1930s. At the onset of the crisis, the four Nordic countries were among the nations with the smallest degree of income inequality among all OECD countries—a feature commonly attributed to their comprehensive welfare states and high taxation.

Aaberge et al.'s (2000) study of what happened to the inequality of household disposable income over this period in each of the four countries has a very clear finding:

> To sum up, we have found that income inequality hardly responded at all to drastically rising unemployment in Finland and was also more or less unresponsive to the less drastic increases in Denmark. But the results for Norway and Sweden suggest that inequality responded to rising unemployment. On the whole, however, we are struck by the low magnitudes of the responses. Unemployment may, at most, have increased the Gini by 2 percentage points. So, in 1993, at the peak of unemployment, these countries probably remain at the top of the international ranking in terms of income equality. (2000: 84)

The authors consider several hypotheses for this remarkable finding: that it is due to generous unemployment benefits replacing labour income; unemployment experienced evenly across all groups; contemporaneous changes in other income sources (e.g. capital and self-employment income) whose effects offset those of changing labour income; and compensating adjustments to labour supply within couples. From their decomposition analyses by income source, Aaberge et al. (2000) conclude that:

> UI benefits have indeed had . . . mitigating effects, but not large enough to explain the development of the income distribution during the years of rising unemployment. . . . Our interpretation . . . is that a recession sets several complex mechanisms in motion, and a large model with interactions between income components

is probably required to understand the evolution of the income distribution during rapidly rising unemployment. (2000: 95)

Although the authors show that inequality rose little among both all individuals aged 20–64 and individuals aged 30–54, their decomposition analysis is restricted to individuals aged 30–54. We conjecture that, if the decomposition analysis had been extended to include older persons, the cushioning impact of the Nordic welfare states in times of recession would have been even more apparent because these groups receive a greater share of income from the government (e.g. pensions and other benefits) compared to the 'prime' age group who are more reliant on the labour market (and unemployment-related benefits).

Aaberge et al. (2000) do not analyse trends in poverty rates or real incomes during the Nordic crisis, but relevant information can be found in a more wide-ranging study of low income in the Nordic countries edited by Gustafsson and Pedersen. In their introduction, Gustafsson and Pedersen (2000: 11) note 'the well known dramatic changes in unemployment' from 1990 and remark that 'the immediate impact of unemployment on the distribution of factor incomes and the poverty share is more or less neutralised by compensations from unemployment insurance or social welfare systems'. They also stress that the sharp rise in public transfers to households, as a ratio to GDP, in the early 1990s could have been even larger in Sweden and Finland had transfer generosity not been reduced. These general observations are documented in subsequent country chapters. Gustafsson (2000: figure 6.2) shows that, in Sweden, the growth of unemployment led to a relatively small increase of poverty in 1993 and the next two years, though the increase was larger when an absolute poverty line was used rather than a relative one. Gustafsson also estimates sharper increases for the Foster–Greer–Thorbecke measures with higher poverty aversion, concluding that 'while the deteriorating labour market did not lead to a significant number of people being poor, the poor became poorer' (2000: 182). Pedersen and Smith (2000: figure 2.1) present annual estimates derived from administrative register data for Denmark and show that the proportion of all persons aged 18–75 years with an income below 50% of contemporary median income was around 10% between 1987 and 1990 but increased in the following three years, even though by only one percentage point. The time profile of poverty rates during the crisis period is almost identical when using a fixed real income cut-off equal to half the average of real median incomes of 1979–95. Pedersen and Smith argue that this picture of aggregate stability masks offsetting changes for different groups: in particular there was a decline in the share of total poverty accounted for by people over 50 combined with an increasing share for some groups of working age. These results underline the point that conclusions about cyclical sensitivity of incomes and the stabilizing role of welfare states depend in part on which groups are considered, in particular whether the population as a whole is included or only people of working age. For more on these issues, see the chapters on Finland (Jäntti and Ritakallio 2000) and Norway (Aaberge, Andersen, and Wennemo 2000), as well as the case study of Sweden in Chapter 6.

1.4.7 Case Study 4: The United Kingdom

Muriel and Sibieta (2009) comprehensively review evidence about how the UK income distribution changed in three UK recessions prior to the GR: those in 1973–5, 1979–81, and 1990–2, of which the early-1980s recession was the deepest of the three. (The impact of the GR is considered in Chapter 7.) The income distribution is defined in terms of the distribution of real equivalized net household income among individuals—a definition corresponding to that used in the official UK income statistics.

Muriel and Sibieta show that median real income levels fell in the first two recessions and remained roughly constant in the third (2009: section 4). Sensitivity of average incomes to the cycle was markedly greater among family types dependent on the labour market for income—reflecting the impact of unemployment and slower earnings growth in recessions—by comparison with groups such as pensioners and lone parents who are much more reliant on benefit income. The pattern of income growth across the middle of the income range was broadly similar across the three recessions: incomes fell by about 1% over the recession for the middle 40% of the distribution (2009: figure 16). The experience of those at the top and bottom of the distribution differed between recessions. In the mid-1970s and early-1990s recessions, income growth for the poorest groups was the same or better than for the middle groups. By contrast, in the early-1980s recession, incomes fell by more. The richest third did better than the middle income groups in the early-1980s and early-1990s recessions (income growth was positive for the richest tenth in the latter case), but the early-1970s recession was different: there was a decline of around 2% or more for the richest third.

The diversity of experience across the distribution between the three recessions means that the picture for inequality trends is not clear cut. Muriel and Sibieta's summary is that:

> Just focusing on the three periods of recession, income inequality did not evolve uniformly over each recession. During the mid-1970s recession, it fell slightly, having been constant beforehand. Then during the early 1980s recession it rose, though this seems to be part of a rising trend throughout the 1980s. During the early 1990s recession, income inequality was flat, having risen substantially

during the late 1980s. Having fallen, risen and stayed constant during these recessions, income inequality has clearly not moved in one single direction during recessions in the past. (2009: 23)

It is clear that '[t]here is no 'rule' for the behaviour of inequality during recessions' (2009: 26).

Muriel and Sibieta (2009) also examine changes in the poverty rate, and are careful to distinguish between changes relative to thresholds defined in relative terms (60-per-cent-of-contemporary-median) and absolute terms (60-per-cent-of-median for the first year of recession). They find that 'though relative poverty has fallen slightly during previous recessions, absolute poverty has tended to rise or stay constant' (2009: 29). The fall in relative poverty was largely because pensioner poverty fell substantially; the rise in absolute poverty was particularly marked for children. These various changes reflect the patterns of real income growth reported earlier. The British experience underlines the point made earlier in the Nordic case about differential and potentially offsetting effects for different groups.

1.4.8 *Microsimulation Modelling and Stress-Testing of Welfare States*

A major macroeconomic shock like the GR puts substantial demands on systems of social protection if it results in a rapid rise in unemployment, as the case study of Nordic countries illustrates, and recent research has used tax-benefit microsimulation models to consider the extent to which different welfare states protect the incomes of those who are affected.

The 'stress tests' considered by Dolls, Fuest, and Peichl (2011) concern a proportional decline in gross household income by five percentage points, and they compare the impact of this being experienced universally by all households ('income shock'), or instead arising through an increase in the unemployment rate among working households ('unemployment shock') characterized by a sample reweighting exercise that assumes that the socio-demographic characteristics of the unemployed do not change with GR onset. Calculations are undertaken for 19 EU countries using EUROMOD, the European tax-benefit microsimulation model.

Dolls, Fuest, and Peichl report that the impact of a shock on the Gini coefficient of equivalized disposable household income depends on the type of shock. The income shock leads to a fall in inequality in all 19 countries, whereas the employment shock increases the Gini in 15 out of 19 countries and decreases it in the other four. The authors remark that the distributional impact depends crucially on which income groups are assumed by the simulation to be hit by higher unemployment rates. If the incidence is among those in the lowest income groups, inequality increases; if more universally experienced, then the impact on inequality is more ambiguous. Income and unemployment shocks both increase the proportion of persons who are poor (relative to a poverty line that is not defined in the paper), but whether the magnitude of the impact is greater or smaller for an income shock again depends on cross-national differences and on who is assumed to become unemployed.

The analysis is extended to include the USA by Dolls, Fuest, and Peichl (2012). This paper highlights again the crucial role that social protection and taxation systems play in protecting incomes in the face of major shocks. Interestingly their measure of the degree of such 'automatic stabilization' is broadly similar in the case of the universally-experienced 5% gross income fall, 38% in the Eurozone countries but only 32% in the USA. For the unemployment shock, however, automatic stabilization absorbs nearly 50% of the shock in Eurozone countries compared to only 34% in the USA. Benefits alone absorb 21% of the shock in Europe compared to just 7% in the USA (2009: 9). At the same time, the authors draw attention to the heterogeneity of automatic stabilization effects within Europe.

Figari, Salvatori, and Sutherland (2011) also consider the impact of the GR, but from a different perspective. Their principal goal is to measure the effects on income for individuals who become unemployed, and to contrast these in detail across selected European states, rather than to summarize the degree of automatic stabilization in an aggregate sense. Their calculations also use EUROMOD, but the focus is Belgium, Spain, Italy, Lithuania, and the United Kingdom, and the analysis concentrates on those who become unemployed (rather than the population as a whole). The unemployment shocks are characterized in a more realistic fashion than by Dolls, Fuest, and Peichl, in the sense that the individuals most at risk of becoming unemployed with GR onset are identified using information from the European Labour Force Survey. (This allows the characteristics of unemployed people to differ before and after onset.) The analysis contrasts measures of 'relative resilience' of social protection system (the ratio of post-shock income to pre-shock income) and 'absolute resilience' (the ratio of post-shock income to the pre-shock poverty line equal to 60% of the contemporary national median).

The headline finding is that 'the factor which plays the major protective role from a large drop in relative income is whether there are other people in the household with earnings' (Figari, Salvatori, and Sutherland 2011: 281). In addition, the authors point to differences in welfare state performance depending on whether the focus is on income replacement or income maintenance relative to a poverty line, and hence also on the nature of the different welfare states. For instance, the authors highlight 'the role for adequate minimum income schemes alongside unemployment benefits. Individuals living in better off households are less well protected in relative terms than those in lower income households where unemployment benefits are characterised or complemented by flat and means tested components, as in Spain, Lithuania and the UK' (Figari, Salvatori, and Sutherland 2011: 281–2).

If instead the focus is on preventing newly unemployed people becoming poor, then it is shown that there is wide variation across these five countries. Here Belgium and Spain perform relatively well: 'support for families with children in the UK helps to cushion the loss of income, but the absolute level of protection is lower than in the other countries' (Figari, Salvatori, and Sutherland 2011: 280). A general lesson, then, is that one needs to look at the social protection system as a whole, and how its various elements interact with each other. One cannot simply focus on unemployment benefits.

A third illustration of how microsimulation models may be used to examine the impact of the GR is the case study by Callan, Nolan, and Walsh (2011) of the public sector pay cuts introduced in Ireland in 2009/10 in the face of the severe crisis. Their study shows once again that distributional impacts of the GR depend on precisely who is affected and where they are in the distribution to start with. Moreover, pay cuts can have quite different effects from increases in unemployment. Public sector workers in Ireland are drawn from the middle of the income distribution rather than the bottom: as Callan, Nolan, and Walsh (2011) point out, compared to private sector workers they are relatively high-skilled, and there has been a public sector pay premium. Unsurprisingly, then, the impact of the package of public sector pay cuts is shown to be progressive (inequality reducing) relative to a counterfactual of a universal 4% cut in pay rates in both the public and private sectors.

1.4.9 Summary of the Evidence

The evidence presented so far relating to past recessions is diverse in nature, but suggests some broad conclusions, as follows:

- Recessions tend to hit incomes throughout the distribution range, but the incidence of income falls depends on which sorts of income are most affected, for example employment income vìs-a-vìs income from savings and investments.

- Poverty rates measured using a threshold fixed in real terms tend to rise in recessions because of the income falls for those at the bottom of the household income distribution.

- Whether poverty rates measured using a threshold that changes with average income also increase depends in part on how average income changes (because this changes the value of a poverty line that is expressed as a fraction of the average). Marked declines in middle incomes can lead to relative poverty rates remaining the same or even decreasing.

- Whether inequality of household income rises or falls in a recession is less clear cut. It depends on the specific pattern of income changes at different points across the distribution, for example the extent to which the incomes of the richest groups fall relative to the middle and the middle relative to the poorest.

- The pattern of income changes across the distribution associated with a recession also depends on country-specific features such as the progressivity of the income tax system, and the nature and extent of income maintenance provided to working and non-working families throughout the income range, and how this social support is provided when there is a recession.

- One might expect that, other things being equal, the more severe the recession, the greater the impact on the distribution of household income, and hence one might also expect the distributional impact of the GR to be greater than the impact of most post-Second World War recessions experienced by OECD countries. This conclusion follows if one summarizes impact in terms of real income levels or absolute poverty rates, but it need not be true if impact is summarized in terms of relative poverty rates or inequality (for the reasons cited earlier about why the direction of change in these aspects is indeterminate). Moreover, other things may not be equal. In particular, the size of the expected change in incomes also depends on the nature of the responses to recessions by governments and households.

1.5 This Time is Different?

Although broad conclusions may be drawn about the distributional impacts of past recessions, there remains the issue of whether this evidence is a reliable guide to the impact of the GR: is this time different? There has been substantial discussion of whether the financial crisis that precipitated the GR was different from previous crises, with a definitive review provided by Reinhart and Rogoff (2009). Although their book has the title *This Time is Different*, the phrase is intended ironically: the themes of the book are that financial crises have been endemic over the last eight centuries and that the financial crisis associated with the GR is not different but, rather, another manifestation of previous crises. But even if the nature and origins of the 2007–8 financial crisis are not substantively different, it may still be the case that the impact on the household income distribution of the recession associated with it (the GR) differs from the impacts of previous recessions.

As Muriel and Sibieta (2009) have pointed out, 'recessions are not uniform events. Past recessions differ from each other in both their causes . . . and their effects' and, also, 'trends in living standards and inequality during previous recessions reflect many other changes in public policy and other socio-economic changes, as well as what we might consider the "direct" effects of recession' (2009: 15).

For instance, the OECD has commented that 'there are reasons to believe that the last cycle was exceptional and that the sustained increases in asset prices, corporate profits and government revenue during the great moderation is unlikely to come back' (OECD 2010c: 228). ('The Great Moderation' is the label given to the period of macroeconomic stability experienced by many countries between the early 1990s and the GR.) The OECD also cites the 'extraordinary revenue buoyancy prior to the crisis' (2010c: 45). In other words, arguably countries were relatively well placed to counter the GR's effects relative to previous downturns in terms of the finances of both governments and firms.

There are a number of other factors relevant to whether this time is different. There have been changes in labour markets and welfare states. For example, greater labour market 'flexibility' may allow countries to recover faster from macroeconomic shocks; so too might more work-orientated welfare benefit systems. (See the 'rising tides' discussion in the previous section for more about these issues.) The trend towards greater financial market liberalization and globalization of national economies may have the opposite effect, by placing greater constraints on governments to act independently. Demography can also matter: with ageing populations and growing dependency ratios, there are additional calls on social protection budgets for funds that might otherwise be spent on macroeconomic stabilization.

Another feature of the GR is relatively high levels of debt which may have made households more vulnerable to the GR than to earlier recessions. (On household indebtedness across EU countries in the late 2000s, see Fondeville, Özdemir, and Ward 2010.) In their discussion of household debt and vulnerability in 2006, the OECD stated that vulnerability appeared not to be rising in an unmanageable fashion, but 'risks remain because sensitivity to shocks has risen' (2006: 136).

Pre-crisis trends in the distribution of income itself may also be relevant. The last three decades have been periods of growing income inequality in many OECD countries, especially at the top of the distribution (OECD 2008). The longer that these higher levels of inequality persist, the greater the chance that societies may accept these levels as 'normal': social tolerance of a marginal increase in inequality and poverty because of a recession might be larger the greater inequality there is in the first place. But the opposite could also be true, with acceptance suddenly turning into indignation, as Hirschman and Rothschild (1973) suggested long ago in the context of developing countries. These are arguments about willingness to tolerate or address distributional issues in recessionary times.

More important, however, is the question: have governments' capacities to stabilize the adverse impacts of recessions through taxes and benefits have been falling over time? If so, one would expect the impact of the GR on household incomes to be greater than in previous recessions, other things being equal.

Evidence relevant to answering this question is provided by the OECD's 2011 study, *Divided We Stand*. Its Chapter 7 examines the nature of tax-transfer redistribution policies across OECD countries over the two decades prior to the onset of the GR, with a focus on households headed by working-age individuals.

The study finds that the degree of redistribution increased in most OECD countries over the two decades before the mid-2000s, a period when market-income inequality was rising. (Redistribution for a country is mostly measured in terms of the difference between the Gini inequality index of household market incomes and the Gini inequality index of household net incomes.) However, although tax-benefit systems became more redistributive,

> they did not stop income inequality from rising (market-income inequality grew by twice as much redistribution) . . . While growing market-income disparities were the main driver of inequality trends between the mid-1980s and mid-1990s, reduced redistribution was sometimes the main source of widening household-income gaps in the ten years that followed. In fact income inequality after benefits and taxes increased *at a faster rate* after the mid-1990s than in the decade before. (OECD 2011f: 263; emphasis in original)

The OECD study emphasizes the greater contribution to changes in redistribution of changes in benefits rather than changes in taxes, pointing to the relevance of not only changes in benefit levels, but also especially changes in the numbers of persons entitled to receipt. On the benefits side, the decline in redistribution was partly driven by benefits not being uprated to the same extent as average earnings growth, but most important was a decline in numbers of persons receiving unemployment benefits (attributable to tighter eligibility rules) even though rates of incapacity benefit receipt also tended to rise. Thus, benefit recipients, mostly found towards the bottom of the income ladder, tended to slip further down. On the other hand, 'at the other end of the income spectrum, tax policy resulted in gains or in comparatively smaller losses' (OECD 2011f: 293). The OECD concludes that:

> Redistributive systems were generally effective at slowing trends towards widening income gaps which were due to falling incomes at the bottom. Tax-benefit systems, however, were less successful at offsetting growing inequality in the upper parts of the distribution, which became a more powerful driver of inequality trends in some countries. Redistribution systems will need to adapt to these new challenges. (OECD 2011f: 293)

In sum, the general tenor of the OECD study is that this time is indeed different—redistributive capacity has been falling over time and so, without adaptations to tax-benefit systems, one would expect the impact on household incomes of the GR to be greater than the impacts of past recessions. (Potential redistribution policy strategies referred to by the OECD include greater targeting of income support, not simply through benefits but also via measures that facilitate and encourage employment and earnings growth in ways that benefit low-income groups in particular, and changes in taxation for those with high incomes.) On the other hand, this conclusion is partial. The OECD analysis focuses on households of working age only, and does not account for redistribution among households headed by an elderly person. Redistribution is measured in terms of inequality reduction, ignoring other aspects of household income distributions such as poverty rates, which also are of interest, as the 'disappointing poverty trends' discussion for the EU in the previous section has shown. Moreover, and as the OECD acknowledges, even if 'this time is different', the distributional legacy of the GR also depends on whether tax-benefit systems are adapted as a result of it, whether in the short-, medium-, or longer terms.

1.6 Summary and Conclusions

The purpose of this chapter has been to review frameworks for thinking about the distributional impacts of the GR employed later in the book and to review empirical evidence from the past.

What do we expect the distributional impact of the GR to be? It is clear that no unambiguous conclusions can be drawn, and for several reasons. First, one needs to differentiate between different types of distributional impact—on average living standards, inequality, and poverty. The evidence we reviewed suggests that recessions reduce income levels generally and lower average income in particular, and raise poverty where this is measured relative to a low-income cut-off that is fixed in real terms ('absolute' poverty). That is, recessions result in a greater concentration of persons at lower real income levels. 'Relative' poverty rates may also increase, depending on how a poverty line defined as a fraction of contemporary median income changes. The impact of the GR on income inequality is unclear. As our review has underlined, the impact depends precisely on who is affected by the crisis and where they are located in the distribution in the first place.

A second reason for a lack of clear predictions is that there is a diversity of experience across countries, related to the specific nature of the GR in each country as well as to variation in systems of social protection, labour market institutions, and so on. We should also not forget country-specific policy measures that may have been introduced as a consequence of the GR. A third complicating factor is that evidence from past recessions may be an unreliable guide to the impact of the GR. Arguably the most important reason for this is the decline in the redistributive capacity of tax-benefit systems between the mid-1980s and the mid-2000s, at least for working-age households (as discussed in the last section), so one might expect less stabilization of the incomes for this group in the face of major economic downturns.

It is only by turning to empirical investigation that we can hope to draw definitive conclusions about the distributional impact of the GR. That is what we do in the rest of this book. In Chapter 2, we describe for 21 OECD countries the nature of the GR and discuss changes in household incomes insofar as we able to do so using the data available. The analysis draws on the decomposition by income source approach that was discussed in this chapter. Chapter 2 also serves to locate the experience of our six case-study countries within this context. Chapters 3–8 provide the case studies for Germany, Ireland, Italy, Sweden, the UK, and the USA. For each country, there is a description of the changes in national output and the labour market in the period around the GR, followed by a much more detailed analysis of distributional outcomes than is possible in Chapter 2. In the final chapter, we consider what may be concluded about the impact of the GR on the incomes of households, drawing a distinction between the short-term and longer-term consequences.

2

The Great Recession and its consequences for household incomes in 21 countries

Stephen P. Jenkins, Andrea Brandolini, John Micklewright, and Brian Nolan, with the assistance of Gaetano Basso

The historical record concerning the distributional impact of previous recessions, reviewed in Chapter 1, shows that outcomes have been diverse across countries. To see whether this is also true for the impact of the Great Recession (GR) requires up-to-date and cross-nationally comparable household survey data for a large number of countries covering the period before, during, and after the recession. Such data are far from being fully available and so, of necessity, our approach to forming conclusions about the GR's distributional impacts on households must be eclectic. We draw on the framework of decomposition analysis that we reviewed in Chapter 1 and on a variety of different forms of data.

Our strategy is first to paint a picture of the likely distributional impact of the GR by examining changes in elements entering the decomposition rather than by looking directly at changes in the overall distribution itself. Although we often do not have household survey or administrative record data about distributions of household income for all of the period in which we are interested, there is a substantial amount of information available on trends in some of the different elements. These data are drawn from a number of different sources and vary in their coverage of both countries and elements. For example, we are able to say much more about changes in labour income than we can about changes in income from capital, and also more about changes in average incomes than changes in inequality or poverty. Thus the chapter provides a first sketch using the data currently available rather than a fully-completed painting. The case studies in Chapters 3–8 start to fill in the canvas for individual countries.

Our first task (Section 2.1) is to describe the nature of the GR itself and how it differed across 21 OECD countries, with a particular focus on the six countries that we consider in more detail in Chapters 3–8. The remaining sections of the chapter seek to assess the distributional impacts of these changes relative to a baseline situation in around 2007, again highlighting cross-country similarities and differences.

Recessions are usually defined by national statistical agencies in terms of changes in Gross Domestic Output (GDP) or in other production indicators. In Section 2.2, we use national accounts data to link the changes in GDP in each country with those in the aggregate incomes of the household sector recorded in the same source. We are also able to analyse the changes in the main types of income received by households. The data reveal the importance of public redistribution in buffering the negative effects of the GR on household incomes in the short term, but do not show anything about how the changes were distributed across households. The distributional aspects are the focus of the remainder of the chapter.

Section 2.3 provides the backdrop to our subsequent examination of changes during the GR in the various elements comprising household incomes. For each of 12 European countries plus the USA, we document the contribution to overall inequality of household income and mean income in 2007 from each of four income sources: labour income, income from benefits and other cash transfers, property and other cash income, and direct taxes.

Having described the baseline, we move to consider what happened to incomes after the onset of the GR via analysis of changes in the prevalence of receipt and the distribution of various income sources. We begin in Section 2.4 with consideration of changes in the distribution of work. Labour income is the principal source of income for most households in most economies and deserves special attention. Changes in labour income can come about via changes in wages or changes in employment. The latter are probably more important in a recession, as the fall in labour demand affects the numbers of people who have any work and the hours worked by those who have jobs. These effects for individuals combine differently within households, implying that the patterns of change in employment rates may differ between individuals and households.

Changes in the distributions of income sources per se are considered in Section 2.5. We start with changes in average wage rates, the other determinant of labour income, and in the distribution of total earnings among employees. We then move to changes in returns on capital assets and in benefit income, components about which we are able to say less. Finally, we draw attention to the links between changes in inflation rates and real incomes, and benefit uprating policies in particular.

In Section 2.6, we first summarize the implications of the analysis of the preceding sections for the distributional impacts of the GR. We are then able to draw on published statistics based on household survey and administrative record data for 2005–9, and in one case 2010, to assess the short-term impact of the GR on average household incomes, on poverty rates, and on inequality in incomes. These data refer to 15 European countries, although for poverty rates and inequality we are also able to present changes in the USA through to 2010. The directions in which countries headed in the years after 2009—the medium-term impact of the GR—depend in part on measures to consolidate government finances in response to the rise in deficits that occurred almost everywhere in 2007–9. The chapter therefore finishes in Section 2.7 with a discussion of the likely distributional impact of these measures.

2.1 How the Great Recession Developed

The decline in GDP in real terms during the GR is shown in Figure 2.1 for each of the 21 countries which we cover in this chapter. The peak-to-trough fall in quarterly figures, as measured by the OECD in data covering to end-2009, is compared with the average change in recessions over the previous 50 years. (In one or two cases the actual trough came later.) Almost everywhere, and in line with the 'Great Recession' label, the fall was substantially larger than the historical average. A second feature of Figure 2.1 is the cross-country heterogeneity in the size of the contraction in GDP: it ranges from none in Australia and little more than 2% in New Zealand to 9% in Finland and nearly 13% in Ireland. Nine countries experienced a fall of 5% or more while nine had a fall of 4% or less. Figure 2.1 also shows the average annual growth rates in real GDP over the 10 years before the GR (these are the numbers given in parentheses after each country's name). These estimates show the extent of the boom that preceded the bust. Austria, with an average growth rate of 2.7% is the median country. Ireland, with a striking pre-GR growth of 6.2% a year is the most extreme case of rise and fall. Finland and Sweden are other examples of higher than average growth followed by a larger than average fall.

The types of macroeconomic shock that provoked the falls in output varied across the 21 countries, from the bursting of a housing bubble in Ireland and Spain, for example, to a collapse in trade in countries such as Germany and Italy, with consequences for household incomes that can be expected to vary depending on the sector of economic activity that suffered the most, for example construction or manufacturing.

The recovery in output from the trough also varied substantially. Figure 2.2 shows quarterly changes in real GDP until late 2011 in the countries that are our case studies in Chapters 3–8. Most of these six countries were among the

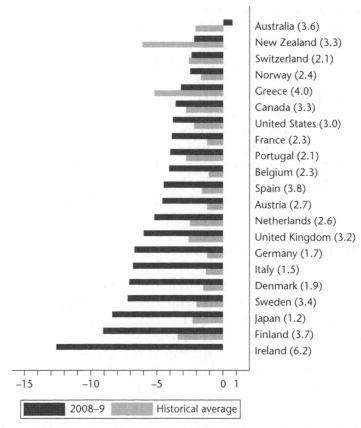

Figure 2.1. Change in national output in the GR in historical context: percentage decline in real GDP from peak to trough compared to the post-war historical average of peak-to-trough changes

Source: OECD (2010*a*: figure 1.9). GDP growth rates over 1997–2007 are from OECD, 'Aggregate National Accounts: Gross domestic product', OECD National Accounts Statistics 2010 (database), http://dx.doi.org/10.1787/data-00001-en [accessed 30 January 2012].

Notes: Australia did not have a recession in 2008–9 but is shown for comparison purposes (its GDP change refers to the period from 2008 Q3 to 2009 Q2). The number of recessions used to calculate the historical average varies across countries depending on data availability and the frequency of recessions. Recessions that occur in the period from *c*.1960 until 2006 are included. No historical average is available for Ireland. The figures in parentheses are the average annual growth rates in real GDP for 1998–2007 (calculated as the value *g* in the formula $R = (1 + g)^{10}$, where R is the ratio of the 2007 figure to the 1997 figure).

most severely hit by the GR of the 21 we consider in this chapter in terms of fall in GDP, but subsequently they displayed a wide range of different experiences. Sweden had a sharp and robust recovery. Germany recovered quite strongly too with the USA not far behind. Recovery was notably weak in the UK and in Italy, and had still not started properly in Ireland by late 2011. If changes in real GDP were our only guide to distributional impact, then we

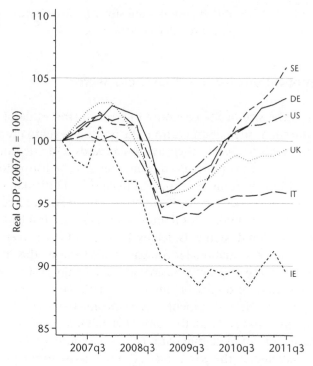

Figure 2.2. Real GDP in 6 countries, 2007Q1–2011Q3 (2007Q1 = 100)

Source: OECD, series LNBQRSA (volume estimates, seasonally adjusted), 'Quarterly National Accounts', 2010, OECD National Accounts Statistics (database), http://dx.doi.org/10.1787/data-00017-en [accessed 8 January 2012].

Notes: The series refer to Germany ('DE'), Ireland ('IE'), Italy ('IT'), Sweden ('SE'), the United Kingdom ('UK'), and the United States ('US').

would expect distributional changes between 2007 and 2011 to be smallest in Germany, Sweden, and the USA, and greatest in Ireland.

The other 15 countries that we study in this chapter also differed considerably in their patterns of recovery. In Denmark, Greece, Japan, Portugal and Spain, output in late 2011 had still not reached the level of the first quarter of 2007, as in the UK, Italy, and Ireland. Following an initial output fall that was relatively modest (see Figure 2.1), Greece experienced a continuous decline during 2010 with GDP by the end of the year over 9% below its early 2008 peak. Portugal saw frail growth in 2010 followed by renewed contraction in 2011. Output struggled to grow in Spain throughout 2010–11. Among the remaining 10 countries, annual growth in 2010 averaged 2.3%, ranging from 0.4% in Norway and 1.4% in France to just over 3% in Canada and Finland (OECD 2011a: annex table 1). At end-2011, the prospects for growth were uncertain in many of the 21 countries, partly as a result of the European sovereign debt crisis that gathered pace during the year, with the OECD commenting that 'advanced economies are slowing down and the euro area appears to be in a mild recession' (OECD 2011b: 7).

2.2 The Implications for the Household Sector

GDP measures the size of the economy in terms of the value of goods and services produced. As such, it differs from the revenues eventually available to resident households to sustain their living standards. On one side, there are incomes that are paid to and received from foreigners, a distinction which is particularly relevant in some countries. In Ireland, in particular, GDP fell by 15.4% at current prices between 2007 and 2009, but 'gross national disposable income', which is the amount of resources available for resident units after netting all international payments, fell by 19.3%, that is 4 percentage points more. On the other side, national income is divided among the 'institutional' sectors comprising the economy. Businesses may retain profits, which coincide with their share of disposable income in national accounts, to sustain investment plans, while government uses its income to provide for services in kind and collective goods. Thus, the same GDP fall may have rather different implications for current living standards between a country where the decline in income is buffered by the government through a rise in the public deficit, and a country where it is entirely transferred to household finances. The national accounts allow us to disentangle these changes, by providing information for the household sector alone (which also includes small sole proprietorship enterprises and non-profit institutions serving households), as distinct from businesses and government bodies.

The importance of this distinction is illustrated in Figure 2.3, which compares the evolution of real GDP with that of real Gross Household Disposable Income (GHDI) in the Euro area (top panel) and the USA (bottom panel). (Real GHDI is obtained using the deflator of the final consumption expenditure of households and non-profit institutions serving households.) Household income appears to be less variable than GDP. During the GR, it stopped rising but did not fall significantly in the Euro area; in the USA, it declined by a smaller extent than GDP and with a lag. The panel for the Euro area also shows that a measure of GHDI augmented by the value of social transfers in kind— 'Gross Household Adjusted Disposable Income', GHADI (not available for the USA)—grew more than GHDI during and after the GR. This evidence suggests that public services did not suffer any cut in real value before the end of 2011, although the situation might change subsequently as a result of the fiscal consolidation packages adopted in many countries of the monetary union. The GHADI data warn us that it is misleading to make inferences about the short-term impact of the GR on living standards from looking at GHDI change

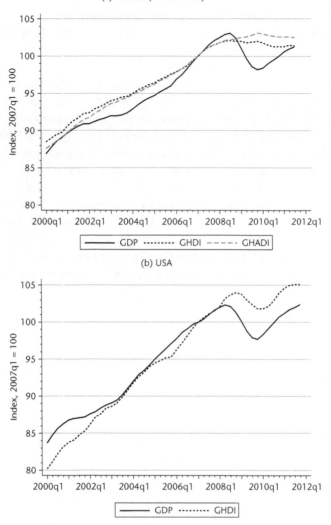

Figure 2.3. Change in real Gross Domestic Product (GDP), real Gross Household Disposable Income (GHDI), and real Gross Household Adjusted Disposable Income (GHADI) in (a) the Euro area (17 countries) and (b) the USA, 2000Q1–2011Q4 (2007Q1 = 100)

Source: Authors' calculations on data from Eurostat, 2012, 'Quarterly national accounts: GDP and main components—Current prices (namq_gdp_c)' and 'Quarterly national accounts: GDP and main components—volumes (namq_gdp_k)', http://epp.eurostat.ec.europa.eu/portal/page/portal/national _accounts/data/database and Eurostat, 2012, 'Quarterly sector accounts: Non-financial transactions (nasq_nf_tr)', http://epp.eurostat.ec.europa.eu/portal/page/portal/sector_accounts/data/database and from US Bureau of Economic Analysis, 2011, 'Integrated Macroeconomic Accounts for the United States: S.3.q Households and Nonprofit Institutions Serving Households (Q)', http://www.bea.gov/ national/nipaweb/Ni_FedBeaSna/Index.asp [both accessed 1 February 2012].

Notes: For the USA, GHDI is calculated as 'Disposable personal income' minus 'Personal interest payments' and 'Personal current transfer payments'. Real GHDI and GHADI are obtained by dividing nominal values by the deflator of the final consumption expenditure of households and non-profit institutions serving households. Households include non-profit institutions serving households. Plotted values are 4-term moving averages centred in the final quarter of the underlying values.

alone, although on distributive issues they are as silent as the GDP data are. In the remainder of this section, we look at changes in both GHDI and its main components for 18 of the 21 countries in our sample (data are missing for Australia, Japan, and New Zealand).

For these 18 countries, the percentage change in real GHDI between 2007 and 2009 is plotted against the corresponding change in real GDP in Figure 2.4. The most striking feature is the prevalent pattern of increases in GHDI despite the almost universal falls in output. Were GHDI to have fallen as GDP did, the data points would be found in the bottom left hand part of the graph below the dashed horizontal line that indicates no change in GHDI. Instead, they lie mostly above this line.

There are increases in GHDI in 12 countries and in seven of these the rise is by more than 2%. Only in Austria, Denmark, Greece, Italy, and the Netherlands did GHDI fall. Notable cases are Ireland, where the 10% contraction in GDP was accompanied by stable total household income, and Sweden and Finland, where household income rose by between 4% and 5% despite a drop in GDP by

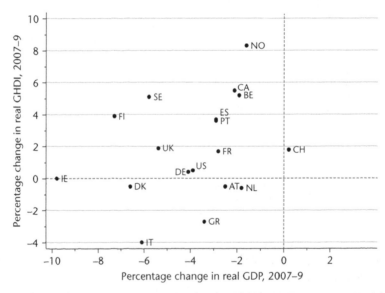

Figure 2.4. Percentage change in real Gross Household Disposable Income (GHDI) and in real Gross Domestic Product (GDP), 2007–9

Source: OECD, 'Detailed National Accounts: Simplified non-financial accounts', 2010, OECD National Accounts Statistics (database), http://dx.doi.org/10.1787/data-00010-en except for Greece and Spain, whose data are from Eurostat, 'Annual sector accounts: Non-financial flows and stocks, Non-financial transactions (nasa_nf_tr)', http://epp.eurostat.ec.europa.eu/portal/page/portal/sector_accounts/data/database [both accessed 30 January 2012].

Notes: Real values for GHDI were derived using the deflator of household final consumption (source: OECD, 2010, 'Detailed National Accounts: Final consumption expenditure of households', OECD National Accounts Statistics (database), http://dx.doi.org/10.1787/data-00005-en [accessed on 28 January 2012].

between 6% and 7%. In contrast, Italy suffered a loss in GDP similar in size to that of the two Nordic countries and a fall of household income by 4%. In part the different dynamics of real GDP and real GHDI during the GR can be explained by the behaviour of their respective deflators. In Belgium, the Netherlands, Denmark, Italy, Portugal, and Greece, the deflator of household final consumption expenditure, used with GHDI, increased less than that of GDP, by between one and two percentage points. In these countries, the terms of trade, which drive the difference between the two deflators, moved in a manner that was favourable to households' purchasing power. The opposite happened in Finland, Norway, and Ireland. The overall picture, however, would not change were we to divide both GDP and GHDI by the same deflator. In general, the household sector appears to have been protected from the impact of the severe downturn of 2007–9, and this is the result of genuinely better trends in households' revenues relative to GDP in nominal terms rather than of a different price index.

Why the household sector did relatively well can be explored by looking at changes in the main components of GHDI. We break down GHDI into six components: (a) 'compensation of employees' (wages and salaries before taxation and social contributions); (b) 'mixed income' (income from self-employment); (c) 'operating surplus' (imputed income from rent for owner occupiers); (d) 'property income' (received dividends and other distributed income of corporations, interest from bank accounts, government bonds and private securities, rents and other current private transfers, all net of the amounts paid); (e) 'current taxes on income and wealth' plus 'social contributions' (social insurance contributions, including those directly paid by employers); and (f) 'social benefits' (all public transfers other than those in kind). (The full detail available on GHDI components is greater than we consider here.) Social contributions in the national accounts, unlike in most household surveys, include those levied on employers in respect of their workers as well as contributions paid by employees. Countries use different combinations of social contributions and taxes and it is therefore appropriate to combine them for our purposes, although whether it is firms or individuals who really bear the burden of employer contributions is open to debate.

The top panel of Table 2.1 shows the percentage real change in each component, while the bottom panel shows the contribution of each component to the total change in GHDI. For example, of the 4.0% fall in GHDI in Italy (final row), 5.2 percentage points were due to a fall in the property income (column 3). By definition, the sum by row of values from column 1 to column 6 equals the value in column 7. The values in the bottom panel are obtained by multiplying those in the top panel by the component's share in total income (not shown). Countries are ranked by the change in total GHDI (column 7).

Compensation of employees (column 1) forms the largest share of GHDI in every country (more than 80% in 2007, on average), although its importance varies considerably. (The variation across countries in shares is a feature of the other income sources too.) It is notable that this component of GHDI fell in real terms in only six countries between 2007 and 2009: Spain, Italy, the UK, Sweden, the USA, and Ireland (in increasing order of magnitude). Given its importance to GHDI, the percentage changes in all countries in the top panel of the table are reflected in the figures in the bottom panel, despite being relatively small in magnitude compared to the percentage changes in some other components of income. As we might expect in a recession, self-employment income ('mixed income', column 2) fell much more generally: there are falls in all but three countries.

The change in rental income imputed for owner-occupied dwellings ('operating surplus', column 3) varied greatly across countries: the biggest declines occurred in the UK, Greece, Spain, and Ireland, all of which are countries in which residential property prices fell considerably between 2007 and 2009. However, the relationship is weak as, in the USA, the operating surplus increased significantly despite a large decrease in house prices (OECD 2011e; ECB 2012). Capital incomes, that is the profits distributed by corporations and

Table 2.1. Components of real Gross Household Disposable Income (GHDI), 2007–9: (a) Percentage change in each component of GHDI and in total GHDI, (b) the contribution of each component to the change in total GHDI (percentage points)

(a) Percentage change in each component of GHDI and in total GHDI

Country	Employee compensation	Mixed income	Operating surplus	Property income and other transfers	Taxes and social contributions	Social benefits	GHDI
	(1)	(2)	(3)	(4)	(5)	(6)	(7)
Norway	6.4	3.1	−0.9	40.6	5.8	9.5	8.3
Canada	1.7	2.5	16.6	−6.3	−5.7	12.0	5.5
Belgium	4.0	−0.8	−3.9	4.6	2.9	10.5	5.2
Sweden	−2.9	−7.0	1.1	10.4	−10.0	4.3	5.1
Finland	0.7	−9.8	4.5	−8.1	−3.9	9.6	3.9
Spain	−0.5	−6.6	−13.7	5.2	−6.3	20.8	3.7
Portugal	3.2	3.6	−1.2	−9.4	5.2	14.8	3.6
UK	−1.5	−6.4	−29.2	4.4	−3.4	16.0	1.9
Switzerland	5.6	−11.9	5.9	−8.9	4.3	6.1	1.8
France	0.9	−6.8	−1.4	0.5	0.5	6.6	1.7
USA	−4.0	−17.2	8.3	−23.3	−16.9	20.2	0.5
Germany	2.0	−7.3	−0.7	−0.7	4.4	7.5	0.4
Ireland	−4.5	−27.6	−6.3	−43.6	−11.1	29.7	0.0
Denmark	0.5	−5.9		−136.4	−1.6	5.2	−0.5
Austria	3.3	−4.0	4.4	−31.6	1.5	7.1	−0.5
Netherlands	5.7	−14.7		−24.1	4.3	8.9	−0.6
Greece	5.2	−5.8	−17.5	−37.9	−0.1	16.7	−2.7
Italy	−0.6	−4.1	4.6	−25.3	−0.3	6.5	−4.0

(b) The contribution of each component to the change in total GHDI (percentage points)

Country	Employee compensation	Mixed income	Operating surplus	Property income and other transfers	Taxes and social contributions	Social benefits	GHDI
	(1)	(2)	(3)	(4)	(5)	(6)	(7)
Norway	6.3	0.2	−0.1	1.8	−2.9	3.0	8.3
Canada	1.5	0.2	1.0	−0.7	1.6	2.0	5.5
Belgium	3.4	−0.1	−0.4	0.7	−1.6	3.2	5.2
Sweden	−3.2	−0.7	0.1	0.8	6.6	1.4	5.1
Finland	0.6	−1.1	0.5	−0.8	1.9	2.8	3.9
Spain	−0.4	−1.7	−1.0	0.3	2.2	4.2	3.7
Portugal	2.3	0.5	−0.1	−1.3	−1.5	3.7	3.6
UK	−1.2	−0.6	−2.6	0.7	1.5	4.1	1.9
Switzerland	5.1	−1.5	0.0	−1.5	−2.4	2.0	1.8
France	0.7	−0.7	−0.2	0.1	−0.2	1.9	1.7
USA	−3.0	−2.6	0.8	−1.9	3.9	3.2	0.5
Germany	1.5	−1.0	0.0	−0.2	−1.9	2.0	0.4
Ireland	−3.7	−4.1	−0.7	−1.9	3.9	6.5	0.0
Denmark	0.6	−1.0		−3.4	1.3	2.1	−0.5
Austria	2.5	−0.6	0.4	−4.3	−0.7	2.1	−0.5
Netherlands	5.6	−3.5		−2.8	−2.9	2.9	−0.6
Greece	2.4	−1.7	−1.7	−5.8	0.0	4.1	−2.7
Italy	−0.3	−0.9	0.5	−5.2	0.1	1.8	−4.0

Source: OECD, 'Detailed National Accounts: Simplified non–financial accounts', 2010, OECD National Accounts Statistics (database), http://dx.doi.org/10.1787/data–00010–en except for Greece and Spain, whose data are from Eurostat, 'Annual sector accounts: Non–financial flows and stocks, Non–financial transactions (nasa_nf_tr)', http://epp.eurostat. ec.europa.eu/portal/page/portal/sector_accounts/data/database [both accessed 30 January 2012].

quasi-corporations to their owners and interests received on financial assets net of those paid on debts ('property income and other transfers', column 4) also generally fell, although there are some very large differences between countries in the percentages changes. Except for Germany, all countries at the bottom of the table—those experiencing the worst dynamics of GHDI— show negative values large enough to contribute to a reduction in GHDI of about two points or more (see panel b). On the other hand, in the UK, Belgium, Spain, and Sweden property incomes rose by between 4% and 10%, and by as much as 41% in Norway.

Taxes and social contributions (column 5) represent a substantial share of GHDI (the mean value was about −45% in 2007) and the changes over 2007–9 often made a significant contribution to the change in GHDI. In 11 countries, these direct taxes and contributions fell or increased less than the total of all other income sources, thus sustaining incomes during the recession. The marked falls in Sweden, Ireland, and the USA accounted for between four and seven percentage points of the GHDI growth. In the remaining countries the average tax burden increased instead: in Germany, Switzerland, and the Netherlands it led to an erosion of income growth by as much as two or three percentage points. Finally, and unsurprisingly, the increase of social benefits (column 6) was very substantial, especially in the traditionally low-spending English-speaking countries but also in Southern European countries, except for Italy. The bottom panel shows that the support to GHDI from social benefits was at least two percentage points, with few exceptions, and exceeded four percentage points in Greece, the UK, Spain, and Ireland. The additional support from public benefits reflects the impact both of automatic stabilizers, such as unemployment benefits, and of discretionary spending undertaken as part of economic stimulus packages (e.g. see OECD 2009: chapter 1), although much of this spending may have come through channels other than the benefit system.

These observations suggest that the protection of household incomes against the collapse of economic activity during the GR was largely provided by the government. Figure 2.5 compares, for each country, the change in total GHDI (top bar) with the change in GHDI if we exclude the change in social benefits (middle bar) and the change in GHDI when we exclude the change in both social benefits and taxes and social contributions (bottom bar). (These values can be obtained by subtracting column 6, and columns 5 and 6, respectively, from column 7 in Table 2.1(b).) In accounting terms, these values show the change in total household income between 2007 and 2009 that would have occurred had total government benefits and direct personal taxes remained at their 2007 values. The nature of this counterfactual exercise needs to be emphasized. On the one hand, the variation of taxes and benefits reflects the government's counter-cyclical action to sustain household income: the aim of the exercise is precisely that of quantifying these effects. On the other hand, by taking the whole variation of taxes and benefits, it is implicitly assumed that it is entirely attributable to the recession. That means that income would not have varied otherwise and that no other factors would have affected taxes and benefits, which is generally not the case (e.g. public transfers could have increased because of a rise in the number of retirees associated with population ageing). Moreover, other aspects of state support that have affected households during the GR are also not removed from the calculations, such as changes to indirect taxation or spending on employment creation. In short, the calculations should be seen only as an accounting exercise.

The exercise is revealing nonetheless. As already noted, the support from benefits was everywhere positive: holding just this element of GHDI at the 2007 value (middle bars) results in the change in household incomes always being less positive or, as is typically the case, negative or more negative than it actually was (top bars). When we also include taxes, we observe that changes in GHDI with social benefits and taxes held at the 2007 level (bottom bars) are negative in the majority of cases. In many countries total household sector incomes would have fallen, or would have fallen more, without the support of

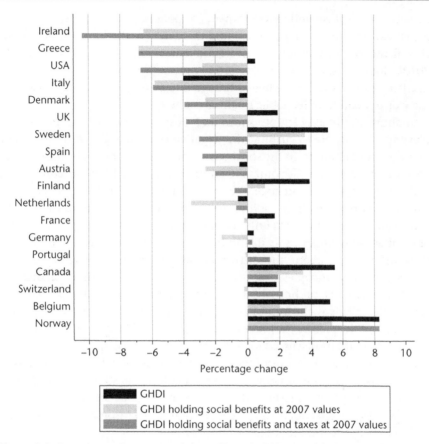

Figure 2.5. Percentage change in real Gross Household Disposable Income (GHDI) and effect of taxes and benefits, 2007–9

Source: OECD, 'Detailed National Accounts: Simplified non-financial accounts', 2010, OECD National Accounts Statistics (database), http://dx.doi.org/10.1787/data-00010-en except for Greece and Spain, whose data are from Eurostat, 'Annual sector accounts: Non-financial flows and stocks, Non-financial transactions (nasa_nf_tr)', http://epp.eurostat.ec.europa.eu/portal/page/portal/sector_accounts/data/database [both accessed 30 January 2012].

Notes: For each country, the top bar shows the percentage change in total gross household disposable income (GHDI) between 2007 and 2009 (the value is zero for Ireland); the other bars show the percentage change in GHDI when holding social benefits at the 2007 value (middle bar) and social benefits and taxes and social contributions at the 2007 values (bottom bar). Data are put into real terms using the same deflator as in Figure 2.3. The countries are ranked by the bottom bar values.

governments through the tax and benefit system. The difference between the top and bottom bars shows the extent of that support, measured as a percentage of the 2007 value of GHDI. It is a huge ten percentage points in Ireland and more than four percentage points in six other countries—Greece, Finland, UK, Spain, USA, and Sweden (in order of increasing size). At the other extreme, in Norway, the Netherlands, and Germany the support was nil, and even slightly negative in Switzerland. Government responses to the downturn have depended on various factors, including the extent of the problem faced and their fiscal positions prior to the crisis and hence their ability to spend (OECD 2010b: 308). Thus, Ireland could afford to use public resources extensively, as it had been in fiscal surplus, whereas Italy had to be more restrained, because of the worse situation of its public finances before the GR.

In short, national accounts show that in most countries public budgets played a crucial role to cushion the negative consequences of the recession for household finances, in the short term. The longer-term implications of the government support to incomes are another story, to which we return at the end of the chapter: by and large, the consolidation of public accounts must be paid for eventually by households. Moreover, this observation holds in aggregate. National accounts data only provide a picture about changes in the total but not about changes in its distribution among households. For more concrete information about the distributional impact of the GR beyond the changes in total incomes, we need to look in more detail at changes in different elements of household income packages using household-level data sources. This is the aim of the sections that follow. It should be borne in mind that the picture they reveal of change in total household income may differ from that just discussed for at least two reasons. First, household survey data will be studied in terms of 'per equivalent person', while the analysis so far has considered totals unadjusted for population size. Second, definitions of income, coverage, and methods differ between national accounts and household surveys. For a reconciliation, see for example Atkinson and Micklewright (1983) for the UK and Brandolini (1999) for Italy.

2.3 The Distributional Baseline at the Time of GR Onset

Before embarking on analysis of each component comprising household income in the sections that follow, we document the contribution of each of the different components to mean income and income inequality in a baseline year, 2007, using decomposition methods proposed by Shorrocks (1982a, b). We are able to do this on a comparable basis for 13 countries: 12 European countries and the USA. We use data from the European Union Statistics on Incomes and Living Conditions (EU-SILC) database and the Current Population Survey (CPS) in the case of the USA. (The EU-SILC data are described by Atkinson and Marlier 2010.) Income is equivalized household net income (see Chapter 1), and refers to annual income for 2007, with two exceptions. For Ireland, income refers to that in the 12 months preceding the survey interview in 2007; for the UK, income refers to that in the period around the time of the survey interview in this year, expressed as an annual amount pro rata.

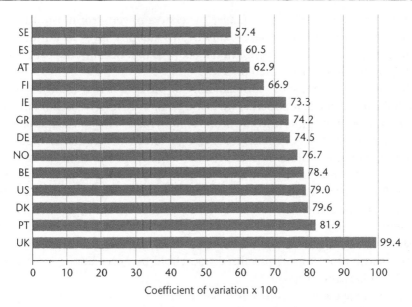

Figure 2.6. Inequality (coefficient of variation) of household incomes in 12 European countries and the USA, 2007

Source: European countries: authors' calculations from EU-SILC. Italy is not included because of data comparability problems. USA: calculations by Jeff Thompson from the Current Population Survey.

Notes: Income is total household net income, equivalized by the square root of household size, distributed among individuals. The data relate to incomes in the year 2007.

Figure 2.6 first illustrates the variation across the 13 countries in the degree of income inequality in 2007 using the coefficient of variation (*CV*), calculated consistently using the data just described. (This inequality index is used because it links with the source decomposition analysis that follows.) Viewed on its own as a summary measure of income inequality, the *CV* is not ideal as it may lack robustness to high income outliers. But, broadly speaking, the country ordering by inequality on the *CV* is what we might expect. For example, Sweden and Finland are among the lower inequality countries and the USA and the UK among those with higher income inequality, although it is surprising that the value for the USA is not higher given other rankings of income inequality across countries (e.g. see estimates of the Gini coefficient from the Luxembourg Income Study data in Table 6.1 in Chapter 6). The different starting points in terms of different levels of inequality and the factors associated with this situation may have affected the nature of automatic stabilization of incomes through the tax-benefit system and the discretionary policy measures introduced as a result of the GR (see Chapter 1 for more discussion).

The estimates in Figure 2.6 relate to a single year, but later in the chapter where we analyse trends over 2005–9 we show that there was no clear trend upwards or downwards in inequality or relative poverty for most of the EU countries around the time of GR onset. This stability gives us a little more confidence in attributing distributional changes that occur in the period after 2007 to the GR and associated policies.

In order to maximize the comparability of the data across countries in our analysis of income components, we distinguish only four household income sources: labour income (income from employment and self-employment), cash transfers (all cash benefits from the government plus transfers such as state retirement pensions), other income (largely income from investments and savings), and direct taxes (income taxes and employee social insurance contributions; treated as negative income). The sum of these four components equals total household net income. Both total income and each of the components is equivalized (by the square root of household size), and we examine distributions of these household income variables among individuals. (Analysis of distributions of unequivalized household incomes among households yields similar conclusions.)

The average income of any particular income group depends on the group-average values of each of the four income sources. Normalizing by overall average income, the 'importance' of each income source for a given income group is given by the share of the group's household income total. In Figure 2.7, we show income shares by component for the richest fifth (panel (a)) and the poorest fifth (panel (b)). Observe that income shares for direct taxes have negative values, by construction. (Receipts of refundable tax credits such as the working tax credit and child tax credit in the UK, and the earned income tax credit and child tax credit in the USA, are counted as cash transfers rather than as offsetting tax payments.) Countries are ranked in ascending order of the share of employment income in total income. Countries with longer bars tend to have larger shares in total income of cash transfers (positive shares) and of direct taxes (negative shares). For each country, the sum of the four shares is 100%.

For the richest fifth, it is clear that the most important component in household income packages is employment income. Its share varies from 105% of the total in Spain to 138% in Denmark. There is also a general tendency for larger (more negative) shares of direct taxes to be associated with larger employment income shares in this income group (the share is –22% in Spain and –65% in Denmark). The share of cash transfers is rather small in every country for this richest fifth, which is unsurprising. Perhaps more unexpected is the relatively small share of other income in all of the countries: the shares range from 3.5% in Portugal to around 11% in Sweden, and 15% in Denmark, Finland, and the USA. To some extent, these estimates may reflect the relatively poor coverage of this component in the EU-SILC household surveys; income data for the three Nordic countries are derived from administrative registers which may have better coverage of top incomes (especially from capital). It may also reflect the

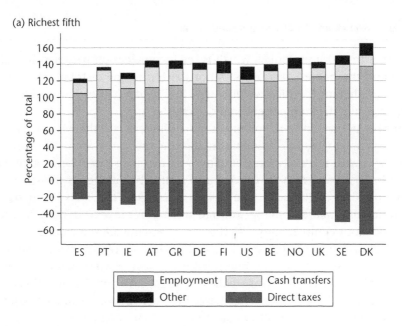

(a) Richest fifth

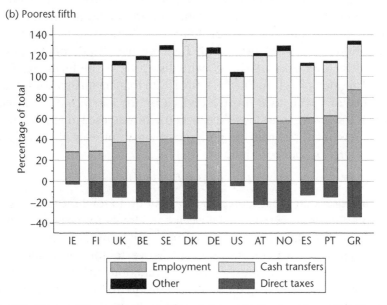

(b) Poorest fifth

Figure 2.7. Shares of income sources (%) in total equivalized net household income, richest and poorest fifths, 12 European countries and the USA, 2007: (a) Richest fifth and (b) Poorest fifth

Sources: European countries: authors' calculations from EU-SILC. Italy is not included because of data comparability problems. USA: calculations by Jeff Thompson from the Current Population Survey. Receipts of refundable tax credits such as the working tax credit and child tax credit in the UK, and the earned income tax credit and child tax credit in the USA, are counted as cash transfers rather than as offsetting tax payments.

Notes: Income is total household net income, equivalized by the square root of household size, distributed among individuals: see text for details. Countries are ranked from left to right in ascending order of the share of employment income in total equivalized household net income. The income shares for each income group in each country sum to 100%.

fact that the 80th percentile, which is the income cut-off between the richest fifth and the poorest four-fifths, is not the top of the distribution. The 'top incomes' literature, which we discussed in Chapter 1, uses much higher cut-offs (typically the 90th percentile and above).

For the poorest fifth, the picture is quite different and there is greater cross-country heterogeneity. At one extreme are the three Southern European countries with relatively large employment income shares (ranging between 61% in Spain and 88% in Greece) and relatively small cash transfer shares (ranging between 50% in Spain and 43% in Greece). The USA is also an outlier, with notably small shares for cash transfers and for taxes (but note the earlier remark about comparability). At the other extreme are the Nordic countries with below-average employment shares but large shares for cash transfers and also direct taxes. Western European countries such as Germany and Belgium lie broadly in between, having smaller shares for cash transfers and direct taxes than the Nordic countries. The shares of other income in total household income are very small in all 13 countries, less than 5% in each case.

Assessing the contribution of income sources to overall inequality is a trickier issue than assessing their contributions to mean income because there are many potential ways of doing this. Various formulae for source contributions have been developed. Here we use the decomposition rule proposed by Shorrocks (1982a, b), who also reviews the literature. That is, the contribution of a given income source, k, to total inequality is given by the covariance of k with total income divided by the variance of total income (which is the same expression as the 'beta coefficient' used in finance to assess the riskiness of an asset held in a portfolio). More intuitively, the contribution of each source, s_k, can be written as

$$s_k = \rho_k(\mu_k/\mu)(CV_k/CV).$$

The expression states that source k's contribution to total inequality is given by the product of the correlation between k and total income (ρ_k), the share of k in total income (the ratio of the source mean to the overall mean, μ_k/μ), and the inequality of each income source relative to total inequality where inequality is measured by the coefficient of variation (CV_k/CV). The formula has the attraction that the contributions sum to 100% and there is a clear interpretation: positive values correspond to sources with a disequalizing contribution to total inequality, and negative values correspond to sources with an equalizing contribution. The greater the magnitude of s_k, the larger the contribution. For estimates of source contributions to inequality based instead on a Gini decomposition rule, see OECD (2011f: chapter 6). The OECD's estimates for the mid-2000s for the different income sources are consistent with what we report here for 2007 using the Shorrocks approach.

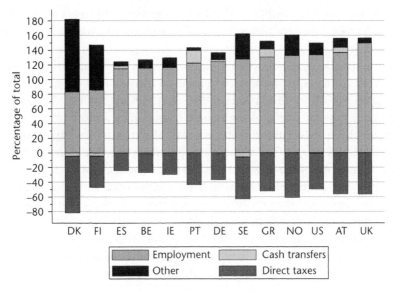

Figure 2.8. Contributions (%) of income sources to inequality of total household income, 12 EU countries and the USA, 2007.

Sources: European countries: authors' calculations from EU-SILC. Italy is not included because of data comparability problems. USA: calculations by Jeff Thompson from the Current Population Survey. Receipts of refundable tax credits such as the working tax credit and child tax credit in the UK, and the earned income tax credit and child tax credit in the USA, are counted as cash transfers rather than as offsetting tax payments.

Notes: Income is total household net income, equivalized by the square root of household size, distributed among individuals: see text for details. The contribution for each country of each income source k is the s_k statistic defined by Shorrocks (1982a, b). The sum of the source contributions for each country is 100%. Countries are ranked from left to right in ascending order of the s_k statistic for employment income.

Source contributions to total inequality in each of the 13 countries are shown in Figure 2.8. The countries are ranked in ascending order of the contributions of employment income, the source which accounts for most of the income inequality in every country, with s_k values ranging from around 80% (Denmark) to nearly 150% (the UK). This is perhaps unsurprising given the generally large shares of employment income in household income (see above), though remember that income shares are not the only factors determining inequality contributions. In all the countries, direct taxes make an equalizing contribution though there is substantial variation in its magnitude. Cash transfers account for virtually none of the observed inequality, and are disequalizing in five countries. In contrast, other income has a relatively large disequalizing contribution, especially in the four Nordic countries and the USA. These large contributions partly arise from the large shares of other income in total income in these countries but this is not the full story. In additional analysis (not shown), we find that the inequality of other income relative to overall inequality (CV_k / CV) is substantially larger in the Nordic countries than other countries, especially in Denmark. We return to this in Section 2.5.

In sum, the decomposition analysis emphasizes the importance of income from work for the distribution of household income and accounting for its inequality. For other dimensions of the distributions such as income levels (and hence poverty rates), other income sources play a more important role. Although these are common features across the countries we have analysed, the analysis also suggests that there are important baseline differences across countries in terms of the different income components, as well as the different levels of overall inequality on which we commented earlier. For example, there is a suggestion that income from savings and investments may play a much more important role in household income in the Nordic countries than in other countries and so, to the extent that these sources are especially affected by the GR relative to (say) employment income, these countries may exhibit different distributional trends after GR onset.

2.4 Changes in the Distribution of Work

The labour market is the main source of income for the household sector, at least for households of working age, as the previous section has shown. So, if we can discern what has been happening to the distribution of work during the GR and afterwards, we have clues to what has been happening to the distribution of household incomes. We draw on a variety of sources, notably OECD statistics derived from household surveys such as the Labour Force Surveys conducted in EU countries.

We begin with a focus on changes in employment. Our interest is in whether people have a job or not (including self-employment) and hence whether they receive labour market income at all. The focus on employment rather than unemployment recognizes that the GR may have induced changes in labour market participation as well as changes in unemployment among economically active individuals. We first consider the distribution of work across individuals and then turn later to its distribution across households. How work is combined within households is important for household incomes over and above individual earnings.

2.4.1 *Changes in Employment Among Individuals*

The change in the employment rate between 2007 and 2009 among people of working age varied a great deal across the 21 countries: see Table 2.2. At one extreme there are six countries with virtually no change in employment rates or even a modest increase: (in order of increasing magnitude) Greece, France, Austria, Switzerland, Netherlands, and Germany. At the other extreme, there are four countries for which the employment rate fell by more than 3 percentage points: Sweden (–3.5), the USA (–4.2), Spain (–6.0), and Ireland (–6.7). These are large falls relative to historical trends in a span of only two years.

In most countries the response of employment to the fall in GDP was smaller than in previous recessions (OECD 2010*a*: 34), although there are clear exceptions as we note below. Moreover, much of the variation across countries in the change in employment is not well explained by the differences in the GDP changes—the correlation between the employment rate changes in Table 2.2 and changes in GDP for the same period is just under 0.5. Commenting on the relationship, the OECD notes that:

> Job losses were unusually large compared with the fall in output in a few countries where a boom-bust pattern in the housing market played an important role in causing the recession, notably Spain, the United States and, to a lesser extent, Ireland (where the fall in output was also especially large). By contrast, the

Table 2.2. Employment rates, level (2007) and change (2007–9), working-age individuals

Country	Level 2007 %	Change 2007–9 (ppt)
Germany	69.0	1.4
Netherlands	74.8	0.9
Switzerland	78.6	0.6
Austria	71.4	0.2
France	64.0	0.2
Greece	61.4	–0.1
Norway	76.9	–0.4
Belgium	62.0	–0.4
Japan	70.7	–0.6
Australia	72.8	–0.9
Italy	58.7	–1.2
Denmark	77.1	–1.4
Portugal	67.8	–1.5
United Kingdom	72.3	–1.6
Finland	70.5	–2.1
Canada	73.6	–2.1
New Zealand	75.2	–2.3
Sweden	75.7	–3.5
United States	71.8	–4.2
Spain	66.6	–6.0
Ireland	69.2	–6.7
Average	70.5	–1.5

Source: OECD, 'Labour Market Statistics: Labour force statistics by sex and age: indicators', (2010, OECD Employment and Labour Market Statistics (database), http://dx.doi.org/10.1787/data–00310–en [accessed 23 February 2011].

Notes: 'ppt' stands for percentage points. Persons of working age, 15–64. The average is unweighted.

employment response to declining output has been unusually muted in a larger number of countries, including Germany, Japan... [and] the Netherlands... where a sharp decline in exports was a major driver of the downturn. (OECD 2010a: 17)

Changes in employment between 2007 and 2011 are shown in Figure 2.9 for the six countries studied in Chapters 3–8. Values in each quarter are indexed relative to the values for the first quarter of 2007. It should be noted that the data refer to total employment and to people of all ages, rather than to the employment rates for people of working age that are the subject of Table 2.2, and this may account for any differences in the picture obtained for 2007–9 for particular countries, for example Sweden. The period covered and the vertical scale of Figure 2.9 is the same as for the changes in GDP shown earlier in Figure 2.2.

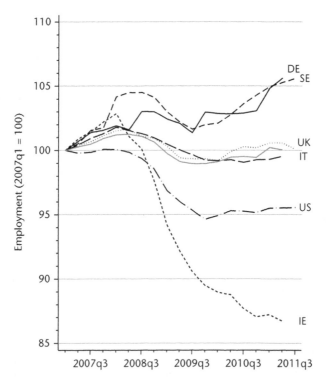

Figure 2.9. Employment levels in 6 countries and all-OECD, 2007Q1–2011Q3 (2007Q1 = 100)

Source: OECD, Main Economic Indicators (database), 2011, 'Labour: Labour force statistics', quarterly employment—all ages, http://dx.doi.org/10.1787/data-00046-en [accessed 19 December 2011].

Notes: The series refer to Germany ('DE'), Ireland ('IE'), Italy ('IT'), Sweden ('SE'), the United Kingdom ('UK'), the United States ('US'), and all OECD countries (the solid grey line).

Comparison of the two graphs tells us more about the relationship between changes in GDP and employment. On the one hand there are similar features, in particular the wide variation across countries. Total employment rose by about 5% in Germany and Sweden, the two countries that also show the largest net increases in output across the same period in Figure 2.2. (Chapter 3 discusses Germany's 'jobs miracle' in the GR and Chapter 6 contrasts the labour market changes in Sweden in the GR with those in the recession of the early 1990s.) At the other extreme, the continued downward trend in employment in Ireland through 2010 and into 2011 stands out, with employment in late 2011 some 13% below the level at the start of 2007. On the other hand, there are some notable differences in the trends shown in the two graphs. For example, there was no sharp fall in total employment in several countries where output fell, reflecting the weak relationship between changes in employment and in output discussed above, and no clear upswing in employment as the economy recovered in other countries, for example Italy but most notably in the USA. The large fall in employment in the USA (much larger than in the four previous recessions) was associated with a much larger rise in unemployment than would have been expected on the basis of the change in GDP and the relationship between unemployment and output in past recessions. (For more about this breakdown in Okun's 'law' during the GR, see OECD 2010a: box 1.1.)

As with employment, the typical pattern in other countries was for unemployment to change less than would have been expected given the past relationship with changes in GDP, although this was not the pattern everywhere. Spain is another exception, like the USA, where unemployment rose and employment fell much more than one would expect (OECD 2010a: figure 1.10) with the employment rate for working age people falling by another 1.2 percentage points between 2009 and 2010 and an unemployment rate in 2010 of 20%. These differences from past recessions in the extent of change in employment (resulting in loss of earnings) and unemployment (leading possibly to unemployment benefit) mean that the distributional impact associated with a given change in GDP may differ from that suggested from the evidence reviewed in Chapter 1.

Employment changes varied a great deal by sex and by age: see Figures 2.10(a) and 2.10(b) which show changes between 2007 and 2009 in employment rates. In all 21 countries, employment rates fell more for men than for women. In ten countries, employment rates for women actually rose over this period. A small rise in participation rates for women for the OECD as a whole was one contributory factor, which could reflect an added-worker effect from the male employment losses (OECD 2011c: 25). The changes for men in Ireland and Spain are striking: a ten percentage point decrease in employment rates, with the next largest change being for the USA with a decrease of nearly six percentage points.

Figure 2.10. Change in employment rates (percentage points), 2007–9, by (a) sex and (b) age

Source: OECD, 'Labour Market Statistics: Labour force statistics by sex and age: indicators', 2010, OECD Employment and Labour Market Statistics (database), http://dx.doi.org/10.1787/data-00310-en [accessed 23 February 2011].

Figure 2.11 gives the quarterly changes in the employment totals for each sex for 2007–11 for our case study countries and their comparison again underlines starkly the differences in the impact of the GR for men and women.

Employment fell between 2007 and 2009 by much more for people aged 15–24 than for people of older ages, and this occurred almost everywhere: see Figure 2.10(b). Those persons both young and male experienced massive falls in employment rates in Ireland and in Spain: by 24 and 20 percentage points respectively between 2007 and 2010 (OECD 2011c: 246–7). Notably, employment rates for persons aged 55+ rose slightly over 2007–9 in more than half of the 21 countries.

The OECD has noted that the concentration during the GR of employment loss on men was unusual compared to earlier recessions and 'probably reflects the sectoral composition of the negative shock to aggregate demand' (OECD 2010a: 21–2), especially the impact of the trade shock on manufacturing and of the bursting of housing price bubbles on construction. The greater impact on the young has followed the pattern of earlier recessions while increases in employment rates among older people is a new pattern, which the OECD suggests may reflect a labour supply response to losses in retirement savings and/or lower availability of early retirement options compared to previous

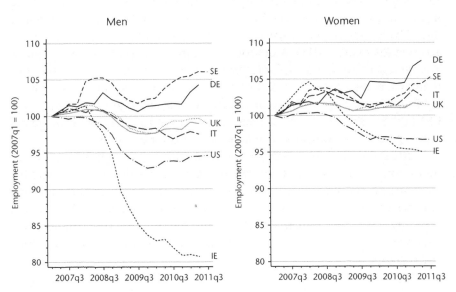

Figure 2.11. Employment levels for men and women, 2007–10, six countries and all-OECD (2007q1 = 100)

Source: As for Figure 2.9.

Notes: The series refer to Germany ('DE'), Ireland ('IE'), Italy ('IT'), Sweden ('SE'), the United Kingdom ('UK'), the United States ('US'), and all OECD countries (the unlabelled solid grey line).

recessions. Attention has also been drawn to the greater impact on the less skilled (OECD 2010*a*: figure 1.3).

2.4.2 *Change in Hours Worked*

Changes in hours worked were another form of reaction to change in aggregate demand during the GR; and fewer hours worked for the same hourly pay means that labour income falls. In countries where reductions in total labour input during the GR took place more through reductions in hours worked than through lay-offs or reductions in hiring, we might expect a more muted impact on the distribution of household incomes. With 'very few exceptions' (OECD 2010*a*: 35), there was a reduction in both employment and in hours during the GR. The exceptions among our 21 countries are Spain (average hours slightly up) and Germany (employment up: see Table 2.2). The precise combination across the peak-to-trough changes in GDP varies substantially across countries, with the role played by lower hours ranging from 'under 20 per cent in Denmark, Portugal and Spain to over 95 per cent in...Norway, Australia [and] Germany' (OECD 2010*a*: 35–6).

As well as reductions in overtime working, a shift from full-time to part-time work is one way that average hours of work may adjust. The part-time share of total employment rose in all 21 countries between 2007 and 2009 for men and in 13 countries for women and by an average of 0.5 and 0.8 percentage points respectively (OECD Employment and Labour Market Statistics database, accessed 29 March 2011). Much of this change was probably involuntary. The typical pattern was therefore for full-time employment to fall by more than total employment. Two of the largest rises in the part-time share between 2007 and 2009 were for the countries where total employment fell most: the USA (a rise in share of 1.6 percentage points for both sexes) and Ireland (a rise of two percentage points for men and 3.4 points for women).

Another way in which average hours may fall is through an increase in short-term working schemes, which have been more widely used in a number of countries. The share of all employees participating in short-term working schemes rose over 2007–9 by more than two percentage points in Belgium, Germany, Italy, and Japan (OECD 2010*a*: figure 1.19). For a more wide-ranging discussion of short-time working schemes during the GR, see Boeri and Bruecker (2011).

2.4.3 *Changes in Employment Among Households*

Up to this point we have considered changes in the distribution of work across individuals rather than across households, but it is household incomes with which we are concerned in this book. If you lose your job or are unable to find a new one, the effect on your household income is cushioned if you live with other persons who have work. On the other hand, if everyone in the household loses their job, then total household income falls more substantially, and the probability of this occurring is increased if people with similarly high risks of non-employment live together. Thus, for example, the very large fall in employment rates among Spanish and Irish young people may have had rather different impacts in the two countries, since adult children are more likely to live with their parents in Spain than in Ireland. (See Iacovou 2010 for information for EU countries about the prevalence of young people co-residing with their parents.)

A key issue, then, is what has been happening to the proportion of households without work. Prior to the GR, employment in some OECD countries was becoming more unevenly distributed across households with members of working age; and the prevalence of household worklessness is more highly correlated across countries with (working age) poverty rates than are individual employment rates (see e.g. Gregg and Wadsworth 1998; OECD 2001; Gregg, Scutella, and Wadsworth 2010).

We can examine household worklessness for all but one of our EU countries (Sweden). Panel (a) of Figure 2.12 shows for 2007 and 2009 the percentage of 18–59 year olds living in households in which nobody worked (when interviewed by the survey). The rates vary substantially across countries, reflecting differences in the strength of national labour markets and the propensity for young people to remain in the parental home (greater in countries such as Greece, Italy, and Spain). In general, the changes in the rates between 2007 and 2009 were modest, which is consistent with the relatively modest changes in individual employment rates in many countries over the same period shown in Table 2.2. In four countries there were small falls in the workless household rate and in only two countries are there increases of more than 1.5 percentage points. The exceptions are Spain and Ireland where there were large rises of 4.6 percentage points and five percentage points respectively.

Changes in workless household rates are plotted against changes in individual employment rates in panel (b) of Figure 2.12. (The figures are based on the same source, Labour Force Surveys, but there are slight differences in the age ranges covered.) The increase in the percentage of people aged 18–59 in workless households in Spain and Ireland was less than the increase in each country's individual non-employment rate, but only by about 1.5 percentage points in both cases. That is, the large falls in individual employment were also accompanied by significant rises in household worklessness in these two countries. The extent to which co-residence can play an income insurance role was limited when the GR increased job loss among older workers (parents) as well as younger workers (currently or potentially co-resident children) and among women as well as men. Labour income losses in the bottom half of the

(a) Percentage of 18–59 year olds in workless households, 2007 and 2009

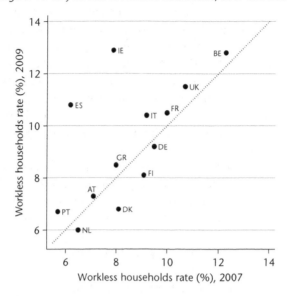

(b) Change in percentage of 18–59 year olds in workless households compared with the change in percentage of individuals non-employed (percentage point changes)

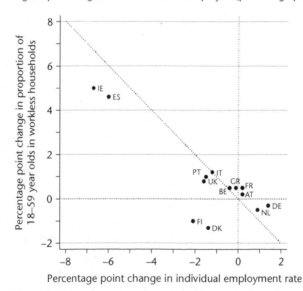

Figure 2.12. Workless household rates in EU countries: (a) Percentage of 18–59 year olds in workless households, 2007 and 2009; (b) Change in percentage of 18–59 year olds in workless households compared with the change in percentage of individuals non-employed (percentage point changes)

Sources: Graph (a) is derived from Eurostat Database 'Population in jobless households' annual data [lfsi_jhh_a], (accessed 24 February 2011). Graph (b) is constructed from numbers in graph (a) and in Table 2.2.

income distribution were therefore likely in Spain and Ireland. These two countries may be contrasted with Denmark and Finland for which there were also relatively large increases in the individual non-employment rate between 2007 and 2009 but the workless household rate fell. Children leave the parental home at younger ages in the Nordic countries than in southern Mediterranean countries; the changes shown in Figure 2.12 for Denmark and Finland may represent a return to the parental home by young people, that is the household composition itself may be adjusting in response to the GR. If so, this is likely to mute the impact of greater individual unemployment on household incomes in these countries.

There is some evidence that the rate of household worklessness also rose in the USA, the country with the third largest fall in the employment rate between 2007 and 2009 (see Table 2.2). We draw on US Bureau of Labor Statistics estimates of the proportion of families with no one in work. (The data refer to families of all ages rather than just to those of working age and the US definition of a 'family' is somewhat narrower than the Eurostat definition of a household as it excludes unrelated individuals.) The fraction of all US families with nobody in work rose from 17.4% in 2007 to 19.6% in 2009, and to 20% in 2010 (Bureau of Labor Statistics 2011a). The rise of 2.2 percentage points between 2007 and 2009 for families of all ages compares with the fall in the individual employment rate among people of working age of 4.2 percentage points (Table 2.2). Among the one in eight families containing an unemployed person in 2010, one third had no employed member.

There is also some evidence for the USA that household formation has been changing as a result of financial pressures, as we have speculated might be the case in Denmark and Finland, with people moving into the same household as their relatives or friends or delaying forming their own household—referred to as 'doubling-up' in the USA. It has been estimated that between 2008 and 2010, the number of multifamily households rose by 11.4% and the number of 25–34 year olds living with their parents rose by 8.4% (US Census Bureau 2010; the size of the bases from which these increases occurred is unclear). The impact of the GR on household formation in the US is analysed in detail by Painter (2010), including what might be expected from the experience of previous recessions. (Doubling-up in the Great Depression was noted by Mendershausen 1946. See also Dyrda, Kaplan, and Rios-Rull 2012 for analysis of US recessions since 1979.) Painter finds sharp increases in over-crowding in households in metropolitan areas between 2005 and 2008, arguing that this shows a substantial amount of doubling-up. See also the case study of the USA in Chapter 8, which includes analysis of changes in average household size across the income distribution.

Doubling-up helps offset the impact of the GR on the distribution of household income but, again, the size of the effect is unclear. Also, the effect on household incomes must be distinguished from the effects on the distribution of a broader concept of well-being that takes into account the changes in household formation that are forced by economic need. A young Finn or young American who used to live alone or with friends may not be happy to return to the parental home.

2.5 Changes in the Sources of Income

The discussion in the previous section referred to changes in whether or not labour market income was being received by households. We now turn to consider changes in labour earnings among recipients. We follow this with consideration of other sources of household income where we have much less information.

2.5.1 Earnings from Employment

The information about average earnings that is most widely available comes from national accounts data and refers to average gross annual earnings per full-time equivalent employee. The adjustment for the number of full-time workers contrasts with our earlier analysis based on the same source of the changes in total 'compensation of employees', shown in Table 2.1. Now we are adjusting for the employment changes, including the full-time share of the total, that we discussed in Section 2.4.

Figure 2.13 compares the changes for 21 countries in this measure of (real) average earnings between 2007 and 2009 with changes over the same period in the employment rate shown earlier in Table 2.2. (There is a small non-comparability in the data: average earnings are adjusted for part-time working but employment rates are not.) In general, average earnings rose—there were small falls only in the USA and the UK, and in Australia in the context of a growing economy (see Figure 2.1). This is likely to have had a dis-equalizing impact on the distribution of household incomes. In terms of the inequality decomposition frameworks discussed in Chapter 1, the rise in average earnings is a clear example of an increase in between-group inequality where the groups are 'earners' and 'non-earners' (assuming no change in average incomes of non-earners).

The rise in average earnings probably reflects a 'selection' effect, with lower-paid workers being more likely to be laid off so that the average among those still in work is higher. That is, it 'may reflect composition effects, with the average... tending to rise in countries where large numbers of youth, low-paid and temporary workers have been laid off' (OECD 2010a: 43). This explanation may be particularly relevant for Ireland and Spain, outlier countries with

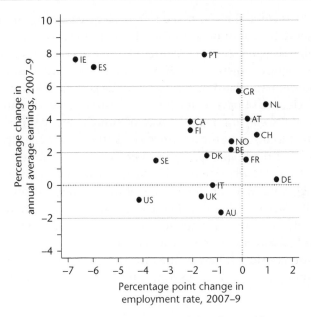

Figure 2.13. Changes in annual average earnings (%) and in employment rates (percentage points), 2007–9

Source: OECD, 2010, OECD Stat Database accessed on 29 March 2011. http://stats.oecd.org/index. php? >labour>earnings (the original source for these data is the National Accounts database: see note to Table 2.1). OECD, 2010, 'Labour Market Statistics: Labour force statistics by sex and age: indicators', OECD Employment and Labour Market Statistics (database), http://dx.doi.org/ 10.1787/data-00310-en [accessed 23 February 2011].

Notes: The change in employment rates is as for Table 2.2. Average earnings are obtained by dividing the total wage bill ('wages and salaries', in the terminology of national accounts) by the average number of employees in the total economy, also multiplying by the ratio of average usual weekly hours worked for full-time dependent employee in their main job to average usual weekly hours worked for all dependent employee in their main job. The resulting estimates correspond to average annual wages per full-time equivalent dependent employee. The method of calculation produces figures that correspond to those for 2008 in OECD (2010a: appendix table J).

an increase in average earnings of between 7% and 8%. However, there is no simple relationship between the changes in average earnings and the changes in employment.

Using the same source, national accounts, Figure 2.14 sets these changes in average earnings over 2007–9 in the context of trends earlier in the decade and extends the analysis to 2010, a year when growth in output had returned in most countries. In a substantial number of countries there was strong real earnings growth in 2000–7, consistent with the widespread economic growth during this period although there are quite a few exceptions. Ireland is a clear example. Among the other 'Anglo' countries, the changes in average earnings during the GR in Canada were more or less in line with the earlier trends, while in the UK, the USA (where growth earlier in the decade had been weak), and in Australia, 2007–9 appears to have marked a change. Only the UK shows any fall in 2010 while the continued rise in average earnings in Ireland may have represented a continuation of a selection effect as employment continued to fall (see Figure 2.9). The Western European countries typically registered less earnings growth over 2000–7 than the Anglo countries, with Belgium and Germany flat-lining in much of the period. The Nordic countries show little evidence of having undergone a change in trend from substantial growth during the GR, although the pace of growth clearly slowed in Sweden and continued to do so in the aftermath in 2010. Greece is a clear outlier in terms of earlier growth among the Southern European countries. The sharp rise over 2007–9 that we have noted in Spain was notably against trend and there is a suggestion that the same is true of the changes in Portugal in 2009. Earnings fell sharply in 2010 in Greece at a time when, as we noted earlier, output also fell. There were also small falls in earnings in Portugal and Spain in 2010, in marked contrast to the changes in 2007–9.

We can also consider trends in the distribution of earnings as well as the average, although we can go beyond 2008 only for a small number of

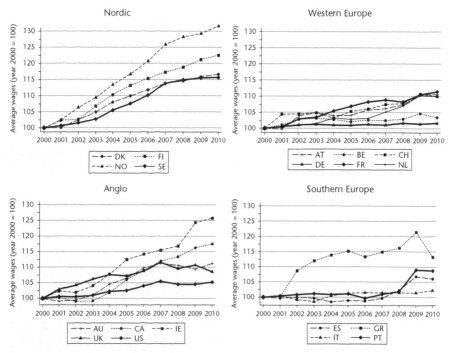

Figure 2.14. Average annual wages per full-time and full-year equivalent employee in the total economy, constant 2009 prices, series normalized to 2000 = 100

Source: http://stats.oecd.org/Index.aspx 'Average annual wages', series CNPMCU [accessed 19 December 2011].

countries and then once again only to 2009: see Figure 2.15. The data all refer to gross earnings for full-time employees but are drawn from a variety of sources and relate to various time periods. (See the notes to the figure; we exclude Japan as the coverage of the data is not comparable.) The source we use provides only ratios so we are unable to show changes in the real values of any quantile. Panel (a) shows the overall inequality of earnings as measured by the ratio of the 90th percentile to the 10th percentile. More detail is shown in panels (b) and (c): changes in top-half inequality (the ratio of the 90th percentile to the 50th percentile) and in bottom-half inequality (the ratio of the 50th percentile to the 10th percentile). The same vertical scale is used for each group of countries, which brings out the differences in earnings inequality across the 20 countries at the onset of the GR—highest in the USA followed by Portugal, higher on average in other Anglo countries and in Southern Europe (except Italy) than in Western Europe, lowest in the Nordic countries. The pre-GR trends differ somewhat between each group. Overall earnings inequality tended to increase among the Anglo countries and the Nordic ones (with the exception of Sweden), display little overall change in Western Europe (with

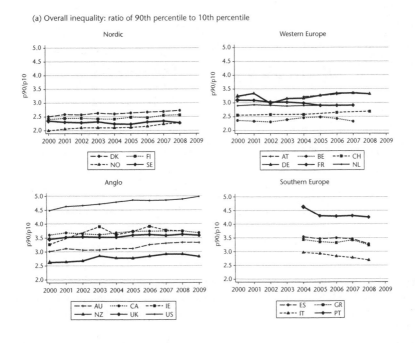

(a) Overall inequality: ratio of 90th percentile to 10th percentile

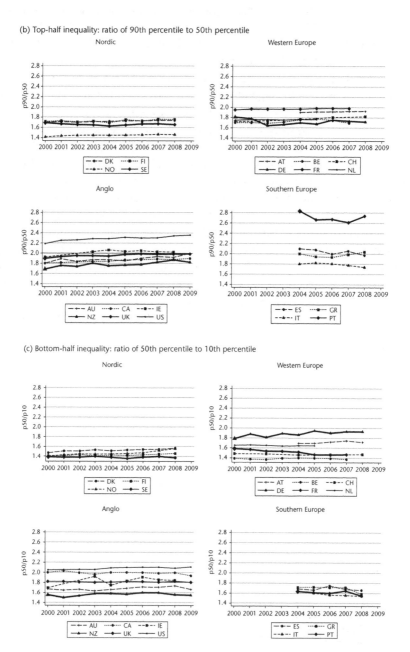

Figure 2.15. Inequality of gross earnings of full-time employees, 2000–9: (a) Overall inequality: ratio of 90th percentile to 10th percentile, (b) Top-half inequality: ratio of 90th percentile to 50th percentile, (c) Bottom-half inequality: ratio of 50th percentile to 10th percentile

Source: http://stats.oecd.org/Index.aspx 'decile ratios of gross earnings' [accessed 30 May 2011].

Notes: Data are derived from household surveys, employer surveys, and administrative registers, and refer variously to gross hourly, gross monthly, and gross annual earnings. The data for France exclude agricultural workers and central government employees.

the exception of a slight rise in Switzerland), and fall or remain unchanged in Southern Europe (where the data do not extend back beyond 2004).

We focus first on the Anglo countries since the data here extend to 2009, with the exception of Ireland. The patterns differ over the 2007–9 period with panel (a) showing a continuing increase in overall earnings inequality in the USA, no change in Australia, and a slight fall in Canada, New Zealand, and the UK. (In the USA, the distribution continued to widen in both the top and bottom half: the ratios of the 90th to 50th percentiles and the 50th to 10th percentiles, shown in panels (b) and (c), were both at their highest values for a decade by 2009.) The experience of the Anglo countries is therefore mixed, but the most striking feature of the graphs is that in no country do we see a sharp change during the GR in overall inequality or in either half of the distribution by comparison with the trends over earlier years of the decade. The data for other countries extend only to 2008, so we can comment just on changes in the first year of the GR. Again, in no country do we see a clear break with earlier trends or changes that are large by the standards of earlier years. We might have expected to see more change given the compositional effects that we surmised earlier to have impacted on average earnings (although note that Figure 2.14 shows that 2009 was the year of the sharp change in average earnings in several countries).

The main messages emerging from this analysis of the earnings of employees, the largest source of household income, are as follows: in general (i) real average earnings (as measured in national accounts) did not fall during the main period of the GR (2008–9) and often rose, and (ii) the immediate onset of the GR was accompanied by little apparent change in the distribution of earnings (as measured in other sources). The case studies in Chapters 3–8 look in more detail at changes in average earnings and in their distribution in individual countries and in some cases are able to analyse the changes to 2010, as well as in the period to 2008–9 that we have considered here.

2.5.2 Income from Capital

The national accounts data discussed earlier in this chapter show the changes in total (average) capital income for the household sector between 2007 and 2009. We do not have information for a range of countries about changes in the distribution of income from capital but, for some countries, we are able to use household survey data to show which income groups received most or least capital income at the start of the GR. We might then be able to predict the direction of the distributional impact of changes in this source of income—the working hypothesis is that the probability of receipt of capital income is unlikely to change much (by contrast with labour income); what will have changed most is the amount received. This analysis extends the baseline description of Section 2.3 by focusing on income from capital (the income sources are more narrowly defined here).

How the probability of capital income receipt varies by income group in 2007 is summarized in Table 2.3 for 12 EU countries plus Norway. Income refers to the total equivalized household net income and the data come from EU-SILC (as described in Section 2.3). We distinguish between rental income from property (imputed income for owner occupiers is not included) in panel (a) and income from interest and dividends in panel (b). The results need to be treated with caution: as mentioned earlier, there may be under-coverage of this type of income in the EU-SILC surveys. (For additional information about selected OECD countries in the mid-2000s, see OECD 2011f, Chapter 6.)

The concentration of capital income at the top of the income distribution is clear. The final columns of Table 2.3(a) and 2.3(b) shows the share of total capital income going to the richest tenth of households and is the basis by which countries are ranked. For rental income the share ranges between 28% (Denmark) and 66% (Austria); for interest and dividend income, the share ranges between 30% (Italy) and 70% in Greece and Finland, with Denmark a clear outlier at 103%. (The explanation for this is not entirely clear to us; Denmark's outlier position was remarked on in Section 2.3.) Thus, although there is quite a lot of variation across countries, the median value of the richest tenth's share is relatively large. In contrast, households in the bottom half of the income distribution receive less than 20% of the total income, for both capital income types, in all but two countries.

We do not have detailed information about changes in rental income during the GR. The 'net property incomes' in the national accounts data

Table 2.3. Share (%) of total household income from rent and from interest and dividends received by decile groups of household income, European countries, 2007: (a) income from rent, (b) income from interest and dividend

(a) income from rent

Row %	Decile group		
	1–5	6–9	10
Denmark	28	45	28
Sweden	21	47	32
Norway	16	45	39
Greece	12	48	39
Portugal	9	46	45
Spain	14	38	48
Italy	13	39	48
Belgium	17	34	49
Germany	15	36	49
UK	9	40	51
Ireland	15	32	53
Finland	11	33	56
Austria	7	26	66

(b) income from interest and dividends

Row %	Decile group		
	1–5	6–9	10
Italy	23	46	30
Germany	24	44	32
UK	19	41	40
Austria	17	42	41
Belgium	19	37	44
Portugal	16	36	48
Spain	14	37	49
Ireland	9	37	54
Sweden	17	29	54
Norway	15	25	60
Greece	3	27	70
Finland	7	22	70
Denmark	–5	2	103

Source: EU–SILC 2008, cross-sectional database. Version 2, 1 August 2010. Data for the Netherlands and France were not available at time of writing.

Notes: The distributions refer to total equivalized net household income among households (SILC variable hx090) for calendar year 2007 except for Ireland and the UK. Income is equivalized by the modified OECD equivalence scale for consistency with the Eurostat statistics summarized in Section 2. The income from rent was computed from variable hy040g; the income from interests and dividends was computed from variable hy090g. Decile group 1 is the poorest; decile group 10 is the richest. Due to rounding, row percentages do not always sum to 100%.

analysed in Section 2.2 include interest from bank accounts and from government bonds as well as rental income. We found that the total of this form of capital income had often risen between 2007 and 2009, although we noted exceptions such as Ireland and Italy (Table 2.1). In contrast, our analysis also showed that distributed income from firms (dividends) received by the household sector typically fell over 2007–9, often by large percentages. We know too that interest rates fell substantially in all countries (other than in Japan where rates were low already): for example short-rate interest rates in the Eurozone fell from 4.3% in 2007 to 1.2% in 2009 and in the USA from 5.3% to 0.9% (OECD 2010c: annex table 34). Therefore households with significant income from dividends and bank interest will usually have seen substantial falls in income received from these sources during the main period of the GR. So applying our working hypothesis in conjunction with the knowledge of the pro-rich distribution of incomes from interest and dividends, we expect these changes to have had an equalizing impact in many countries. Conclusions about the likely impact of changes to rental incomes are less obvious.

2.5.3 Social Benefits and Taxes

As for income from capital, national accounts data show the change in the support received by households from social benefits and the direct tax system and we have shown the importance of this support for total household income during the GR in Section 2.2. The OECD Social Expenditure Database (SOCX) provides a related source of information on this income source for each OECD country. SOCX captures total expenditures on a range of different areas of social policy including retirement, ill-health and disability, the family, unemployment, and housing. The main database at the time of writing extends only to 2007 but Adema, Fron, and Ladaique (2011) provide a partial update covering the period of the GR. As far as total spending on social benefits is concerned, which includes spending on health (in contrast to our earlier analysis of national accounts data), the rises in 2007–9, expressed as a percentage of GDP, represented very sharp increases in relation to the trends in earlier years in many of our 21 countries (Adema, Fron, and Ladaique 2011: chart I.1). For the OECD as a whole, the figure ranged by only 1.1 percentage points during the 16 years 1992–2007, from 19.0% to 21.1%, but jumped by 3.2 percentage points to 22.5% in 2009 (table A.I.1.3). The falls in GDP as well as the rises in social expenditure drove this abrupt change but the latter were more important.

The extent of support given to households during the GR was clearly large, but was it exceptional given the size of the drop in output? The conclusion in OECD (2011c) is that spending on benefits in most countries rose less strongly in response to the decline in output than it had in past recessions. This is explained by the relatively modest increases in unemployment, given the output falls (see Section 2.4), since unemployment is the principal driver of increased benefit expenditure in an economic downturn. And in general the increases in benefit expenditure were in line with the extent of the changes in unemployment, based on past patterns (OECD 2011c: 43). Countries with an exceptionally large rise in unemployment typically had the largest increases in benefit expenditure, notably the USA (as reflected in our earlier analysis of national accounts in Table 2.1).

Although unemployment is an important driver, not all spells of unemployment generate receipt of unemployment benefits. Lack of work is only one of several criteria for receipt. For example, long periods out of work may result in exhaustion of limited-duration unemployment insurance benefit. Figure 2.16 shows estimates of the change in the numbers of recipients of unemployment benefit of all kinds (including both contributory limited-duration insurance benefit and means-tested assistance benefit) during the first and second years of the GR as a percentage of the change in the number of unemployed persons in the year in question. Double-counting of insurance and assistance benefit recipients—in some countries a person could receive both within a year—may explain why some figures exceed 100%. Even allowing for any double-counting, the figures for most countries are well below this level in both years. (It is unclear why the figures for Sweden are quite so low.) There are some marked contrasts in the figures between the countries where unemployment rose most in the GR:

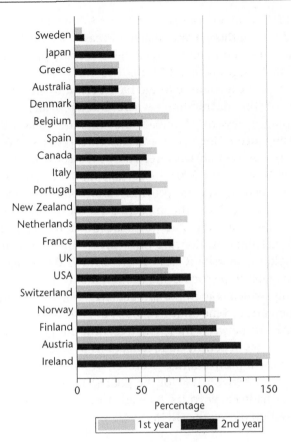

Figure 2.16. Change in number of unemployment benefit recipients as a percentage of the change in the number of unemployed persons by years since onset of GR

Source: OECD (2011c: figure 1.17, panel B).

Notes: Unemployment benefit includes extended-duration benefits and unemployment assistance. Both changes are measured relative to pre-crisis levels.

Spain, USA, and Ireland. In countries where the information is available, the figures are typically lower for young people aged less than 25 than for older age groups (OECD 2011c: 51).

What were the distributional consequences of the changes in benefit expenditure? In our analysis of capital income we established the incidence of that income source in 2007, and then adopted the working hypothesis that the probability of its receipt did not change thereafter. The analogous assumption for the incidence of benefit income during the GR would clearly be untenable, with the sharp rises in unemployment being the main reason. (For other types of benefit receipt, such as retirement pensions, there would be less of a problem.) As Marchal, Marx, and Van Mechelen show, for the working-age population in Europe, 'relative increases in social assistance

71

caseloads did follow to a large extent changes in unemployment in the first crisis years' (2011: 5), though also '[l]arge increases occurred mainly in those countries where the minimum income scheme already played a larger role in the welfare state to begin with' (2011: 5).

The rise in benefit expenditure would have been most concentrated on the bottom half of the distribution—where unemployment will have hit hardest—helping to lessen the impact that the GR would otherwise have had in increasing income inequality and (absolute) poverty. (We have already commented on the cash transfers received by the richest and poorest fifths of the income distribution in 2007 in Section 2.3.) In countries where the unemployment benefit system provided less complete coverage of the unemployed (see Figure 2.16), the impact of the GR can be expected to have been greater. In the case of the USA, we can be firmer in our conclusions about the distributional impacts, drawing on analysis undertaken by the OECD using household survey data (OECD 2011c: figure 1.22). It should be noted that the results refer to persons living in households headed by working-age individuals only, which is an important qualification. The research compared the total incomes of income quintile groups in 2007 and 2009. The share of market income lost between these two years by the poorest fifth that was replaced by increases in benefits (and reductions in taxes) was 89%, falling to about 60% for the top three fifths. However, average real incomes fell in all quintile groups (by between 1% for the poorest fifth and nearly 4% for the middle fifth). Chapter 8 provides a detailed case study of changes in the income distribution during the GR in the USA.

2.5.4 *Inflation, Real Income Levels, and Benefit Uprating*

Changes in the real income levels of households arise through changes in nominal incomes or changes in price levels. We have alluded to this issue at several points in the book, particularly in the context of trends in absolute poverty rates—those calculated using a low-income cut-off held fixed in purchasing power terms—but the point is a more general one.

One of the reasons why real incomes did not fall during the period of the GR is because, in most of the countries that we are considering, inflation rates were falling. This is shown in Table 2.4. For almost all of the 21 OECD countries, the consumer price index rose by more than 3% between 2007 and 2008; the rise was 3.3% for Euro area countries, 3.6% for the UK, and 3.8% for the USA. However, the change between 2008 and 2009 was only 0.3% for Euro area countries, 2.2% in the UK, and –0.3% in the USA. Prices rose again between 2009 and 2010, but not at the rate they had risen by two years earlier.

For certain groups in the population, changes in inflation also lead to changes in nominal incomes. This may describe the case of employees with automatically-

Table 2.4. Change in consumer prices from previous year (%), 2008–10, by country

Country	2008	2009	2010
Australia	4.3	1.8	2.9
Austria	3.2	0.4	1.7
Belgium	4.5	0.0	2.3
Canada	2.4	0.3	1.8
Denmark	3.4	1.3	2.3
Finland	3.9	1.6	1.7
France	3.2	0.1	1.7
Germany	2.8	0.2	1.2
Greece	4.2	1.3	4.7
Ireland	3.1	−1.7	−1.6
Italy	3.5	0.8	1.6
Japan	1.4	−1.3	−0.7
Netherlands	2.2	1.0	0.9
New Zealand	4.0	2.1	2.3
Norway	3.8	2.2	2.4
Portugal	2.7	−0.9	1.4
Spain	4.1	−0.2	2.0
Sweden	3.4	−0.5	1.2
Switzerland	2.4	−0.5	0.7
United Kingdom	3.6	2.2	3.3
United States	3.8	−0.3	1.6
Euro area	3.3	0.3	1.6

Source: OECD (2011*b*: annex table 18).

Notes: Table entries show the percentage change from the previous year in the relevant national consumer price index, i.e. the harmonized index of consumer prices (HICP) for Euro area countries, Euro area, and the UK (where the index is known as the 'CPI'). The Swedish consumer price index includes mortgage interest costs.

indexed pay awards, but this form of labour contract is relatively rare. More important in times of recession is the way in which countries change ('uprate') cash benefit payments to take account of inflation. (How income tax schedules are indexed is also important, but we focus on benefits here.) In many countries, there are no automatic benefit uprating formulae; by contrast, the UK uses formulae that uprate most means-tested benefits automatically each year by an amount that depends on the increase in consumer prices in the previous year.

Marchal, Marx, and Van Mechelen (2011), discussing EU countries, find that 'during the years prior to the crisis, gross benefits generally maintained their purchasing power. In more than a few countries, benefit levels even increased (somewhat) more than consumer prices. Nevertheless, there are some important exceptions, mainly in those countries where no automatic indexation procedure exists' (2011: 8). (The exceptions largely concern new member states.) However, the authors also make the point that having a discretionary uprating process does not necessarily lead to erosion in the real value of benefits. Inter alia, they cite the case of Ireland, which is discussed in more detail in Chapter 4. Marchal, Marx, and Van Mechelen also find that '[i]mmediately after the onset of the crisis, real benefits generally increased. . . . The deceleration in nominal growth [of social assistance benefit levels] seen for 2009–2010 . . . has led in some countries to a small loss in purchasing power. However, this decrease seems very much in line with trends in real benefits in pre-crisis years' (2011: 8). The case of the UK is discussed in detail in Chapter 7. It points to not only the cushioning impact on real incomes of automatic but lagged uprating in times of falling inflation, but also the downward pressures on real benefit levels in times of rising inflation rates (post-2010).

2.6 Changes in Household Incomes in 21 Countries: The Short Term

This section considers the short-term distributional impacts of the GR, focusing on the years of the main economic downturn, 2007–9, but straying on occasion into 2010 as well. The section is in two parts. We begin by reviewing the 'predictions' that arise from the analysis of the chapter to this point. We then analyse what actually happened in 16 countries using the available published statistics on average incomes, inequality of incomes, and poverty. This complements the detailed analysis of household survey microdata in the country case studies in the chapters that follow. Note that the household survey data which we draw on here are typically not the same as those used in the country case studies (Ireland and the USA are exceptions) and this may account for any differences in the results obtained.

2.6.1 *The Implications of What We Have Seen*

First, there will have been considerable heterogeneity in distributional changes across countries, if only because the magnitude and other features of the GR have varied across countries—whether the economic downturn is seen in terms of falls in GDP or reductions in employment. The worst hit countries over 2007–9 of the ones we have considered were Ireland and Spain, with the USA also according to employment decline. Greece has more recently joined the list. The Nordic countries (other than Norway) have also experienced some relatively large changes, for example in household sector income composition and, in some cases, employment rate changes.

Second, marked declines in incomes at the bottom of the income distribution relative to historical trend are unlikely (nor, correspondingly, will sharp increases in absolute poverty rates have emerged). This is because in general total household sector income did not fall between 2007 and 2009, largely due to state support (redistribution from the government sector). This support is concentrated on households in the bottom half of the income distribution, partly by design and partly since the incidence of unemployment is greatest there.

Third, there was a rise in average labour earnings among workers during the GR. This increases the income gap between working and non-working households, which is a factor likely to increase household income inequality, other things being equal. Earnings inequality did not change markedly over the initial GR period relative to trend (nor further into the GR in the few countries where we have data for 2009), which suggests that the GR effect per se will be relatively small.

Fourth, the share of capital income in GHDI, especially distributed income from corporations, generally declined. Since capital income receipt is concentrated among richer households, this will have an equalizing impact on the household income distribution.

In sum, we predict there to have been relatively modest changes in the distribution of household income. Poverty rates may have risen, reflecting falls in real income at the bottom of the distribution that are not fully cushioned by government support. Decreases in median income with the GR will also have reduced how much relative poverty rates may have increased. The change in overall income inequality will have depended on the net effect of offsetting factors such as reduced dispersion in the top half of the distribution (reflecting capital income changes) and increased dispersion in the bottom half (driven by the employment changes). This combination of factors is much the same as described by Mendershausen (1946) in 33 US cities during the Great Depression (see Chapter 1), but of much smaller magnitude, reflecting the smaller size of the GR and also changes in social protection since the 1930s.

The six countries that we study in further detail in the case studies appear to have been hit by the GR to a greater extent than other countries we have considered. A clear exception is Germany, where there was relatively little change. Hence, we expect distributional change in Germany to be muted relative to the other five countries. Ireland is the country among our six for which the macroeconomic downturn was the greatest, and so we might expect the distributional impacts to have been the greatest there. The country case study in Chapter 4 examines the veracity of this expectation in detail.

2.6.2 Changes in Distributions of Household Income, 2005–9

We are able to summarize the distribution of household income in terms of median incomes, income inequality, and both absolute and relative poverty in 15 of our 21 countries—14 EU members plus Norway—using harmonized statistics provided by Eurostat and derived from the EU-SILC data that we used in Section 2.3. At the time of writing, the statistics on the Eurostat website cover 2005–9, extending to 2010 for the single case of the UK. We are thus able to analyse incomes in the main period of the GR, 2007–9, against the background of the immediately preceding years. When we consider inequality and absolute poverty we also draw on published statistics for the USA that extend to 2010, although in this case the definition of poverty and of household incomes is not the same as for the European countries. As before, income is equivalized (this time by the modified-OECD scale) and refers to the calendar year (with the exceptions for Ireland and the UK noted earlier). Table 2.5 provides a summary for the 15 European countries of the changes over 2007–9 for all of the measures and also includes a disaggregation by age, sex, and in one case employment status.

We begin by showing changes in real median incomes in Figure 2.17. Comparing 2009 with 2007, the broad message is similar to that obtained earlier in the chapter in our analysis of total household incomes in the national accounts (Figure 2.4). In general, median incomes rose across the main period of the GR or displayed little change (e.g. Ireland and Italy). Only in the UK was there a clear fall comparing these two years (there was also a slight drop in Spain), although even here if 2006 is taken as the base year there is little change. The fall in median income over 2007–9 implied by the EU-SILC data for the UK is at odds with both the rise shown in national accounts data and, perhaps more importantly (given the different income concept in the national accounts), the survey used in the UK for official estimates of the distribution of household income, which also shows a rise (see Chapter 7: figure 7.3).

In many cases, increases in the median after 2007 followed earlier increases since 2005. The graph also shows that the changes over 2008–9 often were rather different from those right at the start of the GR over 2007–8. The Nordic countries provide a clear demonstration of this—in all four countries median income changed very little over the later period as the GR deepened after initial rises. The same is true in France, the Netherlands, Belgium (where the median in fact fell in 2009), and Greece. The falls over 2007–9 for both the UK and Spain were due to the reductions over 2008–9. Compared to 2008, 2009 seems often to have been a notably different year for median incomes.

Figure 2.18 disaggregates income levels by age, showing the median household income for elderly people (persons aged 60+) as a percentage of the median for individuals aged less than 60. Elderly people tend to have lower median incomes than younger people in all the countries considered, which is not surprising (France is an exception for 2007–9), but the most common pattern is for their relative position to have improved during the GR, in some cases continuing a trend over 2005–7. Older persons have been less exposed to the impact of unemployment on incomes. There are also differences by sex. In

Table 2.5. Changes in real income, poverty rates, and inequality, 15 European countries, 2007–9

Statistic and subgroup	Country														
	AT	BE	DK	FI	FR	DE	GR	IE	IT	NL	NO	PT	ES	SE	UK
Real median equivalent net household income (percentage change)															
All persons	6.2	5.8	2.8	4.4	3.7	1.3	4.8	0.3	-0.5	2.0	5.9	6.1	-1.2	5.9	-5.4
Female aged 18+	6.2	6.2	2.9	5.3	3.2	1.6	3.4	1.1	0.3	2.3	7.6	6.5	-0.2	4.5	-5.3
Male aged 18+	4.4	6.0	2.6	3.2	4.0	0.9	4.5	-0.2	0.6	2.0	6.2	5.8	-2.5	5.4	-5.4
Absolute poverty rate (percentage point change)															
All persons	-1.8	-2.6	0.4	-2.4	n.a.	-0.1	-2.6	-2.1	-0.3	-0.8	-1.9	-2.9	2.0	-0.9	0.7
Aged 0–17 years	-2.2	-1.9	0.2	-2.8	n.a.	1.8	-2.8	-2.0	0.4	-0.4	0.7	-3.2	3.1	-1.1	0.1
Aged 18–64 years	-1.4	-1.9	0.9	-1.1	n.a.	-0.2	-2.0	-1.6	0.9	-0.4	-2.0	-2.3	2.8	-0.3	1.2
Aged 65+ years	-2.9	-5.7	-1.7	-7.0	n.a.	-1.1	-4.4	-5.1	-4.1	-3.3	-5.3	-5.5	-2.9	-2.5	-0.7
Female	-1.8	-3.1	-0.1	-2.5	n.a.	-0.3	-2.5	-2.7	-0.4	-0.4	-3.1	-3.3	1.6	-0.7	0.5
Male	-1.9	-1.9	0.9	-2.3	n.a.	0.1	-2.7	-1.6	-0.1	-1.1	-0.6	-2.7	2.2	-1.1	0.8
Relative poverty rate (percentage point change)															
All persons	-0.3	-0.1	1.5	-0.5	0.8	0.4	-0.2	-2.2	-0.5	-0.2	-0.2	-0.6	1.1	0.7	-1.3
Aged 0–17 years	-0.6	1.1	1.8	-0.6	1.9	2.3	0.0	-0.4	0.0	0.8	2.1	-0.4	1.8	0.2	-2.3
Aged 18–64 years	-0.2	-0.1	1.6	0.5	1.0	0.2	0.0	-1.2	0.6	0.2	-0.5	-0.6	2.6	0.7	-0.3
Aged 65+ years	0.2	-1.8	-0.4	-4.2	-1.3	-0.8	-1.2	-12.1	-4.3	-3.5	-2.7	-1.3	-5.7	0.5	-4.2
Female	0.0	-0.7	1.4	-0.7	0.7	0.2	0.1	-3.4	-0.6	0.4	-0.7	-0.7	0.3	1.3	-1.8
Male	-0.5	0.3	1.4	-0.3	0.9	0.7	-0.6	-1.1	-0.3	-0.8	0.2	-0.6	1.8	0.1	-0.9
Employed (16–64 years)	-1.5	-0.4	1.4	-1.5	-0.2	0.0	-0.3	-0.5	0.5	0.4	0.2	-1.8	2.0	-0.2	-1.6
Not employed (16–64 years)	2.3	-1.7	1.9	2.0	1.8	4.2	1.4	-5.5	0.4	2.0	0.3	1.4	1.6	3.9	-3.5
Gini coefficient (percentage point change)															
All persons	-0.1	-0.9	1.8	-0.9	0.7	-0.9	-0.5	-2.5	0.2	-2.1	-1.5	-2.1	2.6	0.1	-0.2
S80:S20 ratio (percentage point change)															
All persons	0.0	-0.2	0.8	-0.2	0.2	-0.3	-0.3	-0.6	0.1	-0.3	-0.3	-0.5	1.5	0.0	0.0
Aged less than 65 years	0.0	-0.2	0.8	0.0	0.2	-0.2	-0.2	-0.6	0.2	-0.3	-0.3	-0.5	1.9	0.2	0.0
Aged 65+ years	-0.1	0.6	0.7	-0.1	-0.1	-0.2	-0.4	0.5	-0.2	-0.1	-0.2	-0.4	0.1	-0.5	-0.2
Female	0.1	-0.2	0.7	-0.2	0.2	-0.3	-0.2	-0.6	0.1	-0.3	-0.4	-0.6	1.2	0.0	-0.1
Male	-0.1	-0.2	0.8	-0.1	0.2	-0.2	-0.3	-0.4	0.1	-0.4	-0.2	-0.5	1.6	0.0	-0.1

Source: EU–SILC data summaries at http://epp.eurostat.ec.europa.eu/portal/page/portal/statistics/search_database (series ilc_di03, ilc_li22, ilc_li02, ilc_li04, ilc_di11) [accessed 19 December 2011]

Notes: n.a.: not available. Definitions of median and poverty rates are as in Figures 2.17, 2.21, and 2.23. The 'S80:S20' ratio is the ratio of the share of equivalent net household income held by the richest fifth to the share of equivalent net household income held by the poorest fifth.

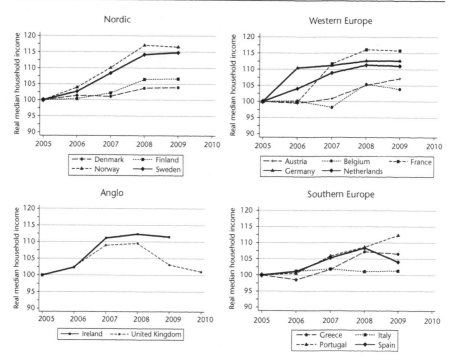

Figure 2.17. Real median equivalent net household income, 15 European countries, 2005–10 (2005 = 100)

Source: EU-SILC data summaries at http://epp.eurostat.ec.europa.eu/portal/page/portal/statistics/ search_database (series ilc_di03 and prc_hicp_aind). [accessed 19 December 2011].

Notes: The data refer to national median equivalized household net income (the equivalence scale is the modified-OECD scale), expressed relative to the corresponding 2005 value. Nominal incomes are deflated to 2005 values using the national all-items consumer price index. Income refers to annual income for a calendar year, with two exceptions. For Ireland, income in year *Y* refers to income in the 12 months preceding the survey interview in year *Y*; for the UK, income refers to income in the period around the time of the survey interview in year *Y*, expressed in annual terms pro rata.

11 out of the 15 countries, median household income over 2007–9 either rose more for women or fell less, although the differences are often small (Table 2.5). This may reflect the better employment experience of women during the GR (see Figure 2.10).

We now turn to income inequality. Estimates of the Gini coefficient are shown in Figure 2.19 while Table 2.5 also provides figures for the 'S80:S20 ratio', which is the ratio of the share of total income of the richest fifth to the share of the poorest fifth. The closer to zero the Gini coefficient is, the more equal the distribution; the closer to 100% it is, the more unequal is the distribution. As already seen in our own estimates using the same data of the coefficient of variation for 12 countries in 2007 (see Figure 2.6), broadly speaking, inequality at the start of the GR was lowest in the Nordic countries,

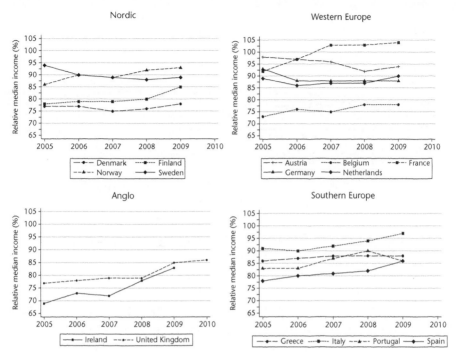

Figure 2.18. Ratio of median income of persons aged 60+ years to median of persons aged less than 60 years (%), 15 European countries, 2005–10

Source: EU-SILC data summaries at http://epp.eurostat.ec.europa.eu/portal/page/portal/statistics/search_database (series ilc_pns2) [accessed 19 December 2011].

Notes: The data refer to national median equivalized household net income. The equivalence scale is the modified-OECD scale. For the definitions of the income reference period, see the note to Figure 2.17.

and highest in the Anglo and Southern European ones, with inequality in Western European countries in between. But what of changes during the GR? If we compare 2009 with 2007, the most common trend is a small fall in the Gini, that is a slight reduction in inequality. This occurs in ten countries and in eight for the S80:S20 ratio (with no change in three other countries). In three countries—Ireland, the Netherlands, and Portugal—the fall in the Gini exceeds two percentage points, which is a reasonably large reduction over a short period. Among the few countries with an increase in the Gini between 2007 and 2009, the change for Spain stands out most: a rise of 2.5 percentage points. Spain and Ireland make for an interesting contrast in view of similarities between the origin and depth of the subsequent downturn in the two countries.

These changes or lack of them between 2007 and 2009 can be put in the context of the changes in the preceding two years, for which the picture is also mixed. In three cases—Norway, France, and Germany—there are some very

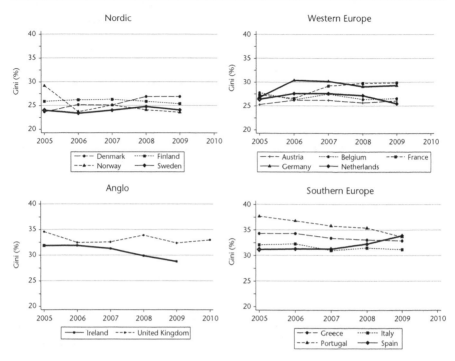

Figure 2.19. Inequality of household incomes, 15 European countries, 2005–10 (Gini coefficient, %)

Source: EU-SILC data summaries at http://epp.eurostat.ec.europa.eu/portal/page/portal/statistics/search_database (series ilc_di12) [accessed 19 December 2011].

Notes: The data refer to distributions of equivalized net household income among individuals (the equivalence scale is the modified-OECD scale). For the definitions of the income reference period, see the note to Figure 2.17.

sharp changes between one year and the next, which may be large enough to call into question the reliability of the data. The large change between 2005 and 2006 for Germany is difficult to assess given inconsistencies between SILC and other sources (Hauser 2008; Frick and Krell 2010). In other cases the year to year changes are more modest, but on a par with what we see between 2007 and 2009. (This is especially the case if one were to make allowance for sampling variability: the changes in either period may not be statistically significant different from zero.) The fall in the Gini in Portugal during the GR continues the trend from 2005 to 2007.

We are also able to draw on information published by the US Census Bureau for inequality of incomes in the USA before, during, and just after the GR. Figure 2.20 shows the Gini coefficient for family income for 2005–10. It should be noted that the definition of income is not the same as for Eurostat's analysis of EU-SILC data, and the US data are not adjusted for differences in family size or composition, and the statistics refer to families rather than households.

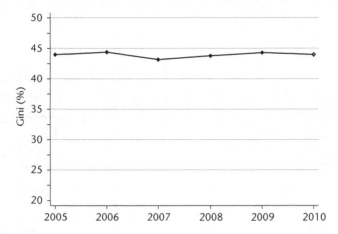

Figure 2.20. Inequality of family incomes, USA, 2005–10 (Gini coefficient, %)

Source: US Census Bureau http://www.census.gov/hhes/www/income/data/historical/inequality/ (F04_2010.xls).

Notes: Figure shows Gini coefficients calculated for the distribution of family money income among families.

Therefore the levels of the Gini coefficient between the European countries and the USA should not be compared; our focus is on the changes over time. These are only modest: the Gini rose by 1.1 percentage points over the main GR years, 2007–9, having fallen between 2006 and 2007 by almost the same amount (1.2 points). The year 2010 saw a slight fall, resulting in a Gini coefficient in that year at the same value as in 2005. The picture of a modest rise between 2007 and 2009 contrasts with the falls which were most common in Europe, but over the years 2005–10 as a whole there was no change. Chapter 8 sets the changes in income inequality in the GR in the USA against the background of trends over a much longer period (more than 25 years).

Changes in average incomes and in inequality of income combine to produce changes in absolute poverty. The estimates of absolute poverty rates that are produced by Eurostat measure the percentage of people beneath a line defined as 60% of national median income in 2005. Table 2.5 shows that there were falls between 2007 and 2009 in 11 out of 14 countries (the information is missing for France). There are falls in all 14 countries for the elderly (defined now as those aged 65+) who everywhere improved their position relative to other age groups, especially adults aged 18–64 who tended not to fare as well as children (0–17 year olds). The movements, including the continuation of earlier trends (see Figure 2.21), in part reflect those already noted in median incomes, but they will also have been driven by changes in inequality in the bottom part of the distribution. The UK and Spain are exceptions, as for median income, registering rises in average poverty between 2008 and 2009, continuing in the case of the UK into 2010.

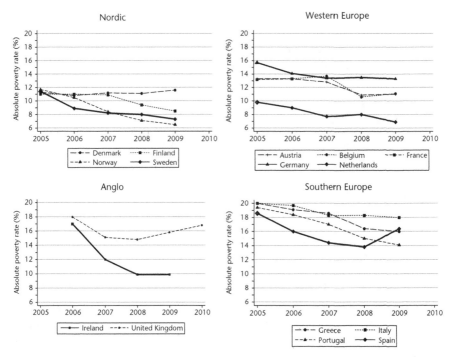

Figure 2.21. Absolute poverty rates, 15 European countries, 2005–10 (percentage of population with a household real income less than 60% of 2005 national median equivalent net household income)

Source: EU-SILC data summaries at http://epp.eurostat.ec.europa.eu/portal/page/portal/statistics/search_database (series ilc_li22) [accessed 19 December 2011].

Notes: The data refer to the percentage of the population 'at risk of poverty'. The poverty line for each country is 60% of 2005 national median equivalized household net income, adjusted for price changes. The equivalence scale is the modified-OECD scale. For the definitions of the income reference period, see the note to Figure 2.17.

We can again draw on published information from the US Census Bureau for information about absolute poverty in the USA, measured as the percentage of persons below the official poverty line. As with the estimates of the Gini coefficient, the levels of poverty cannot be compared with those in the European countries due to differences in definitions. Figure 2.22 shows changes in poverty rates for 2005 to 2010, both for all persons and distinguishing by age and sex. Overall poverty rose by 1.8 percentage points between 2007 and 2009 and rose again by a further 0.8 points in 2010, having changed little over the two years before the onset of the GR. Again, Chapter 8 sets the changes to 2009 against the background of a much longer earlier period. One change in the USA repeats the pattern found for all the European countries—poverty fell between 2007 and 2009 (and also in 2010) for the elderly. There was little change in the (far higher) poverty rate for children, implying that, again as in

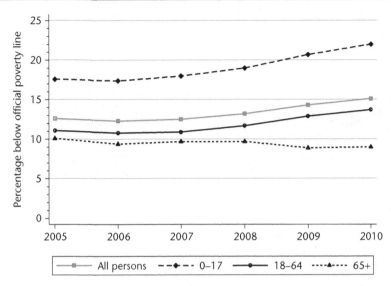

Figure 2.22. Absolute poverty rates, USA, 2005–10 (percentage of persons below official poverty line)

Source: US Census Bureau 'Historical Poverty Tables—People' http://www.census.gov/hhes/www/poverty/data/historical/people.html (tables hstpov2.xls, hstpov3.xls).

Notes: Figure shows percentages with a family money income that is less than the official poverty line.

Europe, adults aged 18–64 fared the least well of the three age groups—and that they experienced a rise in poverty that was larger than that shown for all persons.

Finally, Eurostat also provides information for the European countries about relative poverty rates, defined as the proportion of the population living in a household with an equivalized net household income of less than 60% of the contemporary national median income: see Figure 2.23 and Table 2.5. Echoing the patterns for inequality, the Nordic countries have comparatively low relative poverty rates and the Southern European and Anglo countries have comparatively high relative poverty rates, with the Western European countries in between. When we look at changes in relative poverty rates between 2007 and 2009, the picture is broadly similar to that for trends in the Gini coefficient: for most countries the direction of change is (slightly) downwards. The countries with increases are Denmark, Sweden, France, Germany, and Spain, although the rises are typically small (and Denmark had a fall in 2009). Spain (a rise of 1.1 percentage points) and Ireland (a fall of 2.2 percentage points) are again clear contrasts. The most striking change, taking 2005–9 as a whole, is the large decrease in the relative poverty rate for Ireland from nearly 20% to around 15%. The rate for the UK fell nearly two percentage points between 2005 and 2010 and for Italy by about 1.5 percentage points between

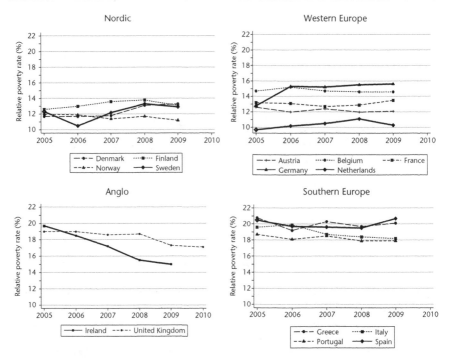

Figure 2.23. Relative poverty rates, 15 European countries, 2005–10 (percentage of population with a household income less than 60% of national median equivalent net household income)

Source: EU-SILC data summaries at http://epp.eurostat.ec.europa.eu/portal/page/portal/statistics/search_database (series ilc_li02) [accessed 19 December 2011].

Notes: The data refer to the percentage of the population 'at risk of poverty'. The poverty line for each country is 60% of national contemporary median equivalized household net income (the equivalence scale is the modified-OECD scale). For the definitions of the income reference period, see the note to Figure 2.17.

2005 and 2009. These perhaps counter-intuitive patterns are investigated in much greater detail in our country case studies.

To summarize for the 15 European countries: (i) the typical pattern was for median households incomes to rise across the main period of the GR, 2007 to 2009, or to change very little, with women and the elderly doing somewhat better than men and younger age groups respectively; (ii) income inequality in general fell slightly; (iii) absolute poverty rates tended to fall slightly, especially for the elderly; and (iv) there were usually small falls in relative poverty rates. In the USA, income inequality rose modestly between 2007 and 2009 but by 2010 was no higher than in 2005; and absolute poverty rose across 2007 to 2010, driven by the change for adults aged 18–64, the elderly experiencing a fall in absolute poverty as in Europe.

2.7 Changes in Household Incomes in 21 Countries: The Medium Term

The distributional consequences of the GR will long outlast the main period of recession itself, as we emphasized in Chapter 1. Much of the analysis in this chapter has focused on the years of the downturn for most countries, 2007–9, occasionally considering 2010. But what can we say at the time of writing (February 2012) about medium-term changes from 2010 onwards, for example in the years to 2015? To answer this question, we need also to take into account the impact of changes in government spending and taxation that are now in progress or are likely in the coming years and which can reasonably be viewed as a consequence of the GR. Chapters 3–8 look at some aspects in more detail; here we provide an overview for many countries that places in perspective the situation in the six that are the focus of the rest of the book.

We have noted the importance of government support for incomes of the household sector between 2007 and 2009. One consequence of this was a worsening of fiscal stance, measured by the government balance (a flow), and a rise in government debt (a stock)—although the direct support of household incomes through the benefit system was not the only, and typically not even the main, reason for these changes. The rise in spending on social benefits between 2007 and 2009 'represented, on average, about 40 per cent of the total rise in government spending' (OECD 2011c: 46); and our own calculations show that the fall in revenues in real terms between these two years was on average almost as large as the rise in total expenditure.

The changes in fiscal stance are illustrated by Figure 2.24 which shows the government balance as a percentage of GDP in 2007 and 2009 for 20 of our 21 countries, sorted on the 2009 values. In 2007, at the start of the GR, only 9 countries were in deficit. All but one were in deficit by 2009. The country excluded from the graph is Norway, an exception due to its oil wealth, with a large government surplus of 17.5% of GDP in 2007 and 10.7% in 2009. Norway apart, the change in government balance averaged –6.7 percentage points of GDP. However, the change for individual countries varied widely from less than –1% in Switzerland and about –3% in Austria and Germany to –13% of GDP in Spain and –14% in Ireland, figures which indicate a massive worsening in fiscal stance.

The changes over time are shown in more detail in Table 2.6 which focuses on the six countries that are the subject of the country chapters that follow, again ranked by 2009 values. There is very great variation in experience across them, both in 2007–9, as already illustrated in commenting on Figure 2.24, and in subsequent years (the numbers for 2011–12 are estimates). Like Ireland,

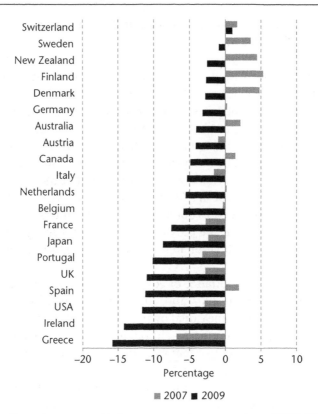

Figure 2.24. General government balance expressed as a percentage of GDP, 2007 and 2009

Source: OECD 2011*b*: annex table 27.

Notes: The graph does not include Norway, for which the statistics are +17.5% for 2007 and +10.7% for 2009.

the UK and the USA had double-digit deficits in 2009 while Sweden had the smallest deficit of any country with a negative balance. The collapse of Irish government finances, following a bank bailout, and the consequent Eurozone and IMF assistance, is reflected in the figure for 2010. This aside, deficits in 2010–11 tended to stabilize and start to come down. This was the pattern in other countries too, as summarized by the 20 country averages at the bottom of the table. At the same time, government debt as a percentage of GDP continued to increase, albeit at a slower pace than before: the figure for the (again unweighted) 20 country average was 64% in 2007, 79% in 2009, and is estimated by OECD to have been 90% in 2011 (OECD 2011*b*: annex table 32, general government gross financial liabilities).

In most cases, a substantial part of the government deficits that emerged in the GR is not explained by the usual fall in tax receipts and rise in automatic stabilizer spending that accompanies the downturn of a recessionary cycle—

Table 2.6. Government balance as a percentage of GDP, 2007–12

	2007	2008	2009	2010	2011	2012
Sweden	3.6	2.2	–0.9	–0.1	0.1	0.0
Germany	0.2	–0.1	–3.2	–4.3	–1.2	–1.1
Italy	–1.6	–2.7	–5.4	–4.5	–3.6	–1.6
UK	–2.8	–5.0	–11.0	–10.4	–9.4	–8.7
USA	–2.9	–6.6	–11.6	–10.7	–10.0	–9.3
Ireland	0.1	–7.3	–14.2	–31.3	–10.3	–8.7
20 country average	0.1	–1.7	–6.6	–7.0	–5.1	–4.2

Source: OECD 2011*b*: annex table 27.

Notes: the 2011 and 2012 figures are estimates. The 20 country (unweighted) average is for the countries shown in Figure 2.24.

and it will not be removed by economic growth in the upswing. These 'structural' parts of the deficit are due to expenditure on stimulation measures following the crisis, expenditure on servicing the higher levels of debt brought about by the GR, and the impact of the recession in reducing productive capacity (OECD 2010*c*: 45). To avoid an unsustainable further expansion in debt, many OECD governments at the time of writing are now reducing or planning to reduce their structural deficits. Estimates both of the size of the structural deficit and the extent of 'fiscal consolidation' required to remove it are subject to debate, and of course to changes in circumstances. (There is also debate on the appropriate speed of adjustment.) But as of May 2011, the OECD estimated that even to stabilize the level of government debt as a percentage of GDP by 2025, large improvements in the government balance of the order of between 6% and 8% of GDP would be needed in Greece, Ireland, Portugal, and the UK, and between 10% and 11% of GDP in the USA and Japan (OECD 2011*a*: 226), with smaller improvements elsewhere. At the other extreme, however, the OECD considered that little or no fiscal consolidation would be required in Sweden. So the extent of consolidation of government finances that the OECD believed to be required varies enormously, with extreme cases of both types included among the six countries that are the focus in the rest of this report.

What are the implications for the distribution of household income of governments' efforts to reduce their structural deficits resulting from the GR? This depends on how the consolidation of finances is achieved, as well as on the speed at which it takes place, besides of course the pace of economic recovery. Information on the form of planned consolidation to 2015 was collected from member countries by the OECD in Autumn 2010 (OECD 2011*d*). By no means all countries had clear plans at that time, but Table 2.7 shows the four expenditure and revenue measures most commonly mentioned among the 30 countries surveyed. (Changes expected as a result of the economic upswing, e.g. lower expenditure on unemployment benefit,

Table 2.7. The four most frequently cited areas of expenditure and revenue reported by OECD member states as part of their fiscal consolidation plans, Autumn 2010

Expenditure		Revenue	
Area	Number of countries	Area	Number of countries
Welfare	18	Consumption taxes	20
Health	15	Tax expenditures	14
Pensions	14	Income taxes	12
Infrastructure	13	Tax on financial sector	8

Source: OECD 2011*d*: figure 1.21, p. 46, and figure 1.28, p. 53.

Notes: 30 countries were surveyed of which not all had fiscal consolidation plans. The headings are those given in the source document. 'Welfare' appears to be a broad heading covering all public cash benefits including universal benefits.

were excluded.) On the expenditure side, the most frequent mention of 'welfare' (this appears to be a much broader concept than the term is often used to imply) and health reflect the importance of these areas in government expenditure. On the revenue side, the emphasis on increases in consumption taxes is notable.

Some of these measures, and others not listed in the table such as public sector wage cuts or freezes (e.g. noted in Ireland and Italy in Chapters 4 and 5) and reductions in public sector employment, will lead to direct changes in household incomes. Other measures will not, but may have a significant effect on the standard of living. Increases in consumption taxes are an obvious example: the purchasing power of money incomes will fall, but the incomes themselves will be unaffected in the first instance. (General equilibrium effects may eventually reduce incomes through changes in employment in industries affected by the tax increases.) This serves as a reminder of the limits of an exclusive focus on household income as a measure of economic welfare when assessing the distributional impact of the GR—see our caveat in Chapter 1.

We limit ourselves in this chapter to commenting on the likely direction of impact. As far as average incomes and absolute poverty rates are concerned, all measures that lead to direct changes in money incomes will have a negative effect in the first instance, although the increase in absolute poverty might be limited by the precise nature of the change, for example a public sector wage freeze might include exemptions for the most lowly paid jobs. As far as inequality of money incomes or of consumption and levels of relative poverty are concerned, it is virtually impossible to sign the direction of impact without the details of the policy change. For this reason, we do not attempt to summarize the effect of possible measures that could be used to consolidate public finances as in OECD (2010*c*: table 4.8). Cuts in public transfers ('welfare' in Table 2.7, which appears to be a broad heading covering all public cash benefits including universal benefits) could be progressive if targeted on better-off households or regressive if undertaken across the board. The impact of a public wage freeze would depend on the concentration of public sector workers across the distribution of household incomes (possibly highest in middle-income households). The direction of effect of an increase in income tax on the inequality of after-tax incomes depends on a variety of factors including the combination of change in different marginal rates and the tax-free threshold. An impact of an increase in indirect taxation, for example Value-Added Taxation, will vary according to whether particular goods and services are exempted and may also depend on whether households are ranked by their income or their spending.

In the country case study chapters that follow, we are able to estimate for some of them the extent of the distributional impact of actual or planned measures to improve public finances, even when the changes do not affect money incomes. The focus of the chapters is, however, on the period immediately after the GR's onset, that is the short term rather than the medium or longer term.

3

Country case study—Germany

Markus M. Grabka and Joachim R. Frick

The Great Recession of the late 2000s had a significant, but fortunately only temporary, impact on the German labour market and economy as a whole. By the last quarter of 2010, nominal GDP had already returned to pre-recession levels and unemployment had reached its lowest levels since reunification. Scholars have described this striking resilience of the German labour market as 'Germany's jobs miracle' (Krugman 2009). In this chapter, we describe the impact of the Great Recession (GR) in Germany on individual and household income as well as on employment. We show that both employment and income levels remained fairly stable during the GR, although the use of overtime declined. We also find evidence that the income distribution temporarily became more concentrated. Furthermore, based on subjective indicators of people's concerns about the German economy and about their own financial situations, we find that while the recession produced a general sense of uncertainty about the economy, it had no identifiable effect on personal financial concerns. Finally, we explain the surprising positive development of the German labour market during the GR in detail, highlighting the central role of short-time compensation programmes, other forms of flexible labour arrangements, and the German government's aggressive stimulus packages. The price for these programmes will still have to be paid in the future, however, given that increased public debts will have to be balanced by cutbacks in social security and public benefits.

3.1 Selected Macro-Level Information

Germany's export-oriented economy was severely affected by the GR. Real GDP fell by 4.7% in 2009 against the previous year, the strongest decline since the Second World War: see Figure 3.1. Not even the oil crisis of the early 1970s produced a comparable downturn in the German economy, although its effects are still present in the collective memory. At that time, real GDP fell by only 1.0%.

Fortunately, the GR resulted in only a rather short-lived macroeconomic slump in Germany. In the last quarter of 2010, nominal GDP had already surpassed pre-recession levels. Thus, within less than three years, the German economy was already out of the recession (Federal Statistical Office 2011).

One reason for this quick recovery was a surge in the global demand for German exports. The sector affected most severely by the GR was manufacturing—the sector that had been driving growth in Germany before the start of the recession and also one with high cash reserves. There are also indications that firms in this sector lacked skilled workers just before the start of the GR (Aricò and Stein 2011; Burda and Hunt 2011).

Figure 3.2 presents time-series data on the number of registered unemployed in Germany. Over the last 20 years, unemployment has followed an inverse U-shaped path. After reunification, the number of unemployed more than doubled from about 2.5 million to more than 5 million in 2005 (corresponding to an unemployment rate of 12.1%). The relatively strong economic situation in Germany from 1999 to 2002 led to a temporary break in this long-term trend of increasing unemployment. Since 2005, unemployment has declined dramatically, in parallel with the implementation of several sweeping labour market reforms (such as the Unemployment II benefit introduction). Unemployment in

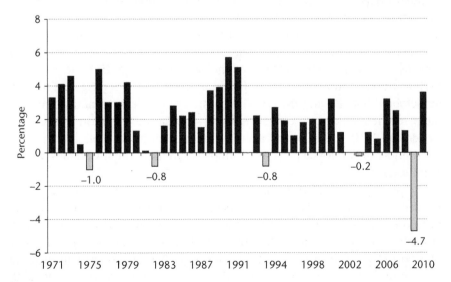

Figure 3.1. Change (%) in real GDP year-on-year

Source: Federal Statistical Office (2010). West Germany prior to 1992.

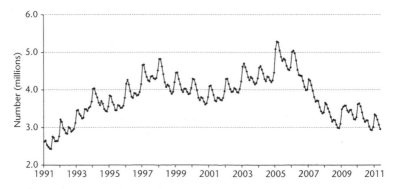

Figure 3.2. Number of registered unemployed, 1991–2011 (millions)
Source: Statistik der Bundesagentur für Arbeit (2011).
Note: Monthly data, with year labels centred over the value for January of each year.

Germany reached a low point in October 2008 with fewer than 3 million unemployed (an unemployment rate of 7.6%). The GR put a temporary stop to this development in 2009, slightly increasing the number of unemployed by 0.5 million (corresponding to a 0.7% increase in the unemployment rate). Since then, unemployment has begun to decline again. In March 2011, the German unemployment rate was the lowest since reunification, at roughly 7%.

Unfortunately there are no reliable time-series data on discouraged workers in Germany. Thus we are not able to contextualize this positive trend through comparison with developments in the hidden labour force. However, the number of employed persons in Germany provides a useful figure that moves in more or less the opposite direction to the unemployment figures: see Figure 3.3. Disregarding any seasonal effects, the number of employed persons remained fairly stable over the period 2002 to 2006 at about 39 million workers. Subsequently, employment increased, reaching 40.8 million in October 2008. During the GR, the number of workers stagnated. Employment reached its lowest point in February 2009 at 39.8 million workers. By November 2010, the recovery of the German economy had already brought the number of employed persons to almost 41 million, the highest level since reunification.

The principal aim of this chapter is to describe the impact of the GR on household incomes. Significant macroeconomic shocks have occurred before in Germany, which provide the possibility of analysing their incidence and any differences in the effects that they had. The most important macro shock of recent German history was reunification in 1990. Although reunification constituted a major turning point in the German economy, wage inequality had already begun to increase in the 1980s but only at the top of the

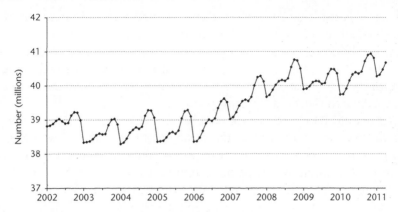

Figure 3.3. Number of employed people, 2002–11 (millions)

Source: Statistik der Bundesagentur für Arbeit (2011).

Note: Monthly data, with year labels centred over the value for January of each year.

distribution, as shown by Dustmann et al. (2009), based on a 2% sample of social security records. These authors argue that changes in the education and age structure explain a substantial part of the increase. Wage inequality rose most substantially in East Germany during the first five years after reunification (Franz and Steiner 2000) and at the top of the distribution (Gernandt and Pfeifer 2007). In contrast, de-unionization in Germany played an important role at the bottom of the distribution, at least in the 1990s. Gernandt and Pfeifer (2007) also argue that wage inequality has risen in particular for low-skilled workers and those with low tenure or entrants. Antonczyk et al. (2010) argue that the general increase in wage inequality could also partly be explained by cohort effects and institutional changes in Germany, the latter being of particular relevance for low-skilled workers. An overview of a number of empirical studies investigating wage inequality in Germany is presented by Gernandt and Pfeifer (2007).

The effect of reunification on market as well as post-government income has been analysed by Schwarze (1996); Grabka et al. (1999); and the German Council of Economic Experts (2006); among others. These papers present evidence that income inequality in the western part of Germany was barely affected by reunification. Prior to reunification, pre-tax and transfer inequality was lower in East Germany than in the West. However, in the early to mid-1990s this pattern shifted, and pre-tax and transfer inequality became significantly higher in the East, as is still the case today. Inequality in West Germany remained surprisingly stable after reunification but started to increase in the late 1990s. Significant increases in income levels at the very top of the distribution played an important role in this (Bach et al. 2009), which is in line with findings of Piketty and Saez (2006) for a number of Western countries. When looking at post-tax and transfer income, we find a robust picture of much lower inequality in East than in West Germany. This is the result of a continuous redistribution process within Germany from West to East (Fuchs-Schündeln et al. 2010). Inequality of post-tax and transfer income became more unequal over the last ten years, while real mean net household income remained flat in Germany over this period.

After reunification, the East German labour market performed much worse than in West Germany, with an unemployment rate that was twice as large. This pattern still persists today. However, a policy instrument used widely during the transition process became important again during the GR, namely short-time compensation programmes. This was in addition to generous unemployment and pension benefits and massive public infrastructure programmes. Thus, one might argue that the experience gained with structural breaks in the East German economy made it easier to deal with the effects of the GR.

3.2 Data Sources and Variables Used

The analysis that follows of the effects of the GR at the individual and household level is based primarily on micro data from the German Socio-Economic Panel (SOEP). The SOEP is a representative panel study of individuals in private households in Germany. It started in 1984 and the same individuals and households are interviewed annually. There were 22,000 adult respondents in 2009. The SOEP has nine different subsamples to allow detailed analysis of various subgroups of the population such as migrants or high-income households. The main topics surveyed include demography, the labour force, health, housing, income, and subjective well-being. For more details, see Wagner et al. (2007).

The main measure used here is current net household monthly income. At the time of writing, the SOEP provides annual income figures only up until the 2009 income year, collected during interviews in the 2010 wave of the survey. However, current monthly income figures are available for 2010 as well. Information on current income is collected in the month of the interview. The majority of the household interviews take place in the first quarter of each observation year. In 2010, almost three out of four interviews were completed by April.

One should keep in mind the disadvantages associated with current monthly income. There is a tendency to underestimate irregularly derived incomes (capital incomes or one-time payments such as Christmas pay or holiday bonuses)—at least in Germany. (For a discussion of the British case, see Böheim and Jenkins 2006.) Furthermore seasonal effects such as changes in employment status during a calendar year cannot be considered, which may be of particular relevance in this report. Another aspect is the consideration of non-monetary income components such as imputed rents, which play a significant role in the German context (Frick and Grabka 2003). Summing up, if current net monthly household income is used for research on income distribution, there is a tendency to underestimate both income levels and the extent of inequality compared to estimates based on annual income figures. However, the long-term trends estimated using the two measures are similar, at least in Germany. This is part of the reason why the Canberra Group advises that annual income figures be used in inequality research (Expert Group on Household Income Statistics 2001).

Another income concept used in this chapter is current monthly gross individual income from the respondent's main job, which consists of all wages and salaries from dependent employment (without any one-time payments such as holiday pay or bonuses, but including overtime) and income from self-employment. Earnings from a second job are not included in this measure. This income concept refers to the month prior to the interview.

Alternative data sources such as the Mikrozensus, or the German part of the European Statistics of Income and Living Conditions (EU-SILC)—both administered by Federal Statistics of Germany—are not used here due to the lack of up-to-date information in the respective public use files. The annual Mikrozensus would have the advantage of a very large number of observations, given that 1% of the population is required to participate in this survey, corresponding to about 800,000 individuals. The German part of the EU-SILC not only lacks current data but also possesses well-known disadvantages with respect to representativeness (Hauser 2008). (See Chapter 2: Section 2.6, for analysis of household incomes in Germany that draws on the EU-SILC.)

3.3 Individual-Level Analysis

An economic downturn is usually associated with a reduction in labour demand, or at least this was the case in past recessions in Germany. But in the case of the GR, there is no evidence of a significant change in labour market attachment in the SOEP survey data: if one separates the population of working age (16–64 years) into those employed and those not employed at the time of the interview (generally in the first quarter of the year), no large change can be observed: see Figure 3.4. Between 2006 and 2010, there was a modest decrease in the percentage of the population outside the labour force from almost 41% to 36%. For 2009, the year when the GR hit its deepest point in Germany, only a minor increase was registered.

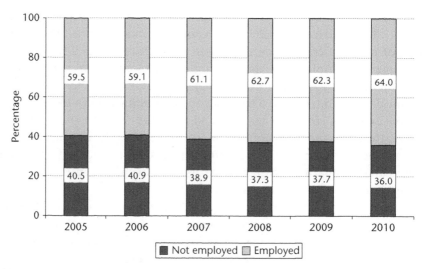

Figure 3.4. Percentage of adults aged 16–64 employed and not employed, 2005–10

Source: SOEP v27. Figures for 2010 are provisional. Classification is based on self-reporting by respondents at the time of the interview.

Note: Individuals of working age (16–64 years).

Table 3.1. Current labour market attachment (% of total adult population), 2005–10

Attachment	2005	2006	2007	2008	2009	2010
Full-time	36.5	36.1	36.5	37.7	37.5	37.2
Part-time	9.4	9.3	10.1	10.1	10.0	10.7
In education or training	2.5	2.4	2.3	2.3	2.4	2.2
Marginal or irregular	4.6	5.1	5.1	5.7	5.9	5.6
Not employed	47.1	47.1	45.9	44.3	44.3	44.4
Of which: officially registered unemployed	8.1	8.4	7.8	6.8	7.1	6.9
Number (thousands)	69,119	69,296	69,595	69,783	69,769	69,190

Source: SOEP v27. Figures for 2010 are provisional. Population: adult individuals in private households of all ages.

Note: Classification is based on self-reporting by respondents. Part-time is usually defined as a working time of fewer than 35 hours per week. Marginal employment corresponds to a job with a maximum wage of €400 per month.

Current labour market status is further differentiated in Table 3.1, which refers to adults of all ages. The percentage of persons who were full or part-time employed increased slightly in 2007, and again between 2007 and 2009—by 0.9 percentage points, taking the two groups together. There was also a rise of 0.8 points over 2007–9 in the percentage of persons reporting marginal or irregular work. (These rises are consistent with the small increase in the employment rate over 2007–9 for persons of working age that is shown in labour force survey data for Germany in Chapter 2: Table 2.2.) The percentage not employed and the percentage who reported that they were officially registered as unemployed both fell slightly between 2006 and 2007. Reflecting the rises in employment, the overall percentage not employed fell again in 2008. Between 2008 and 2009, there was a just a slight rise in the share of registered unemployed from 6.8% to 7.1%, which is line with the aggregate unemployment figures shown in Figure 3.2.

One possible explanation for these findings—a lack of any sharp negative impact of the GR on employment—could be a change in working hours and the use of overtime and working hours accounts. In Table 3.2, we present information on average working hours and overtime hours for those individuals who were employed in the current and previous month. Again, the figures mainly refer to the first quarter of each observation year in the SOEP.

The GR did not induce any substantial change over the observation period, at least according to SOEP data. For example, those who stated having been employed full-time worked approximately 44 hours per week on average in all 6 years under consideration. Only the mean length of overtime declined slightly from 2009 to 2010. (One should keep in mind that 2010 SOEP information in this chapter is provisional because of the preliminary nature of the weighting factors.) Note that respondents are asked to include overtime in their current working hours.

The rather small effect of the GR shown by the SOEP data is surprising in light of the literature citing pronounced changes in hours worked among the employed in Germany during the GR (Burda and Hunt 2011; German Council of Economic Experts 2010). One potential explanation is that the SOEP only collects information in the first quarter of each year. The GR entered its most

Table 3.2. Mean actual working hours and use of overtime, by current labour market attachment (adult individuals in private households), 2005–10

Attachment	2005	2006	2007	2008	2009	2010
Actual working hours per week						
Full-time	43.8	44.2	44.6	44.1	44.2	43.9
Part-time	24.6	24.7	24.9	24.8	25.1	24.7
In education or training	40.5	40.9	39.9	39.9	40.9	40.2
Marginal or irregular	13.1	14.2	13.8	14.6	13.0	12.4
Total	37.8	38.0	38.1	37.8	37.6	37.0
Mean length of overtime in hours in the last week						
Full-time	2.5	2.7	2.9	2.7	2.6	2.0
Part-time	1.2	1.5	1.3	1.4	1.3	1.5
In education or training	0.9	0.9	0.7	1.0	1.0	1.0
Marginal or irregular	0.2	0.3	0.3	0.3	0.3	n.a.
Total	1.9	2.2	2.2	2.1	2.0	1.8
% of employed with overtime in the last week						
Yes	45.9	50.1	49.7	49.8	47.0	39.9

Source: SOEP v27. Figures for 2010 are provisional.

Note: Classification is based on self-reporting of respondents. Part-time is usually defined as a working time of fewer than 35 hours per week. Marginal employment corresponds to a job with a maximum wage of €400 per month.

severe phase after the first quarter of 2009 and was already slowing down by the first quarter of 2010.

Although the mean hours of overtime decreased only slightly, a much more pronounced effect of the GR can be observed for the share of employees who worked some amount of overtime, shown in the last line of Table 3.2. Almost 50% of all workers stated that they worked overtime in the pre-crisis years; this figure declined to 47% in 2009 and reached roughly 40% in 2010. This result is also consistent with other research (e.g. Aricò and Stein 2011).

The general pattern of overtime compensation in Germany has changed over the last ten years. While payment for overtime was more prevalent in the 1990s in Germany, the percentage of employees who stated receiving over-time pay in 2010 had dropped to only 10%. Half of those who worked overtime in 2010 received time off in compensation, 20% received partial time off in compensation, and the remaining 20% got no compensation at all (estimates derived from SOEP data; not shown here).

The change in the pattern of overtime compensation is only one aspect of a more general trend toward more flexible work arrangements in Germany over the last ten years. One facet that is part of this development is the growing percentage of fixed-term labour contracts, especially among new entrants to the labour force (Federal Statistical Office 2010). Another factor affecting flexible labour arrangements is the increasing prevalence of working time accounts and a fairly new, but less frequently used, option called 'working-time corridors' (*Arbeitszeitkorridore*) (Bispinck 2006; Burda and Hunt 2011).

The reported actual working hours and the mean amount of overtime could not be broken down here by industry or other characteristics. However, the GR did not leave export-dependent sectors of the German economy unscathed, in particular the manufacturing industry, the mechanical engin-eering, and the automotive industry (Aricò and Stein 2011). The manufactur-ing industry, for instance, shrank by almost 20% during the GR (Möller 2010). As Möller (2010: 330ff.) argued, the 'crisis primarily hit strong firms in eco-nomically strong regions' and 'especially those firms were hit by the world recession that had the most severe recruitment problems before the crisis', which is one of the most likely explanations for the German jobs miracle. Given that these firms were in a relatively good financial situation before the GR, they were also able to hoard labour for at least a few months, and thus decided to retain their skilled workers in order to have them available when demand picked up again (Aricò and Stein 2011; Bargain et al. 2011).

The typical workers affected by the GR were male and working full-time, mainly in southern Germany and without vocational training (Rosemann and Kirchmann 2010; Bargain et al. 2011), while in previous recessions, women, older workers, and workers in part-time jobs were most severely affected. The one group hit both by previous recessions and the GR were persons aged under

25, who experienced increased unemployment rates. However, one should keep in mind the relatively small overall increase in unemployment in Germany during the GR.

One policy instrument that was reactivated and expanded to preserve these industries is short-time compensation (STC). The basic idea of STC is that a firm with financial difficulties—due, for example, to a slump in demand—can apply for financial aid from the Federal Employment Agency to prevent the need for layoffs. In return, the firm has to reduce working hours and pay.

STC has a long tradition in Germany. First established in the 1950s to preserve employment during cyclical downturns, it was used heavily during the process of economic transition in East Germany after reunification. While STC plans are designed to last for 6 months in non-recession periods, from late 2008 to early 2009, they were lengthened to 24 months. STC is beneficial not only for employers but also for employees. STC payments in Germany have the same replacement rate as regular unemployment benefits: 60% for single workers and 67% for workers with dependents. Employer costs are also subsidized extensively. In the first six months, the employer has to pay only 50% of social security contributions and beginning at the seventh month, all social security contributions are reimbursed. In some cases, employers do not even have to cover wages—for example, if workers are undergoing training. For more details about the German STC programme, see Vroman and Brusentsev (2009); Will (2011); and Brenke et al. (2011).

The STC programme was heavily used in Germany during the GR (Figure 3.5). The peak level of more than 1.4 million employees in STC was

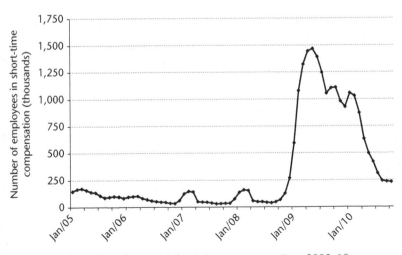

Figure 3.5. Number of employees in short-time compensation, 2005–10

Source: Statistik der Bundesagentur für Arbeit (2011): Arbeitsmarkt in Zahlen, Kurzarbeit—Zeitreihen, Nürnberg.

reached in early 2009 (this corresponds to about 5% of all employees who are subject to social insurance contributions). About 50% of all employees in STC reduced their working hours by up to a quarter. The mean length of STC was less than six months (German Council of Economic Experts 2010) and within less than 18 months the number of employees in STC had fallen to pre-recession levels. STC was used primarily in the manufacturing sector, for almost 1.2 million employees, and especially in large manufacturing firms (Brenke et al. 2011).

The fact that the STC programme only lasted for a few months for the majority of employees in such industries (respondents in the SOEP who stated having received STC in 2009 reported a mean duration of about 16 weeks) is a potential explanation of why survey estimates such as those derived from the SOEP did not show any significant changes in working hours or overtime, at least at the time of the interview.

STC clearly helped to stabilize private consumption in Germany during the GR. When analysing real gross monthly labour income, again one cannot find any notable impact of the GR: see Table 3.3. For workers employed full-time in the private sector, mean income from this source remained relatively stable between 2005 and 2006. Between 2006 and 2008 there was a small decrease of about €100. However, the 2009 figure had almost returned to pre-crisis levels. Mean earnings in the public sector, which were not significantly affected by the GR, show considerable stability for the whole period. But, overall, for all employees in the private as well in the public sector, no major changes occurred (Brenke and Grabka 2011).

Table 3.3. Real mean gross monthly labour income (Euros, 2005 prices), private and non-private sectors, 2005–10

Attachment	2005	2006	2007	2008	2009	2010
Private sector						
Full-time	2,894	2,901	2,846	2,807	2,863	2,855
Part-time	1,194	1,164	1,119	1,106	1,142	1,146
In education or training	602	568	567	592	566	599
Marginal or irregular	549	470	512	446	549	497
Total	2,311	2,309	2,213	2,200	2,213	2,225
Public sector						
Full-time	2,876	2,821	2,855	2,838	2,833	2,835
Part-time	1,537	1,574	1,574	1,532	1,556	1,588
In education or training	726	700	620	581	682	700
Marginal or irregular	406	481	502	621	666	383
Total	2,421	2,373	2,373	2,389	2,361	2,360

Source: SOEP v27. Population: adult individuals in private households.

Note: Income is in current prices and includes income from self-employment. Classification is based on self-reporting of respondents. Part-time is usually defined as a working time of fewer than 35 hours per week. Marginal employment corresponds to a job with a maximum wage of €400 per month.

Summing up, Brenke et al. (2011) argue that without the extensive use of STC in combination with other flexible labour arrangements, unemployment in Germany would have risen much more steeply during the GR than it did.

3.4 Household-Level Analysis

The assumption is made typically in welfare analysis that household members pool and equally share all economic resources. Thus, what may at first appear to be an adverse economic situation at the individual level may be less of a problem when the household level is analysed. First, we look at the changes in the proportions of households with different patterns of labour market attachment. Here, we focus on households with a working-age head (aged 16–65 years), and distinguish between the number of workers in the household at the time of the interview: see Figure 3.6. At first glance, the GR seems to have had no notable effect. Households with no members in the labour force make up less than 21% of the sample in all years. Comparing the figures over time, and bearing in mind the macroeconomic indicators of the labour force in Germany, we also see an increase in labour market attachment over time. In 2010, only 18% of all households reported that no one was working.

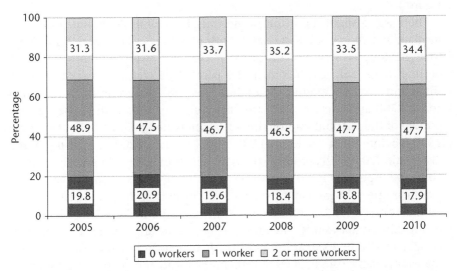

Figure 3.6. Distribution of numbers of workers per household (%), among households with a head of working age (16–65 years)

Source: SOEP v27. Figures for 2010 are provisional. Population: adults (16 years and older) in private households. Classification is based on self-reporting by respondents at the time of the interview.

Household labour force structure does not tell us how economic resources are distributed within the household. And non-labour income also needs to be included in the analysis. Thus we now turn to consider current net monthly equivalized household income. The evolution of income inequality in Germany in a longer-term perspective has been described, for example, by the German Council of Economic Experts (2009); Frick and Grabka (2010); and Biewen and Juhasz (2010). After reunification, Germany was character-ized as a country with below-average inequality compared to other OECD countries. However, since 2000, there has been a strong increase in inequality. Relative income poverty rose by more than 40% up to 2005, with almost 15% of the population below the poverty threshold. Between 2005 and 2008, poverty remained fairly stable in Germany. A comparable development could also be seen in standard inequality indicators such as the Gini coeffi-cient (German Council of Economic Experts 2009).

The statistics just cited are based on annual income data, which we noted earlier are not available in the SOEP for 2010 at the time of writing. Hence we first present here estimates of the distribution of household income that are based on (real) current net monthly household income: see the top half of Table 3.4. (The distribution is of individuals and income is equivalized by the square root of household size.) The last two columns in the table summarize the changes over the full period, 2005–10, and the changes between 2007 and 2009. The mean, median, and 10th and 90th percentiles are plotted in Figure 3.7.

There was a slight dip in mean monthly income in 2008, but not in the median, and then small increases in both measures in 2009 and 2010. (Note that previous economic downturns in Germany were accompanied by a decline in median real income.) The percentage changes over 2007–9 are small and positive, around 1% to 2%. The 10th percentile (P10) remained above €700 and showed no sharp changes, consistent with support at the bottom of the distribution from the social safety net, falling by about 5% over 2005–8 before rising to a level in 2010 equal to that of 2005. At the top of the distribution, the 90th percentile (P90) fell a little in 2008 before rising again in 2009 and especially in 2010 with the recovery of the economy. Overall, the picture is one of little change over 2007–9. The bottom half of the table shows estimates based on the annual net income measure to 2009. The data shows reasonably similar trends. The lowest values for mean, median, P10, and P90 are all recorded in 2008, as for monthly income (other than the median), but there are notable rises in 2009 of €500 in the mean and €650 in the median—increases of 2.2% and 3.5% respectively.

There was little obvious change in any of the commonly used income inequality indices—the Gini coefficient and the generalized entropy meas-ures—in 2008 or 2009, whether one focuses on monthly or on annual

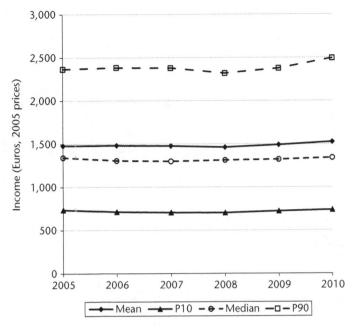

Figure 3.7. Current net monthly household income (Euros, 2005 prices), 2005–10

Source: See Table 3.4

incomes. If anything, the GR appears to have led to a small decrease in income inequality: for example, the Theil coefficient for monthly income fell by 3% between 2008 and 2009. However, looking at 2005–10 as a whole, the Gini coefficient for monthly income increased slightly, from 0.263 to 0.273, an increase of about 4%, while the generalized entropy measures showed an increase of 7% to 8%, which continues the overall trend described by Frick and Grabka (2010). The inequality figures based on annual income data also show little movement to 2009, with the Gini coefficient remaining essentially unchanged over 2007–9.

Finally, we consider the changes in the poverty rate, the estimates of which are also shown in Table 3.4. Poverty is defined here as living in a household with an equivalized net household income of less than 60% of the contemporary median for the total population. Between 2008 and 2009, the poverty rate defined on the basis of monthly income fell by 1.1 percentage points to 13.1%, having increased by 0.6 points between 2007 and 2008. In 2010, the poverty rose again by about one percentage point to 14.0%. This is against a background of median monthly income remaining roughly constant between 2008 and 2010 at about €1,300. However, when calculating poverty rates on the basis of annual incomes, this rather positive picture is somewhat altered: there is an increase in the poverty rate of 1.1 percentage points between 2008

Table 3.4. The distribution of real net equivalized household income (Euros, 2005 prices), 2005–10

	2005	2006	2007	2008	2009	2010	% change 2005–10	% change 2007–9
Current net monthly household income								
Mean	1,481	1,484	1,478	1,463	1,492	1,525	3.0	0.9
P10	738	715	707	704	724	738	0.0	2.4
Median	1,342	1,307	1,299	1,313	1,322	1,340	-0.1	1.8
P90	2,368	2,386	2,381	2,321	2,379	2,495	5.4	-0.1
Poverty rate (%)	13.6	13.2	13.6	14.2	13.1	14.0	2.9	-3.7
Gini	0.263	0.273	0.271	0.270	0.270	0.273	3.8	-0.4
Generalized entropy indices:								
Mean log deviation	0.117	0.126	0.124	0.124	0.122	0.125	6.8	-1.6
Theil	0.122	0.136	0.137	0.132	0.128	0.131	7.4	-6.6
Half CV-squared	0.158	0.187	0.210	0.197	0.167	0.171	8.2	-20.5
Percentile ratios:								
P90/P10	3.21	3.33	3.37	3.30	3.28	3.38	5.3	-2.7
P90/P50	1.77	1.83	1.83	1.77	1.80	1.86	5.1	-1.6
P50/P10	1.81	1.83	1.84	1.83	1.82	1.81	0.0	-1.1
Annual net household income								
Mean	21,908	21,863	22,025	21,754	22,250	n.a.	n.a.	1.0
P10	9,794	9,873	10,045	9,632	9,841	n.a.	n.a.	-2.0
Median	19,134	18,988	19,151	18,960	19,619	n.a.	n.a.	2.4
P90	35,532	35,676	35,526	35,477	35,742	n.a.	n.a.	0.6
Poverty rate (%)	15.4	14.6	15.0	15.2	16.3	n.a.	n.a.	8.7
Gini	0.294	0.288	0.292	0.294	0.293	n.a.	n.a.	0.3
Generalized entropy indices:								
Mean log deviation	0.150	0.142	0.149	0.150	0.150	n.a.	n.a.	0.7
Theil	0.172	0.155	0.163	0.165	0.167	n.a.	n.a.	2.5
Half CV-squared	0.500	0.244	0.302	0.278	0.306	n.a.	n.a.	1.3
Percentile ratios:								
P90/P10	3.63	3.61	3.54	3.67	3.63	n.a.	n.a.	2.5
P90/P50	1.86	1.88	1.86	1.87	1.82	n.a.	n.a.	-2.2
P50/P10	1.95	1.92	1.90	1.96	1.99	n.a.	n.a.	4.7

Source: SOEP v27. Figures for 2010 are provisional.

Note: The population covered is individuals in private households. The equivalence scale is the square root of the household size. The poverty line is 60% of contemporary median income.

and 2009. These conflicting findings may be the result of the different income reference periods. Whereas monthly incomes provide a snap-shot, annual incomes better cover all income changes occurring within a given year.

We continue the analysis by differentiating the sample according to household type (Table 3.5). The pattern of income distribution is in line with those reported in the literature. Observe, for example, that lone parents as a group have clearly below-average incomes, while couples without children are mainly at the top of the distribution (Frick and Grabka 2010). Taking the period 2005–10 as a whole, there seem to be no clear changes attributable to the GR. All income statistics based on net monthly household income remain relatively stable over time for the household types examined here. There is only a small and temporary drop in real net income in 2008, which is rather similar across household types (apart from the small group of 'other households', which consists mainly of multi-generational households). Another rather small change can be observed for the poverty rate. While single people and childless couples aged less than 65 years show a small increase in relative income poverty between 2007 and 2009, for all other household types this indicator falls slightly, even for those of working age. The small increase in relative poverty for the two household types mentioned may be the result of a somewhat higher risk of unemployment during the GR. Although families with parents of working age may also be confronted with a higher risk of unemployment, at the same time a new family transfer might have buffered the effect of the GR. On 1 January 2007, the 'parents' money' (the *Elterngeld* programme) came into effect. This transfer is for parents with a newborn child and amounts to 67% of the last gross earnings of the parent who stays at home. This new transfer might have played a part in damping the effect of the GR for at least some families in Germany (Grabka and Frick 2010).

The relatively small impacts of the GR on the level and distribution of net household income are the result of not only effective labour market policies but partly also the effect of strong buffering from the German tax and transfer system. In a simulation study, automatic stabilizers absorbed 48% of a proportional income shock in Germany, compared to only 32% in the USA (Dolls et al. 2012). The higher effectiveness compared to the USA is also true of other EU countries such as Denmark, Belgium, and Hungary, with values similar to or higher than those for Germany.

3.5 Additional Indicators

Germany experienced not only a crisis in export-oriented firms but also a banking crisis. Thus the GR may also have produced significant changes in the financial assets of private households, given that it started as a financial

Table 3.5. The distribution of current real net monthly household income (Euros, 2005 prices) by household type, 2005–10

	2005	2006	2007	2008	2009	2010
Mean						
Single householder < 65 years	1,451	1,421	1,418	1,371	1,409	1,410
Single householder ≥ 65 years	1,339	1,327	1,318	1,290	1,336	1,399
Couple, no children, < 65 years	1,799	1,805	1,811	1,848	1,853	1,881
Couple, no children, ≥ 65 years	1,559	1,515	1,508	1,458	1,495	1,553
Lone parent	1,037	1,041	1,023	997	1,039	1,030
Couple with children	1,456	1,488	1,477	1,463	1,496	1,539
Other households	1,363	1,293	1,299	1,407	1,335	1,364
10th percentile (P10)						
Single householder < 65 years	600	557	577	547	589	575
Single householder ≥ 65 years	700	689	674	657	668	683
Couple, no children, < 65 years	875	835	885	862	859	882
Couple, no children, ≥ 65 years	849	835	817	796	826	850
Lone parent	577	557	556	531	514	543
Couple with children	800	787	792	797	809	827
Other households	648	660	561	612	674	679
Median (P50)						
Single householder < 65 years	1,300	1,280	1,251	1,220	1,262	1,248
Single householder ≥ 65 years	1,200	1,181	1,155	1,126	1,142	1,155
Couple, no children, < 65 years	1,626	1,601	1,683	1,658	1,652	1,699
Couple, no children, ≥ 65 years	1,414	1,322	1,361	1,313	1,322	1,307
Lone parent	955	905	885	867	917	907
Couple with children	1,342	1,321	1,334	1,313	1,349	1,386
Other households	1,250	1,218	1,228	1,407	1,190	1,294
90th percentile (P90)						
Single householder < 65 years	2,500	2,461	2,406	2,251	2,336	2,366
Single householder ≥ 65 years	2,200	2,165	2,146	2,059	2,234	2,311
Couple, no children, < 65 years	2,828	2,853	3,063	2,985	2,974	2,941
Couple, no children, ≥ 65 years	2,404	2,338	2,310	2,253	2,313	2,549
Lone parent	1,674	1,636	1,565	1,592	1,673	1,634
Couple with children	2,250	2,273	2,223	2,205	2,336	2,403
Other households	2,100	1,969	1,945	2,182	2,196	2,026
Poverty rate (%)						
Single householder < 65 years	23.9	23,9	24.2	26.1	24.9	25.2
Single householder ≥ 65 years	16.7	15.3	18.9	18.9	18.3	17.9
Couple, no children, < 65 years	7.5	8.5	6.5	7.3	6.8	7.7
Couple, no children, ≥ 65 years	7.4	7.5	7.6	8.3	7.1	8.1
Lone parent	34.6	33.9	36.1	36.6	34.8	37.9
Couple with children	10.4	9.6	9.8	9.7	8.8	9.4
Other households	20.2	14.9	21.6	17.8	17.2	21.4
Population share (%)						
Single householder < 65 years	11.4	11.8	11.9	12.3	12.4	12.2
Single householder ≥ 65 years	7.0	7.4	7.4	7.5	7.8	8.1
Couple, no children, < 65 years	16.4	16.0	15.9	16.1	16.2	16.1
Couple, no children, ≥ 65 years	11.4	12.0	12.4	12.5	12.8	13.5
Lone parent	7.6	7.5	7.6	8.0	7.7	7.7
Couple with children	44.2	43.2	42.8	41.7	41.6	40.6
Other households	2.1	2.1	1.9	1.9	1.7	1.7

Source: SOEP v27.

Note: The population covered is individuals in private households. The equivalence scale is the square root of the household size. The poverty line is 60% of contemporary median income. Households are classified according to the age of the household head.

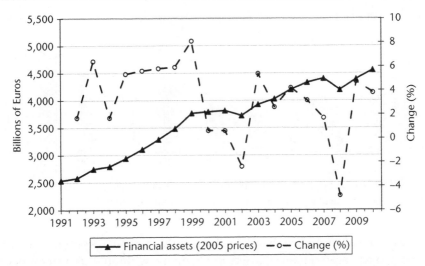

Figure 3.8. Total real financial assets of private households in Germany (billions of Euros, 2005 prices), and change compared to the previous year (%)

Source: German Bundesbank (2011). Data on financial assets refer to October of each year.

Note: Households including non-profit organizations.

crisis (Buiter 2007). Total real financial assets increased almost continuously from reunification in the early 1990s: see Figure 3.8. There were only two periods in which real financial assets stagnated or decreased. The first occurred after the turn of the Millennium with the bursting of the 'New Economy' bubble. However this had a relatively small effect on aggregate financial assets. The second period was the GR. The GR led to a temporary decline in aggregate real gross financial assets of about 4% (corresponding to €200 billion in 2005 prices) between late 2007 and the first quarter of 2009. Since then, however, financial assets reached pre-crisis levels with values of more than €4,500 billion (in 2005 prices) in the fourth quarter of 2010.

Given the much higher inequality of net worth compared to net household income in Germany (Frick and Grabka 2009), it can be assumed that the very rich were affected most by the GR. Here, we focus on high net worth individuals (HNWI), who are defined as those having investable assets of US$1 million or more, excluding primary residence, collectibles, consumables, and consumer durables (Capgemini and Merrill Lynch Global Wealth Management 2011). The number of HNWI in Germany is estimated to have fallen by just 1.9% between 2007 and 2008, corresponding to a decline of 16,000 individuals: see Figure 3.9. However in the subsequent two years, 2009 and 2010, their number reached pre-recession levels with growth rates of 6% and 7.2%, respectively. The number of HNWI in 2010 amounted to more than 900,000 individuals, or more than 1% of the total population in Germany. On

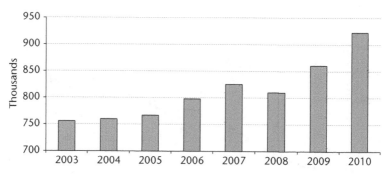

Figure 3.9. Number of high net worth individuals (thousands), 2003–10
Source: Capgemini and Merrill Lynch Global Wealth Management (2011).

this basis, it can be argued that the GR was only a temporary occurrence with respect to aggregate financial assets in Germany, with only short-term book losses, at least for the very wealthy. One explanation why the GR did not have a more significant effect may be the quick and resolute reaction of the German government in stabilizing the banking sector with its 'bank rescue package' (Weber and Schmitz 2011).

We can also consider micro-level information about the savings behaviour of private households and this supports the findings based on the data on HNWI: see Table 3.6. Private consumption makes up a large percentage of German GDP, and any shift towards savings could impair the aggregate economic situation. Over the period 2005 to 2010, more than half of all households in the SOEP reported that they had put money into savings in the month prior to the interview. The amount saved declined slightly between 2009 and 2010. The real mean amount saved is astonishingly stable over time for the total population, with a value of about €200 per household per month. This corresponds to an average savings rate of more than 11% in Germany in 2009 (Federal Statistical Office 2011). This aggregate savings rate for private households has also remained stable over the years since 2002, with a share of between 10% and 11%. When looking at those households who reported

Table 3.6. Savings behaviour of private households, 2005–10

	2005	2006	2007	2008	2009	2010
Percentage of households that saved in previous month	57.5	55.3	56.2	55.7	56.5	53.5
Mean amount saved per household (€)	205	203	203	202	204	201
Mean amount saved among households who save (€)	354	367	363	367	365	357

Source: SOEP v27. Figures for 2010 are provisional. Euro figures are in 2005 prices

Note: The population covered is individuals in private households.

putting money into savings on a regular basis, the real mean amount also remained stable at about €350 for all years. (Of course, there were significant differences across the income distribution in the amount saved: see Brenke 2011.)

In addition to the objective indicators just presented, the SOEP also provides information about subjective measures such as financial concerns. Subjective indicators could be interpreted as early indicators of a general shift in mood of the broader population and a potential increase in general uncertainties. This could be of particular relevance given that the majority of results we have presented indicate a relatively stable situation in Germany during and immediately after the GR, while medium- and long-term effects cannot, by definition, be described.

We therefore present three subjective measures here: see Table 3.7. The first indicator relates to 'general economic development', which in the past typically reflected the general economic situation in Germany. Between 2005 and 2007, the percentage of respondents who reported being very concerned fell by half to just 25%. In 2009, the figure increased to almost 45%, presumably as a result of the GR. However, in 2010, the general economic situation in Germany improved, and the percentage of individuals with concerns dropped again to roughly one-third of the adult population.

In contrast to the rather volatile figures on concerns about the general economic situation, the figures on respondents' concerns about their own financial situation remain relatively stable over time. Around a quarter of all adults report being very concerned, while half responded that they were at least somewhat concerned about their own financial situation. Furthermore, concerns about job security tended to decline in parallel to the macro-indicator of registered unemployment in Germany. Almost half of the employed

Table 3.7. Concerns about various life domains

	2005	2006	2007	2008	2009	2010
Concerns about *general* economic development (% of total adult population)						
Very concerned	54.7	44.6	25.4	25.7	44.5	35.5
Somewhat concerned	40.6	48.4	59.2	61.1	49.4	56.1
Not concerned at all	4.7	7.0	15.4	13.2	6.1	8.4
Concerns about *own* economic situation (% of total adult population)						
Very concerned	27.4	27.4	25.4	22.0	24.4	23.6
Somewhat concerned	50.4	48.8	49.1	50.8	53.0	49.0
Not concerned at all	22.1	23.8	25.5	27.2	22.6	27.4
Concerns about job security (% of employed population)						
Very concerned	21.3	18.6	17.4	15.8	16.6	15.9
Somewhat concerned	41.7	40.1	39.8	37.5	39.7	36.8
Not concerned at all	37.0	41.3	42.8	46.8	43.7	47.3

Source: SOEP v27. Figures for 2010 are provisional. Population: adults (17 years of age and older) living in private households.

population in 2010 stated that they had no economic concerns at all. It appears that the GR increased concerns about the general economic situation, but had little effect on respondents' concerns about their own economic situation. This rather surprising contrast might be partly explained by media coverage. While the German media tended to dramatize the general economic situation during the GR, most people did not experience negative impacts on their personal financial situation. This might also be a result of the government's rapid and aggressive response to the GR. Finally, another explanation might be that the social safety net or at least the existence of basic social care in Germany provides security even in times of severe economic downturn.

3.6 Conclusions

The GR led to a strong but only temporary decline in real GDP as well as in aggregate financial assets in Germany. However, this economic downturn had only small effects on the labour market. The overall number of employed persons decreased temporarily, while the number of registered unemployed rose by only around 0.5 million.

These rather small effects on the job market can be explained in part by the government's highly successful policy interventions aimed at reactivating and broadening the STC programme, which was used heavily in those industries hit hardest by the GR, namely the manufacturing sector. At its peak, more than 1.4 million persons profited from the STC programme, which thus stabilized private consumption and overall domestic demand. In addition, flexible labour market arrangements such as working time accounts, reductions in overtime, and other instruments creating more internal flexibility for firms that have been introduced over the last ten years also contributed to the success story, especially among those firms hit hardest by the GR. Herzog-Stein et al. (2010: 13) estimate that 'working time reductions secured some 1.1 million jobs, labour hoarding, with the acceptance of lower hourly productivity, some 2 million'. Furthermore, the German economy's quick recovery on the back of business investment and strong export growth made an additional contribution to this positive story (OECD 2011d).

Burda and Hunt (2011) emphasize the role of expectations in this context. There were rather pessimistic expectations prior to the GR, which resulted in low hiring in the boom phase between 2004 and 2008. Thus 'weak employment growth in the boom accounts for 41 per cent of the missing employment decline in the recession' (Burda and Hunt 2011: 38). During the GR, however, there were expectations of a fairly quick recovery; hence firms retained employees in order to have skilled and experienced employees once the recession was over (Aricò and Stein 2011).

In consequence, we observe only small effects of the GR in the SOEP data, whether in terms of gross labour income or net total household income. We do not see any substantial changes in household income levels or their distribution. The relative poverty rate based on current net monthly income decreased slightly in 2009, but the rate based on annual net household income data increased by one percentage point. Subgroup analyses show a rather small increase in relative income poverty for single persons and childless couples aged less than 65 years.

However, a price for the GR still has to be paid in the near future. The German government passed two laws to sustain the economy in November 2008 and January 2009 (Konjunkturpaket I and II). This legislation included, for example, reductions in contributions to the statutory unemployment insurance, the government grant to the statutory health insurance, and a car scrapping scheme. (The last of these measures protected the automotive industry from a severe slump and entitled new car buyers to a €2,500 premium for the trade-in of an older car.) In addition, the government initiated public investments in infrastructure and in building renovation. The total amount spent by the government is estimated to have been about €80 trillion in 2009/10. A significant part of this was new liabilities. The additional burden will have to be paid for in the future, through increased taxes or reduced public spending. Government plans point to a reduction in public spending on low-income families in particular as well as a general cut in public expenditures. The medium-term effects of the GR will therefore most likely appear in the future.

In response to the GR, government expenditures have been financed increasingly on the basis of new debt: see Figure 3.10. The same phenomenon occurred after German reunification, when total public debt increased from less than 40% of GDP in 1990 to 60% in 1997. Since then total public debt had

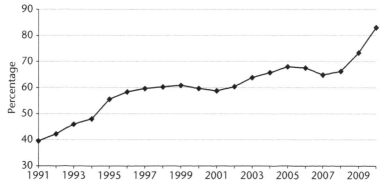

Figure 3.10. Public debt as a percentage of GDP, 1991–2010
Source: Deutsche Bundesbank 2011.

remained fairly stable at roughly 60% of GDP for more than ten years, amounting to 65% in 2007. The level of public debt has risen significantly since 2008. In 2010, debt amounted to more than 83% of GDP, which is well above the Maastricht criterion of 60%. In parallel, the public deficit was almost 4% of GDP in 2009 and close to this figure again in 2010. Due to the quick recovery of the German economy, the expected deficit in 2011 is only 2.5% of GDP.

The fiscal consolidation plans of the German government are aimed primarily at reducing welfare expenditures—more so than in other OECD countries—to keep the public deficit below 3% of GDP in the years to come (OECD 2011d). This policy will also be accomplished by a new fiscal rule called 'the debt-brake', with the aim of permanently limiting the federal government's structural deficit to a maximum of 0.35% of GDP from 2016 onwards (OECD 2011d). To achieve this target, the government already plans to cut back social security and unemployment benefits and to reduce parental and housing benefits. The resulting savings are estimated to amount to 1.13% of GDP in 2011–14 (OECD 2011d). There are also a number of new taxes under discussion or already enacted, such as a nuclear fuel tax and a financial transactions tax.

It can be assumed that such new taxes will be passed on directly to consumers. Private households will therefore be burdened by new taxes together with the reductions in social security and social benefits already enacted. The latter will affect the bottom of the income distribution most severely, and so it seems that income inequality in Germany will therefore increase further in the years to come. This may be exacerbated by other laws enacted independently of the GR, such as a reduction in inheritance tax exemptions and a flat tax on capital income, both of which privilege the top of the income distribution.

4

Country case study—Ireland

Brian Nolan, Tim Callan, and Bertrand Maître

Ireland, with a population of only four million people and accounting for an insignificant proportion of the OECD's economic activity, none the less represents a particularly interesting case study with respect to the distributional impact of the Great Recession. In the first instance this is because the recession itself had a more negative impact on national output in Ireland than in any other OECD country, as the analysis in Chapter 2 brought out. Furthermore, this dramatic downturn followed a decade of exceptionally rapid growth, including an unbridled property price boom. As a consequence, the fall in GDP from 2008 onwards went together with a bursting of the property bubble, a collapse in asset values and a banking crisis of unprecedented proportions, and a ballooning fiscal deficit. This toxic combination meant that, by late 2010, despite substantial increases in taxation and expenditure cuts, the Irish government was no longer able to borrow on international financial markets at acceptable rates and as a Eurozone member had to be 'bailed-out' by the EU and IMF (following on after Greece and followed by Portugal).

The scale of the recession after a decade of unprecedented economic growth, the size of the fiscal deficit and required retrenchment, the widespread impact of asset price falls, and the scale of the banking crisis all mark Ireland out as an outlier in terms of macroeconomic fluctuations, and likely to be particularly illuminating as to their distributional impact. As we show in this chapter, the evidence suggests that while GDP per head (in constant price terms) has fallen to levels previously seen a decade earlier, and many households have seen significant real income losses, the overall pattern of market income changes taken together with the tax and social security policy response in the first phase of the recession hit the better-off proportionately more than those on low incomes, so that commonly-used summary indicators of income inequality declined. However, survey data for 2010 suggests that this was followed by a sharp increase in income inequality.

4.1 Employment and Earnings

The so-called 'Celtic tiger' boom lasted from the mid-1990s to 2007, with the late 1990s in particular seeing Ireland with the highest rates of economic growth in the OECD. This was accompanied by a remarkable increase in employment levels, with the total number in employment rising from about 1.2 million at the start of the boom to close to 2 million by 2004 and 2.15 million by 2007. This meant that by 2007 over 60% of the adult population were in employment, and only 3% were unemployed. Substantial net immigration was also seen during this period for the first time, with return of previous emigrants notable in the early part of the boom and an inflow from the new member states of the European Union after 2004, the net inflow reaching an annual peak of almost 70,000 towards the end of the boom.

The immediate impact of the Great Recession (GR) was to reduce the overall employment rate to 55% by 2009 and 53% by 2010. The full-time employment rate fell from 50% to 41%. For those remaining in employment average hours of work per week fell for men from 41 to 39, and more modestly for women from 31.6 to 30.8, as part-time working increased and overtime was cut back. Net emigration also returned, both of Irish citizens and recent arrivals from Eastern Europe, with a net outflow of about 35,000 in the 12 months to 2010 and 60,000 estimated for the following year.

Focusing on the conventionally-measured working-age population of individuals aged 15–64 years, the decline in employment was very heavily concentrated among young men. The employment rate for men aged 20–24 fell from 75% to 47% between 2007 and 2010 whereas, by contrast, for men aged 35–44 the decline was only from 86% to 76%. Women aged 20–24 also saw a substantial decline, from 67% to 53%, but still much less than among men; women aged 45–54, remarkably, saw almost no fall in their employment rate (of about 64%). Unemployment rates correspondingly soared for younger men, rising for those aged 20–24 from 8% to 32% and for those aged 25–34 from 5% to almost 20%; the increase for men aged 45–54, from 4% to 13%, while still pronounced, was considerably less. Younger women experienced increases in unemployment that were substantially lower than for young men but greater than for mid-career or older women.

What happened to earnings and earnings dispersion among individual employees against this background? It is worth noting first that during the boom years, Ireland did not experience the pronounced increase in earnings inequality and widening gap between high versus low levels of education seen in many other OECD countries in recent decades (OECD 2008). Strong demand for low-skilled employees appears to have kept up their returns, while returns for the highly educated were limited by strong increases in supply, via an increasing flow of new graduates, return migrants and immigrants from other EU countries (Barrett, FitzGerald and Nolan 2002; McGuinness, McGinnity, and O'Connell 2008; Nolan, Voitchovsky, and Maître 2010). This meant that while mean and median hourly earnings rose by one-third in real terms, conventional measures of earnings dispersion show a considerable decline from the mid-1990s to 2007: the ratio of the top decile to the bottom decile, for example, fell from 4.8 to 4 (Nolan, Voitchovsky, and Maître 2010). The immediate impact of the recession on average earnings varied across employees and sectors; the earnings series produced by the Central Statistics Office based on responses from employers show average hourly earnings for industrial workers in industry declining in 2008, but all employees in industry saw an increase. The EU-SILC Survey of households shows average gross hourly earnings among employees continuing to increase in nominal terms from 2007 to 2008, as the crisis had its first impact, and again from 2008 to 2009: see Table 4.1. A new employer-based series produced by the Central Statistics Office covering all employees also shows an increase in 2009. As consumer prices fell in the latter year this meant that average hourly earnings actually rose quite sharply in purchasing power terms, by almost 9%.

Focusing on the dispersion in hourly earnings among employees, the ratio of the top to the bottom decile (P90/P10) was not substantially altered by the recession, with the ratio of the median to the bottom decile (P50/P10) and the ratio of the top decile to the median (P90/P50) both unchanged. While survey data for 2010 are not yet available for analysis, data on average hourly earnings produced from employer surveys by the Central Statistics Office show a

Table 4.1. Gross hourly earnings, 2004–9

Measure	2004	2007	2008	2009
In nominal terms (€):				
Mean	15.6	19.1	20.0	20.8
In real terms (€, 2004 prices):				
Mean	15.6	17.1	17.2	18.7
P10	7.4	7.7	7.7	8.4
P50	12.8	13.6	13.6	14.9
P90	27.1	30.7	30.4	32.7
Dispersion: percentile ratios				
P90/P50	2.1	2.3	2.2	2.2
P50/P10	1.7	1.8	1.8	1.8
P90/P10	3.6	4.0	3.9	3.9

Source: Analysis of EU-SILC Ireland microdata. Price deflator is Consumer Price Index available from the CSO at http://www.cso.ie/statistics/consumpriceindex.htm

decline of 2% comparing 2010 with 2009, with average weekly earnings falling by slightly more.

While the number of persons in employment—and thus in receipt of income from employment—fell in 2008 and 2009, as shown by the labour force survey figures quoted earlier and by the EU-SILC household survey, the numbers relying on social welfare payments correspondingly rose. Administrative data on the number of recipients of weekly social welfare payments (thus excluding universal child benefit paid monthly, as well as one-off payments) shows that the total number of recipients rose by 14% in each of the years 2008 and 2009, and more modestly again in 2010. This increase was primarily in unemployment-related schemes, where the number of recipients came close to trebling between 2007 and 2010. Taking both those in receipt of payments and their dependants into account, by 2010 the total number of beneficiaries of weekly social welfare payments approached 2.2 million (out of a total population of 4.2 million), up from 1.6 million in 2007.

These labour market changes at an individual level produced the pattern across households shown in Table 4.2 in terms of the proportions of working-age adults in the household actually in work. For households where the 'head' (or more correctly in EU-SILC what is termed the 'household reference person') is aged under 60, the percentage with no-one in work rose by two percentage points in 2008 and by a further 3.5 percentage points in 2009 to reach 17%. There was an even sharper fall, of nine percentage points, in the percentage with all working-age adults in the household in work, as the proportion with some but not all of those in work also rose.

4.2 Income Inequality and Poverty

We now turn to the implications of these changes in employment and welfare recipiency for household incomes and their distribution. The scale of the

Table 4.2. Percentage of working-age adults in work, by age of household head, 2004–9

Working-age adults in work	2004	2007	2008	2009
Household head aged below 60 years				
None	13.2	11.5	13.4	16.9
Some	39.5	35.9	37.2	39.5
All	47.3	52.5	49.4	43.9
Household head aged 60 years or more				
None	69.3	68.8	67.7	72.5
Some	16.5	14.5	14.8	13.2
All	14.2	16.6	17.5	14.3

Source: Analysis of EU-SILC Ireland microdata.

impact of the GR on national income, in the context of extremely rapid growth over the previous decade, must be emphasized: by 2010 GDP per head in nominal terms had fallen by close to one-fifth compared with 2007, and in real terms it was back to levels seen a decade earlier. However, as brought out in the analysis in Chapter 2, the impact on the household sector was much more muted, because much of the decline was felt in the company sector and because of the response of social transfers. The point of departure in terms of Ireland's level of income inequality (on which see Nolan and Maître 2000; Nolan, Maître, O'Neill, and Sweetman 2000; Nolan and Smeeding 2005) is also worth noting. Before the onset of the GR, summary measures of income inequality such as the Gini coefficient, Atkinson's inequality measure, the Theil coefficient, and the P90/P10 ratio—published for example by Eurostat and by the OECD in *Growing Unequal* (2008)—show that Ireland was above average within the EU-27 and the OECD. The Gini coefficient for Ireland around 2005 was 0.32, compared with a simple average of about 0.30 within the EU-27, putting Ireland on a par with countries such as Spain, Italy, the UK, and Poland, as well as among OECD countries Australia, Canada, and New Zealand. That level of inequality is consistent with relatively low social protection spending (as a proportion of national income) and low redistributive impact of income transfers together with direct taxes, arising in particular from low spending on public pensions, which in turn reflects both a low share of older persons in the population and the flat-rate nature of the social security pension system.

In terms of the institutional structures more broadly, Ireland is aligned with what is generally termed the Liberal welfare regime and has a level of income inequality similar to most of the other countries in that grouping. This remained the case over the years of the 'Celtic Tiger', when summary inequality measures were rather stable with only a modest increase towards the end of that boom (see Figure 4.1). In terms of decile shares, over the boom years there was some increase in the share going to the top 10%, but this was mostly balanced by a decline for others in the top half rather than further down the distribution. Trends right at the top of the income distribution may be better captured by data from the income tax system, and estimates of the share of total income going to the top 1% from that source do suggest a sharper increase (Nolan 2007).

Ireland's economic boom was also notable for a substantial increase in married women's labour force participation, but this did not have a disequalizing effect on the household income distribution because it was as common for women married to lower-earning as to high-earning men. Social welfare support rates initially lagged behind average earnings, especially net of tax as direct taxes were cut, but subsequently made up much of that ground, as larger increases were awarded in annual budgets in the latter years of the boom.

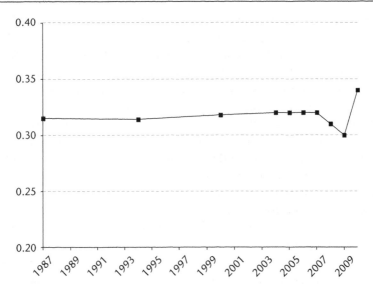

Figure 4.1. Trends in inequality in Ireland: Gini coefficient of equivalized net household income, 1987–2010

Source: Calculated by the authors from survey microdata from ESRI 1987 Survey, Living in Ireland Survey 1994–2001, and EU-SILC 2003–9; 2010 estimate based on CSO (2011). Figures for 1987–2009 use the modified OECD equivalence scale. The CSO calculation for 2010 uses a slightly different equivalence scale which if applied to earlier years yields Gini coefficient estimates that are a little lower than does the OECD scale; a small adjustment has therefore been made to the CSO figure on this basis. (The series for the Gini published by the CSO shows the same upward jump in 2010.)

While substantial in real terms, those increases in social welfare were still exceeded by the increase in average net household income (before or after equivalization to take household size and composition into account), to which increasing numbers of earners in the household also contributed.

Turning to the period from the onset of the GR, the impact on average household incomes and on the distribution was striking. Here we rely on the SILC household survey, the only annual source of data on household incomes available for Ireland, carried out by the Central Statistics Office with a sample of about 6,000 households and designed to produce data to report to Eurostat in the EU-SILC framework. (In contrast with the situation for Germany, Italy, and Sweden in Chapters 3, 5, and 6, we are using the same source of household survey data that was drawn on in the comparison of household incomes in European countries in Chapter 2: section 2.6.) Whereas EU-SILC income data for most other EU countries use the previous calendar year as the income reference period, Ireland uses the 12 months prior to the interview date, with interviewing carried out throughout the year, and thus data are more up to date. At the time of writing, detailed results from the 2009 survey have been published and the microdata up to that year have been analysed for this chapter, so that is where our discussion concentrates. Preliminary headline results for 2010 have also been published (Central Statistics Office 2011) and will be described. However, since only limited information has been released as yet and unit record data are unavailable, it has not been possible to explore them in any depth.

Table 4.3 shows that average net equivalized income continued to rise in 2008 but fell by over 5% in 2009, with the median falling by 7%; similar trends were seen for gross income, before direct taxes and social insurance contributions were deducted. Changes in the composition of total income coming into households in the survey, underlying these declines in the average, are also shown: there is a decline in the share of total income coming from employment in both 2008 and 2009 (with much of that fall in self-employment income) while investment income also falls, with a sharp rise in the importance of cash social transfers and a marginal decline in direct tax and social contributions as a share of net income.

To see where in the income distribution these changes will have had their effects, Table 4.4 compares the composition of net income in 2007 and 2009 for those in the bottom 30% of the distribution, the next 50%, and the top 20%. Focusing first towards the bottom, there was relatively little change for

Table 4.3. Mean and median net and gross equivalized household income, and composition of net income, 2004–9

	2004	2007	2008	2009
	€ (nominal)			
Net				
Mean	24,366	30,319	31,064	29,300
Median	21,271	25,844	26,857	25,543
Gross				
Mean	31,231	37,908	38,467	36,356
Median	26,082	30,254	31,328	29,157
	€ (2004 prices)			
Net				
Mean	24,366	27,145	26,715	26,385
Median	21,271	23,138	23,097	23,001
Gross				
Mean	31,231	33,939	33,082	32,738
Median	26,082	27,086	26,942	26,256
	% of total net income			
Employment income	91.8	84.5	82.8	79.7
Investment income	7.4	11.0	10.1	8.7
Cash transfers	16.1	17.3	19.0	22.8
Other	5.0	5.3	5.4	6.1
Direct taxes and social insurance contributions	−20.3	−18.0	−17.3	−17.2
Net income	100.0	100.0	100.0	100.0

Source: Analysis of EU-SILC Ireland microdata. Price deflator is Consumer Price Index available from the CSO at http://www.cso.ie/statistics/consumpriceindex.htm

Table 4.4. Shares of income sources in net household incomes (%), by income group, 2004–9

Income source	Bottom 30%		Middle 50%		Top 20%	
	2007	2009	2007	2009	2007	2009
Employment income	20.2	18.8	78.1	70.1	106.0	106.2
Investment income	6.6	4.9	10.2	8.2	12.8	10.2
Cash transfers	65.6	66.5	18.4	26.4	5.00	7.3
Other	9.2	11.2	6.1	6.2	3.6	4.7
Direct taxes and social insurance contributions	–1.6	–1.4	–12.7	–10.9	–27.4	–28.3
Net income	100.0	100.0	100.0	100.0	100.0	100.0

Source: Analysis of EU-SILC Ireland microdata.

the bottom 30%: two-thirds of its income already came from social transfers in 2007 and this went up by a modest one percentage point, with a corresponding fall in income from employment and investment. For the net 50% of the distribution the changes were more pronounced: income from employment fell by eight percentage points and investment income by two percentage points, with a sharp rise in the share coming from cash transfers and a fall in the share of income tax and social contributions. For the top 20%, there was much more stability in income composition, with some decline in investment income and increase in the share of income tax and social contributions.

Focusing on the distributional implications, the share of income going to each decile group and summary inequality measures for net equivalized income (using the square root of household size equivalence scale) are shown in Table 4.5. Strikingly, it is the share of the top 10% that sees most change, falling from close to 25% before the crash to 23.2% by 2009, whereas the shares of each of the bottom five decile groups rose, so the share going to the bottom half of the distribution went up by 1.3% of total income. This is reflected in a decline in the summary measures of inequality, with the Gini coefficient for example down to 0.30 by 2009, a decline of 6%. (Indeed, the distribution for 2009 Lorenz-dominates that for 2007.)

Up to that point, then, the impact of the recession was equalizing rather than disequalizing, indeed quite considerably so. In addition to the most immediate effects impacting substantially on income towards the top (via profits and income from capital and self-employment), the nature and phasing of the policy response via the tax and social welfare systems is particularly important in this case. As we discuss in the next section, increases in taxation dominated in 2008 and 2009 and were rather progressive in character, whereas from 2010 reductions in social welfare were also implemented, which will have affected the shares of those towards the bottom.

Table 4.5. Decile group shares (%) and inequality indices (net equivalized household income), 2004–9

	2004	2007	2008	2009
Share (%) of:				
Bottom 10%	3.0	3.2	3.4	3.4
2nd	4.4	4.6	4.8	4.9
3rd	5.4	5.6	5.8	6.0
4th	6.8	6.7	6.9	6.9
5th	8.1	7.9	8.1	8.1
6th	9.4	9.1	9.2	9.2
7th	10.7	10.6	10.6	10.6
8th	12.4	12.5	12.3	12.6
9th	15.0	15.2	14.8	15.1
Top 10%	25.1	24.7	24.3	23.2
Inequality indices:				
P90/P50	1.94	1.99	1.94	1.95
P50/P10	2.25	2.11	2.01	1.99
P90/P10	4.38	4.20	3.91	3.87
Gini	0.327	0.322	0.311	0.302

Source: Analysis of EU-SILC Ireland microdata.

The headline results for 2010 suggest that this, and other factors, contributed to a dramatic increase in inequality in that year, with the Gini coefficient rising from 0.30 to over 0.34—see Figure 4.1. This increase may also reflect the impact of lump-sum payments to those retiring, notably from the public service where early retirement was incentivized to reduce the pay bill, since these lump sums are counted as income in the year received. It will take some time before the medium-term impact of the GR on income inequality becomes clear, but it is highly significant that the initial inequality-reducing impact in the Irish case has not been sustained.

To give some indication of the impact of the recession on different types of person and household, Table 4.6 shows how changes in mean income differed by household type, and for persons classified by age and gender. Each comparison reveals a dramatic difference between older persons and the rest of the population: between 2007 and 2009 those aged 60 or over and their households saw substantial increases in average net income in real terms, of 10% or more, while other households, and both adults of working age and children, saw declines of 3% to 6%. This reflects the impact of declines in employment and in income from self-employment on those of working age and their families, together with the remarkable extent to which pensioners have been insulated from the effects of the crisis in income terms.

As well as the overall impact of the recession on the distribution of income, the impact on incomes towards the bottom, in other words on income poverty, is of particular interest from a policy perspective. With the widely-used relative approach to deriving an income poverty threshold, incorporated for

Table 4.6. Mean real net equivalized income (Euros, 2004 prices), by household and person type, 2004–9

Household and person type	2004	2007	2008	2009	Change 2007–9 (%)
Aged less than 60 years					
Single adult	21,439	24,438	24,156	23,003	−5.9
Single adult with children	11,690	14,671	14108	14,174	−3.4
2 adults, no children	27,610	32,590	31,613	30,989	−4.9
2 adults with children	23,623	27,599	27,470	25,793	−6.5
Aged 60+ years					
Single adult 60+	12,509	14,801	17,627	16,756	+ 13.2
2 adults 60+	19,133	21,813	22,971	24,750	+ 13.5
Age/sex					
Child (aged less than 18)	22,479	25,358	24,966	24,090	−5.0
Man (18–59 years)	27,618	30,348	29,357	28,912	−4.7
Woman (18–59 years)	26,240	28,960	27,931	27,866	−3.8
Man (60+ years)	19,197	21,430	23,248	25,090	+ 17.1
Woman (60+ years)	17,357	20,295	45,134	22,387	+ 10.3

Source: Analysis of EU-SILC Ireland microdata; price deflator is Consumer Price Index, CSO: http://www.cso.ie/statistics/consumpriceindex.htm

example into the EU's set of commonly-agreed social inclusion indicators, a threshold of 60% of median equivalized income in the country in question is often employed. In the case of Ireland, relative income poverty measured in this fashion increased in the earlier years of the Celtic Tiger boom, despite the sharply rising levels of employment and incomes from work, largely because those remaining reliant on social transfers fell behind. Much of this ground was made up in the latter part of the boom, so that by 2005–7 Ireland's relative income poverty rate was above the EU- and OECD-averages but not an outlier, see Table 4.7.

The immediate impact of the GR was to reduce this relative income poverty measure: in 2007, 20% of persons were in households below 60% of median equivalized household income, and this fell to 19% in 2008 and 17.5% in 2009. This reflects the factors already adverted to in discussing the increasing share of total income going to the bottom deciles in the distribution—relating to the incomes most affected, the nature of the policy response, and timing—

Table 4.7. Poverty indicators, 2004–9 (% of individuals)

Measure	2004	2007	2008	2009
Income poverty rate, poverty line = 60% of contemporary median equivalized income	23.7	20.3	19.4	17.5
Income poverty rate, poverty line = 60% of 2006 median equivalized income	n.a.	20.3	20.5	20.6
Lacking at least 2 of 11 deprivation items	n.a.	11.8	13.8	17.3

Source: Analysis of EU-SILC Ireland microdata.

as well as the nature of this poverty measure (on which see the discussion in Chapter 1). Those towards the bottom of the income distribution were already heavily reliant on social transfers as the main source of income, since the households involved largely comprise older persons and those of working age who, for a range of reasons, are not in sustained employment. The increase in unemployment and corresponding decline in income from employment, which was the most obvious effect of the recession, will thus have left many of them unaffected. The evolution of income support rates for the unemployed, pensioners, and others relying on social protection is also important. These cash transfers are not formally indexed to prices or wages; instead any increases are entirely at the discretion of the government of the day, generally announced along with taxation changes in the annual budget statement. Support rates provided in weekly social transfers were actually increased for 2009, as discussed in more detail in the next section. These increases in income support took place at a time when, most unusually, poverty thresholds framed in purely relative terms were going down since average (median) incomes across all households were declining. So the relative position of those relying on social transfers improved considerably, serving to offset the impact of increasing numbers relying on those transfers. These factors are reflected in the changes in composition of those falling below relative income poverty thresholds: in 2007, 9% of those below the 60% relative income threshold were unemployed, but this was up to 13% by 2009; the proportion made up of those who are retired fell by about the same amount. Headline results for 2010 show that the relative income poverty threshold fell by 10%, much more rapidly than in 2009, and despite this the percentage of persons falling below it rose by about 1.5 percentage points. This increase was concentrated among children and working-age adults, with the rate for older persons unchanged.

In such a situation it is useful to also look at what happened to poverty rates calculated using income thresholds that remain constant in purchasing power terms rather than moving in line with average incomes—often referred to as 'anchored' poverty thresholds. Taking a low-income cut-off in 2007 as 60% of median income and subsequently moving in line with the consumer price index, the percentage of persons falling below that threshold was stable to 2009, in contrast to the fall in relative income poverty over those years, and headline results suggest it rose sharply in 2010.

It is also relevant to note trends in deprivation over these years, as captured by a range of non-monetary indicators included in the same household survey. These showed increasing levels of deprivation in 2008 and a sharper rise in 2009. Taking 11 deprivation items used in monitoring poverty in Ireland, the percentage reporting deprivation on two or more items rose from 12% in 2007 to 14% in 2008 and 17% in 2009. The largest increases were seen for items such as being able to afford an afternoon or evening out or to replace worn-out furniture. Headline results for 2010 show a further sharp increase in deprivation, with 22.5% reporting deprivation on two or more of these items.

4.3 The Tax and Transfer Policy Response

One component of the immediate impact of the Great Recession, as described earlier, was to plunge Ireland into fiscal crisis. Changes to direct taxes and social transfers constituted one of the main planks in the government's response, and will have had a significant influence on the overall redistributive impact of the crisis: these are announced in the annual budget statement from the Minister for Finance towards the end of each year, to apply for the following calendar year. The response was rather tardy, only beginning in late 2008 when introducing the budget for 2009, which brought in a new income levy charged on gross income that increased with income and had none of the allowances or reliefs that apply in the standard income tax system. Remarkably, social transfer rates were actually increased at that point, by about 3%, despite falling inflation and the fiscal situation (though support for the newly-unemployed aged less than 21 was cut and the universal early childcare supplement payment for children under 6 was abolished). At that point, the scale of the recession was not yet fully appreciated and the stated aim was to protect the most vulnerable, but prices were falling and holding rates unchanged would have sufficed to increase their purchasing power. A special 'emergency' budget in April 2009 then doubled the rates for the income levy so that it ranged from 2% to 6% of gross income, and the long-standing health levy was also doubled to 4%. These tax and welfare changes are those that will have impacted by 2009, and will thus have affected the household survey data analysed in the previous section.

The budget for 2010 then announced reductions in nominal rates of social welfare support, of the order of 4%, for recipients of working age but not for pensioners. Unemployment payments for those aged 21–25 were also sharply reduced. In addition, the rates of universal child benefit were cut by 10%, although those dependent on social welfare received a compensating increase in their weekly payment. In the Budget for 2011, further cuts in welfare for those of working age, again of about 4%, were implemented and child benefit was again cut by 10%, this time with no compensation for welfare recipients. The income and health levies were restructured and combined into a new universal social charge, and income tax was increased via reduced credits rather than raising rates. The complex set of changes in taxes and transfers over the period 2009–11 are summarized in Table 4.8.

Table 4.8. Tax and social transfer changes in response to the crisis, budgets 2009–11

Budget 2009
- income levy introduced
- 3% rise in welfare payment rates

Supplementary budget April 2009
- Levy rates doubled (to 2/4/6), health levy doubled (to 4)
- PRSI ceiling raised
- Christmas bonus abolished
- Early childcare supplement halved, to be abolished
- Cuts in payment rates for unemployed under 21

Budget 2010
- Cuts in welfare for working age of 4%
- Larger cuts for 21–25 year olds
- Child benefit cut by 10% with compensation for welfare recipients

Budget 2011
- Cuts in welfare for working age of 4%
- Child benefit cut by 10% with no compensation for welfare recipients
- Universal social charge—combining income and health levies
- Increases in income tax via reduced credits
- Cuts in public service pensions
- Restricting tax reliefs on employee pension contributions

The distributional impact of these tax and welfare changes can be analysed using the SWITCH tax-benefit simulation model (about which see for example Callan et al. 2009). The results presented in Figure 4.2 relate to the impact of tax and welfare changes over the entire period 2009–11 taken together and, as is customary in such redistributive analyses, they are benchmarked to the average change in earned incomes over the period, which in this case most unusually was a decline of 4%.

As we have seen, the two budgets introduced in 2009 focused for the most part on increasing taxes, and this produced a highly progressive pattern of gains and losses, with considerable increases in the share of income going to lower parts of the distribution and substantial falls for the top end of the income distribution. Subsequent budgets for 2010 and 2011 implemented cuts in social transfers for those of working age, which impacted on lower income groups, but also further increased direct taxes. The overall impact of tax and welfare changes over the period was thus still highly progressive, as shown in Figure 4.2, with the percentage losses for the bottom 20% being only about one-third of those for the top 20%. While every decile group saw a decline in income due to the combined effects of tax increases and cuts in social transfers these were least towards the bottom, reflecting the extent to which policy sought to insulate those relying on pensions in particular from the impact of the recession.

Another policy response to the fiscal crisis which had immediate implications for household incomes and their distribution focused on public sector pay. The public sector, broadly defined, accounted for about 17% of total

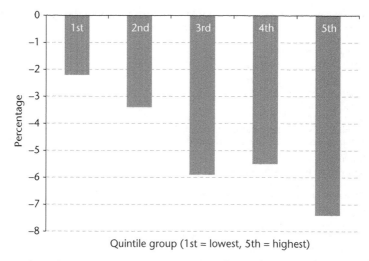

Figure 4.2. Distributive impact of tax and welfare changes by household net income quintile group: percentage loss, 2009–11

Source: Analysis of EU-SILC data using SWITCH tax-benefit model.

Note: losses for each quintile group are shown against a wage-indexed benchmark of −4% change over the period—see text for details.

employment before the onset of the recession, and pay accounts for a very large share of current public expenditure, so cuts were seen as potentially playing a major role in fiscal correction. In addition, public sector pay rose rapidly during the boom and the public/private sector premium appears to have widened significantly (Kelly, McGuinness, and O'Connell 2009*a*, *b*). (The public sector covers a very broad occupational mix, including substantial numbers of routine non-manual and manual workers.) A public sector pension levy was introduced in 2009, which charged rates of between 5% and 10% on earnings above €15,000. The budget for 2010 then announced reductions in public service salaries of 5% on the first €30,000, 7.5% on the next €40,000, and 10% on the next €55,000 of salary. (Importantly, retired public servants receiving pensions linked to pay in the grade did not have their pensions cut in line with that pay.) The impact of the pension levy and pay cut taken together on the total disposable income of different decile groups can be simulated using SILC survey data distinguishing these employees, and is striking. As there are few public sector employees in the bottom four deciles, the net impact on them is close to zero. The proportionate fall in disposable income then rises steadily as one moves up the distribution, from an average fall of 0.5% for the fifth and sixth decile groups up to 3% for the top decile group. This reflects both the position of public sector workers in the distribution and the fact that the pay cuts were structured to have greater impact as the pay level involved rose.

4.4 Projection for the Post-2009 Period

The likely distributional impact of the increases in direct tax and social contributions and cuts in cash transfers implemented in 2010 and 2011 have been included in our analysis based on the SWITCH tax-benefit model for Ireland in the previous section. The same model can also be used to carry out a broader simulation or projection exercise which attempts to incorporate not only the tax and social transfer changes implemented but also the key changes in macroeconomic variables, notably the proportion in employment and the average return to employment, to 2011 and look at what the shape of the income distribution and key income poverty indicators might then be. This is done by changing the structure and parameters of the direct tax and social welfare systems to reflect the policies actually implemented, as already examined in the previous section, but in addition also changing the weights applied to different households to reduce the numbers in employment and increase the numbers unemployed or inactive; this aims to align aggregate employment and unemployment rates with best estimates of the actual situation in 2011, while taking into account the types of household most likely to be affected by increased unemployment or inactivity (in terms of age and education level).

Taking 2008 as the base year, the model has been used to simulate household incomes and produce key distributional indicators for 2011. The results show the share of the top decile group falling substantially by almost two percentage points and the next decile group from the top seeing a marginal fall, with the corresponding gains in income share being spread throughout most of the rest of the distribution; the Gini coefficient thus declines. Relative income poverty rates also fall in the simulation, with the percentage below 60% of median income down by about two-thirds of a percentage point and a much more pronounced fall in the proportion below 50% of the median. These simulation results are consistent with the results of the 2009 SILC survey, but not with the sharp rise in inequality in 2010 shown in the headline results for that year described above. As made clear, it is only when further details and the microdata from that survey become available that it will be possible to get behind those headline figures, and investigate in depth the reasons for the divergence between them and the pattern suggested by the simulation exercise.

4.5 Inequality, the Recession, and the Medium Term

The analysis presented in this chapter has focused on the way the Great Recession has affected household incomes and their distribution, but in conclusion it is also worth noting that it will also have impacted on the distribution of wealth. Wealth held in forms other than housing is highly concentrated, in Ireland as elsewhere (see Jäntti, Sierminska, and Smeeding 2008 for a comparative analysis of wealth distribution in a number of OECD countries), so the effects of the collapse in the value of financial assets and non-residential property will be felt disproportionately towards the top. In the Irish case the banking crisis led to shares in the domestic banks effectively losing their value, so holders of those specific financial assets will have been particularly hard hit, and are likely to have been more dispersed through the income distribution. However, the key feature of the GR for Ireland was the collapse in property prices, in a country with very high home ownership (of about 80%) and with housing being the main asset for most wealth-holders. With house prices down by up to half since their 2007 peak, those who bought property towards the height of the boom with borrowed money and who are now in negative equity are in a very difficult position. Overall, the recession may well have seen the distribution of wealth among those who hold some become more unequal, although the gap between those with and without wealth may have narrowed.

Looking to the future, the macroeconomic and fiscal prospects for Ireland over the medium term—the next four to five years—are fraught, with major implications for income inequality and socioeconomic inequality more broadly. The commitment to reduce the fiscal deficit to 3% by 2015 (from over 14% at its peak) is at the core of the agreement between Ireland and the IMF/EU associated with the autumn 2010 bail-out, and will entail major cuts in public spending combined with some further increases in taxation. Public sector numbers will be reduced, but the prospects for a sustained upturn in private sector employment are not good, despite strong export performance. The likely distributional implications of retrenchment in spending on public services are difficult to establish when the nature of the cuts is not yet clear, but their salience highlights the importance of going beyond the cash income of households to obtain a comprehensive picture of their economic circumstances and the medium- to long-term distributional impact of the recession. In a similar vein, an intergenerational perspective is especially important: those already retired may be spared the worst effects, those in the workforce will carry the burden of substantial extra taxation and reduced cash and non-cash support, but the young seeking to enter the workforce for the first time or already unemployed may be the most seriously affected if unemployment fails to come down from its current very high levels for young people. Out-migration is already a significant feature, as it has been in previous Irish recessions, but the extent to which these young migrants will be in a position to return to Ireland having obtained valuable experience, as they did in the 1990s, crucially depends on the resumption of economic growth at a level sufficient to lead to substantial and sustained net job creation.

5

Country case study—Italy

Andrea Brandolini, Francesco D'Amuri, and Ivan Faiella

When Lehman Brothers announced its bankruptcy on 15 September 2008, the Italian economy was already sliding towards recession. The panic in global financial markets and the dramatic collapse of the world trade turned a mild downturn into the most severe recession experienced by Italy since the Second World War. The sharp drop in foreign demand rapidly propagated to the rest of the economy owing to the intense subcontracting relations and the tightening of lending conditions by banks (Bugamelli, Cristadoro, and Zevi 2010). From the cyclical peak in August 2007 to the trough in April 2009, industrial production dropped by 27.2% and GDP by 7% (Istat 2011a: 10–11). Employment fell, but with a lag: it continued rising until April 2008 but, as the crisis deepened, firms began to reduce working-time and to freeze job turnover (Cingano, Torrini, and Viviano 2010). By August 2010, the number of workers employed had diminished by 770,000, a fall of 3.3%, according to the Labour Force Survey (LFS).

In Italy, the Great Recession (GR) has been largely a 'real' phenomenon. That is, it was triggered by the drop in world trade and demand while the worsening of business confidence and domestic financing conditions played only a secondary role (Caivano, Rodano, and Siviero 2010). The banking sector did not need any major injection of public money, and the deterioration of the government deficit, far smaller than in many rich countries during the GR, was largely driven by falling tax revenues and growing expenditures to sustain non-financial firms and households. The housing market did not experience the bust that occurred in other countries such as Ireland or Spain: the number of transactions did go down but housing prices only marginally declined (Panetta 2009). The low share of more risky assets in household portfolios, high real wealth holdings, and low indebtedness reduced Italian households' exposure to the turmoil in financial markets, and helped them to smooth out the impact on consumption expenditure of falling incomes. Also, household demographic structure helped cushion the effects of the GR. Before the crisis about a quarter of disposable income was from pensions and two-fifths of all persons lived in households receiving some pension income. The family provided economic support to many young job-losers still living with their parents (Mocetti, Olivieri, and Viviano 2011), consistent with the role of the family observed in many southern European welfare states (Ferrera 1996).

The GR amplified the 'growth problem' already manifest in the Italian economy, whose roots are mainly to be found in the supply side (Ciocca 2003; Brandolini and Bugamelli 2009). Between 1998 and 2007, Italian GDP grew by an average 1.5% per year, or by 1.1% on a per capita basis, which is by far less than in previous decades or in other advanced economies. Employment went up more than macroeconomic conditions would have justified, largely thanks to the greater 'flexibility' introduced in the labour market by legislative changes and contractual agreements (Brandolini et al. 2007). About two-fifths of the 2.8 million additional salaried jobs created between 1997 and 2007 were on a fixed-term basis. Moreover, the number of 'quasi-employees'—individuals who work for single customers in their premises but are formally self-employed to reduce social security contributions and employment protection—rose considerably. Increased flexibility was accompanied by substantial wage moderation, with real wages per full-time employee rising annually by 0.5% between 1997 and 2007. Real earnings at first employment progressively decreased (Rosolia and Torrini 2007; Rosolia 2010). According to national accounts, the gross disposable income of consumer households increased by 0.4% per year on a per capita basis and, in 2007, its value was only slightly higher than in 1992. Although income inequality and poverty rates have barely changed since 1993 (Brandolini 2009), a widespread sense of impoverishment and a growing concern for rising inequalities have dominated the public debate (Boeri and Brandolini 2004).

The impact of the GR on Italians' standard of living must be seen in the context of a stagnating economy, with household finances strained by modest income growth and increased occupational insecurity, and a very limited capacity of the government to raise expenditure due to the public debt. The stimulus from economic policies and automatic stabilizers was among the lowest across advanced economies. Yet, on the basis of the available information, it appears to have been sufficient to prevent a radical deterioration in key income distribution indicators during the recession and the subsequent modest economic recovery. Now that an intensive and painful attempt to consolidate public finances is beginning, it is an open question whether this deterioration can continue to be avoided.

The aim of this chapter is to assess how economic conditions have changed among Italian households during the GR. We review some available data in Section 5.1. However informative, they do not include detailed information on incomes at the household level. For this reason, in the following sections we simulate income changes due to labour market dynamics, the main channel through which the GR has affected income distribution in Italy. The building blocks of this microsimulation model (imputation of income from labour and pension, entitlements to benefits for job-losers, transitions in the labour market) are illustrated in Section 5.2. This section also outlines the main income support schemes existing in Italy and describes how transition probabilities in the labour market have differed between people during the crisis. The simulation results for the income distribution among working-age individuals and among house-holds, respectively, are discussed in Sections 5.3 and 5.4; Section 5.5 concludes.

5.1 Income and Living Conditions During the GR

The GR hit the household sector considerably: real gross disposable income fell by 4.1% between 2007 and 2009, according to national accounts. This result was driven largely by the fall in interest and dividends and other property income. Without these changes, household disposable income would have remained virtually stable. (These figures refer to the 'consumer household sector' and hence differ from those discussed in Chapter 2: excluded are both 'non-profit institutions serving households' and 'small unincorporated enterprises with fewer than 5 employees'.)

From tax records (Dipartimento delle Finanze 2010), we may infer the changes during the GR in the distribution of personal pre-tax income net of interest and (a large part of) dividends, which are mostly subject to flat-rate withholding taxes. (Capital gains and losses are also excluded.) The population coverage of these data is good (the 41.5 million tax files filed in 2009 cover about 85% of all residents older than 19 years) and the trend over time in total pre-tax income appears to be broadly in line with that estimated in national accounts, after properly matching income components.

Excluding non-positive incomes, as information is missing in 2007 (in 2009 they added up to 575,000 tax files), the effects of the recession show up more in the fall of the number of taxpayers (–1.1%, compared to a rise by 1.3% in the number of people older than 19 years) than in the decline of their mean income (–0.4%). The drop was concentrated at the bottom of the income distribution, while real incomes increased in the middle and, to a lesser degree, at the top. This is shown in Figure 5.1, which reports the cumulative changes in the real values of the mean and the nine percentiles P10, . . . , P90 for the GR period (2008–9) on the right, and the five years prior to the GR (2003–7) on the left. (See the note to the figure for details about the estimation of distributive statistics.) The overall impact of the GR on the distribution among taxpayers of pre-tax positive incomes was modest and ambiguous: the Gini index of inequality decreased slightly from 0.459 to 0.455, while the ratio of P90 to P10 went up from 12.7 to 13.6. The share of total income held by the top 1% of taxpayers declined by half a percentage point, from 9.5% to 9.0%, whereas the income share of the other taxpayers in the top 10% did not change. (The same conclusion holds after adjusting data as suggested in the top income literature: see the estimates for Italy by Alvaredo and Pisano 2010.) In the five years before the GR, mean income rose by 4.4%, with relatively few differences across deciles, except at the bottom, where we find 'marginal' taxpayers with highly variable and often occasionally low incomes. During those five years, the Gini index fluctuated between 0.453 and 0.460.

Italy's income distribution appears to have been hardly affected by the GR. Yet, this impression of stasis, which extends to the years before the GR, fades away when we divide taxpayers into three groups: employees, pensioners, and a residual group comprising self-employed people and all other taxpayers. In 2009, these groups accounted for 51%, 37%, and 12% of all taxpayers, respectively. (This classification is the only one possible if one uses existing tabulations of tax statistics, and is based on taxpayers' declarations, regardless of their actual main source of income.) As is clear from the bottom charts in Figure 5.1, patterns of change differ significantly for these three groups. Real pre-tax incomes of employees fell during the GR, as well as in the previous five years, across the entire distribution: in both periods, the proportionate decline shrinks as we move from the bottom to the top of the distribution, implying rising within-group inequality. In contrast, pensioners' incomes show a steady and fairly homogenous increase in both periods, the only exceptions being the worse trends in P10 and P20 between 2002 and 2007. The third group mostly comprises self-employed taxpayers and, unsurprisingly, has by far the most variable incomes: the relatively sustained growth between 2002 and 2007 is followed by a sharp reduction between 2007 and 2009. Variations are greater for P30 and P40 than for percentiles at either extreme of the distribution, but within-group inequality rose during the GR according to all commonly-used inequality indices.

The apparent stability of the distribution of pre-tax incomes hides important re-rankings across main categories of taxpayers but, *prima facie*, the GR seems to have affected only the incomes of self-employed taxpayers, whereas employees' and pensioners' incomes continued virtually unaltered along the trends observed before the GR (negative and positive, respectively). The greater sensitivity of incomes from self-employment shows up in the composition of the top 1% of taxpayers, where the proportion of self-employed fell from 17% to 14% between 2007 and 2009.

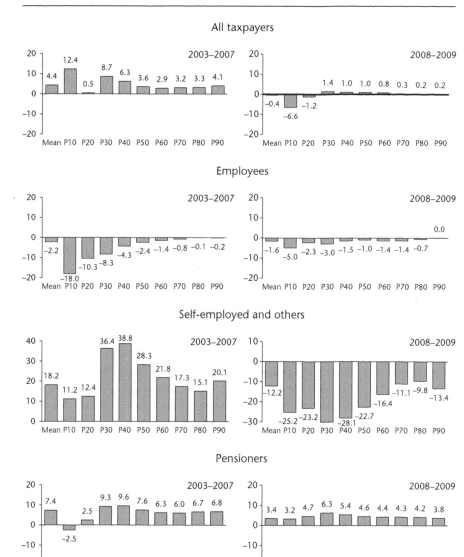

Figure 5.1. Changes (%) in real annual pre-tax income: mean and deciles, by period

Source: Authors' estimates from tabulations in Dipartimento delle Finanze (2010 and previous years). Taxpayers are classified on the basis of their declarations, regardless of whether their primary source of income coincides with the income characterizing the category to which they belong. Estimates calculated using INEQ, software designed by Frank Cowell (LSE), assuming a piecewise linear distribution except for a Paretian top interval (open interval in the few cases where the algorithm does not converge). Incomes are divided by the deflator of the final consumption expenditure of households. In all the charts, the vertical axes use a scale that spans 40 percentage points.

These tax data provide important and timely insights about income distribution changes during the recession. Tax evasion aside, there are two main problems with these data, however. First, they do not provide any information about changes in the distribution induced by variations in the income earned on financial assets. As a consequence of the drop in profitability and the lowering of interest rates, the flow of interests and dividends received by households plummeted by over 40% from 2007 to 2009, accounting for much of the fall in household disposable income during the GR, as mentioned above. If these components are included in the income definition, we may expect some narrowing of the distribution, since financial wealth tends to be more concentrated at the top of the distribution than labour and transfer income are. Using data from the Bank of Italy's Survey of Household Income and Wealth (SHIW) for 2006 (the survey is conducted every two years and no data are available for 2007), we may see that the fall in earned interest and dividends is indeed estimated to be larger for higher income groups (Figure 5.2 (a); interest and dividends in 2009 are approximated by reducing their value in 2006 by the corresponding average decrease measured in national accounts). However, the size of the drop is probably too small (less than 1% of income from labour and pensions) to affect income distribution in a perceptible way. (This may reflect the underreporting of this income component.)

Changes in asset values may also have important consequences for living standards as capital gains or losses tend to affect household consumption behaviour (Guiso, Paiella, and Visco 2006; Bassanetti and Zollino 2008). Between 2007 and 2009, households experienced considerable capital losses on risky financial assets, as shown by the fall by about a third of the Total Return Index for the Italian stock exchange estimated by Morgan Stanley Capital International, which is an equity price index embodying full reinvestment of dividends. Conversely, housing prices rose slightly, by almost 1%. Capital gains and losses are usually excluded from the concept of disposable income, but it is worth estimating their allocation along the income range. Using again data from the SHIW for 2006, we may approximate capital gains by applying the changes in the previous asset price indices to the holdings of risky assets and dwellings in 2006. By construction this calculation ignores changes in the stock of owned assets, but it indicates that, between 2006 and 2009, capital losses on risky assets and capital gains on houses tended to be proportionally larger for richer decile groups of the distribution of equivalent income from labour and pensions. The net effect on the distribution of total income is unclear, however, in the absence of more precise simulations: see Figure 5.2(b).

The second problem with the tax data is that they refer to individuals and cannot account for income pooling within households. Unfortunately, household-level income data are available only up to 2008, both in the SHIW and in

(a) Interest and dividends received

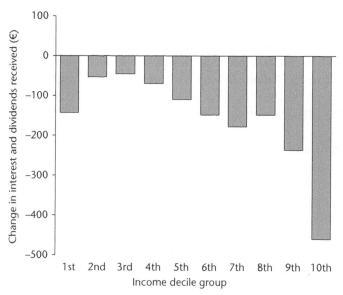

(b) Capital gains on risky and housing assets

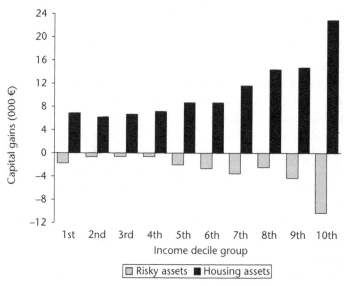

Figure 5.2. Changes in (a) interest and dividends received, and in (b) capital gains on risky and housing assets, 2006–9, by income decile group

Source: Authors' estimates from SHIW data (Version 6.0, February 2010). Households are ranked by the sum of labour and pension income.

Istat's Statistics on Income and Living Conditions (SILC), except for the few aggregate figures for the 2010 wave of SILC (covering income earned in 2009) released by Eurostat in December 2011 and discussed in Chapter 2. To investigate the redistributive role of the family in some depth, which is crucial to understand the distributive implications of the GR in Italy, in the next sections we employ microsimulation methods.

Before turning to microsimulation, we gauge what happened to household poverty and hardship drawing upon the statistics from the SILC (Eurostat 2011; Istat 2011*b*), the Istat's expenditure survey (Istat 2011*c*), and the Istat's multipurpose survey (Istat 2011*d*): see Table 5.1. The SILC survey is carried out by Istat in the last quarter of each year and collects information on current living conditions together with information about incomes earned in the previous calendar year. According to the most recent SILC wave, between 2007 and 2009 the proportion of low-income people did not vary much—if anything, it slightly fell—when the poverty line is set at either 60% of the contemporary equivalent median income, or anchored in real terms at 60% of the equivalent median income in 2004. Eurostat's material deprivation composite index worsened between 2007 and 2008, but the decline was partly reversed in 2009 and 2010. Some indicators of deprivation deteriorate slightly during the GR but others exhibit little change. Turning to Istat's estimates based on households' consumption expenditure, the relative poverty rate has increased slightly without, however, departing from the flat trend observed since the late 1990s: the rate of 13.8% estimated for 2010 is roughly the same rate observed for 2000. A rising tendency is somewhat more noticeable for the absolute poverty rate which went up from 4.1% in 2007 to 4.9% in 2008 and to 5.2% in 2009–10. Finally, indicators of self-assessed economic condition, gathered in Istat's multipurpose survey, show only a modest worsening during the GR: the spike in 2008 can hardly be linked to the economic crisis, as the survey is carried out in February and has been since 2005. The deterioration of households' subjective evaluation of their economic situation predates the GR.

To sum up, all the available information on pre-tax income, consumption expenditure, deprivation indicators, and self-assessed economic conditions, consistently suggests a limited impact of the GR on inequality and poverty, despite the considerable fall in mean income. However, there are indications that this aggregate outcome may have been associated with substantial differences in the experience of different groups, largely linked to different trends in labour and pension incomes. Note that similar movements also characterized the 15 year period prior to the GR, when substantial stability of inequality and poverty indices was accompanied by an improvement of the relative position of the households of self-employed workers, managers, and, to a lesser extent, pensioners, and a worsening in relative position of the households of white-collar and, especially, blue-collar workers (Brandolini 2009).

Table 5.1. Poverty and hardship indicators, 2002–11 (%)

Indicator	2002	2003	2004	2005	2006	2007	2008	2009	2010	2011
Income-based indicators										
Low-income headcount ratio (SHIW) (1)	20.0	–	20.7	–	19.2	–	21.5	–	–	–
Low-income headcount ratio (SILC) (2)	–	19.1	18.9	19.6	19.9	18.7	18.4	18.2	–	–
Low-income headcount ratio (fixed real line) (SILC) (3)	–	–	18.9	20.0	19.7	18.3	18.3	18.0	–	–
Expenditure-based indicators										
Relative poverty headcount ratio (4)	12.4	12.0	13.2	13.1	12.9	12.8	13.6	13.1	13.8	–
Absolute poverty headcount ratio (5)	–	–	–	4.1	3.9	4.1	4.9	5.2	5.2	–
Material deprivation indicators										
Eurostat material deprivation index (6)	–	–	14.3	14.3	13.9	14.9	16.1	15.6	15.9	–
Inability to make ends meet (6)	–	–	15.7	15.2	15.2	16.1	18.1	16.6	16.8	–
Arrears on mortgage or rent payments (6)	–	–	3.8	3.4	3.5	3.8	4.3	2.9	3.3	–
Arrears on utility bills (6)	–	–	10.4	10.5	10.9	10.4	13.6	11.0	10.5	–
Arrears on hire purchase installments or other loan payments (6)	–	–	3.1	3.2	2.7	3.2	1.9	3.0	2.6	–
Inability to afford one week annual holiday away from home (6)	–	–	38.6	39.1	38.8	39.1	39.8	41.0	39.8	–
Inability to keep home adequately warm (6)	–	–	10.7	10.6	10.1	10.4	11.3	10.6	11.2	–
Inability to afford a meal with meat or fish every second day (6)	–	–	7.0	6.3	5.6	6.2	7.5	6.2	6.7	–
Inability to face unexpected financial expenses (6)	–	–	26.6	27.9	27.5	32.0	31.6	33.1	33.3	–
Lack of money for food (7)	–	–	5.3	5.8	4.2	5.3	5.8	5.7	5.5	–
Lack of money for medical expenses (7)	–	–	12.1	12.0	10.4	11.1	11.3	11.1	11.0	–
Lack of money for necessary cloths (7)	–	–	17.6	17.8	16.8	16.9	18.5	16.9	16.9	–
Lack of money for transports (7)	–	–	7.9	8.5	7.0	7.3	8.3	8.7	8.3	–
Self-assessed economic condition indicators										
Dissatisfaction with own economic situation in last year (8)	–	–	–	–	47.5	46.3	53.7	50.6	49.3	49.5
Worsening of own economic situation relative to previous year (9)	40.5	47.6	–	45.9	43.4	41.0	54.5	50.0	43.3	43.7
Insufficient own economic resources in last year (9)	35.1	40.0	–	41.6	42.9	41.9	49.4	45.5	42.9	42.7

Sources and notes: (1) authors' estimates from SHIW data (Version 6.0, February 2010): share of individuals with equivalent income below 60% of the median equivalent income (square root equivalence scale); (2) Eurostat (2011): share of individuals with equivalent income below 60% of the median equivalent income (modified OECD equivalence scale); (3) Eurostat (2011): share of individuals with real equivalent income below 60% of the median equivalent income in 2004 (modified OECD equivalence scale); (4) Istat (2011c) and previous releases: share of households with equivalent expenditure below the relative poverty threshold (Carbonaro equivalence scale); (5) Istat (2011c) and previous releases: share of households with expenditure below the absolute poverty thresholds; (6) Eurostat (2011): share of deprived persons; (7) Istat (2011b) and previous releases: share of deprived households at least once in previous 12 months; (8) Istat (2011d) and previous releases: share of dissatisfied persons aged 14 years or older; (9) Istat (2011d) and previous releases: share of dissatisfied households.

5.2 The Microsimulation Model

The analysis of tax data shows that, during the GR, income trends varied across the different sources of income and the number of taxpayers with positive incomes fell, possibly as a consequence of reduced job opportunities. Mocetti, Olivieri, and Viviano (2011) observe that the recession led to an increase in the jobless household rate that is lower than expected, and that the negative shock in the labour market was partly absorbed within the family, as job losses mostly related to young people still living with their parents. These considerations suggest that accounting for the trends in the labour market goes some way towards understanding the distributive consequences of the GR.

To this end, we build a microsimulation model to estimate the variations in income brought about by labour market flows during the GR. We take the Istat's Labour Force Survey (LFS) as the basis for the simulation model and impute income data from the SHIW to LFS respondents. The LFS is the primary source for monitoring the Italian labour market, contains detailed socioeconomic variables for a very large representative sample, and is available on a quarterly basis (Ceccarelli et al. 2006). We use more than 700,000 observations, relative to the fourth quarter of each year in the simulation period 2006–10. (Hence, the yearly figures discussed below actually refer to the structure of the population as of the respective last quarters.) We first account for transitions in the labour market, and we then estimate the entitlement to benefits in the case of job suspension or separation. Finally, we impute income from labour or pension to workers and retirees. These procedures are described below and summarized in Table 5.2.

5.2.1 *Labour Market Transitions During the GR*

Between 2007 and 2010, total employment decreased by about 2%. About half of the reduction was due to the termination of fixed-term contracts which were not replaced. Hours worked decreased by more than the fall in number of employed workers, due to a drop in overtime work and an increased reliance on short-time work subsidy schemes (explained below). On average, the probability of exiting employment in quarter t, conditional on being employed in quarter $t–4$, rose from 6.6% in 2006–07 to 6.9% one year later, and to 7.2% in 2008–10; the probability of the opposite transition, from non-employment to employment, touched a minimum in 2008–09 (8.8%), down from around 10% in the previous two years, and it returned to 9.2% in 2009–10.

Table 5.2. Estimation of income sources and simulation strategy

Variable	Input	Estimator	Covariates	Simulation	Output for 2006–10
Working status	LFS 2006–2010				Observed
Wage income	LFS 2009–2010	Linear regression on subset defined by 6 strata (2 sexes × 3 geographical areas). Dependent variable in 2009 Euro.	Age, education, sector of activity (dummies)	Fit of regression parameters augmented with a stochastic component (random variate drawn from normal distribution with 0 mean and variance equal to the mean squared error of regression).	Simulated on data observed in 2009
Self-employment income	SHIW 2006–2008	Linear regression on subset defined by 6 strata (2 sexes × 3 geographical areas). Dependent variable in 2009 Euro, top-coded at P1 and P99.	Age, education, sector of activity (dummies)	Fit of regression parameters. Fitted values calibrated to replicate percentiles of donor distribution.	Simulated
Pension income	SHIW 2006–2008	Linear regression on subset defined by 6 strata (2 sexes × 3 geographical areas). Dependent variable in 2009 Euro, top-coded at P1 and P99.	Age, education (dummies)	Fit of regression parameters. Fitted values calibrated to replicate percentiles of donor distribution.	Simulated
Unemployment and CIG benefits	Administrative information and LFS 2009–10	–	–	Calculated applying formal entitlements rules to eligibility criteria and wages estimated from the LFS.	Simulated

Notes: All estimators use survey weights. LFS: Istat's Labour Force Survey. SHIW: Bank of Italy's Survey on Household Income and Wealth.

These job transitions are the drivers of the income distribution changes in our simulations. As the LFS utilizes a rotating panel in which individuals are interviewed in two consecutive quarters and in the same two quarters one year later, we study transitions at a 12-month interval using the longitudinal version of the LFS database. This entails a loss in sample size but avoids the misclassifications typically associated with recall questions (Bowers and Horvath 1984; Poterba and Summers 1986).

To account for transitions from employment to non-employment and vice versa in the period 2006–10, we estimate a heteroskedasticity-robust linear probability model $y_{it|y_{it-4}=1} = \alpha + \beta X_{it-4} + \epsilon_{it}$, where y_{it} for individual i in quarter t is missing if the individual was non-employed in t–4, 1 if the individual is non-employed in t, and 0 otherwise. The explanatory variables (X) are all measured at t–4, and include the usual socio-demographic characteristics (sex, education, area, marital status, and age summarized by five ten-year age groups) and job-related characteristics (sector, qualification, type of contract), plus a set of quarter dummies controlling for seasonal factors and year dummies capturing the change in average transition probabilities taking place during the crisis. Most parameter estimates are statistically different from zero.

As shown by the results reported in column 1 of Table 5.3, job separation probabilities significantly increased during the GR: by 0.3 points in 2007–8, 0.6 in 2008–9, and 0.7 in 2009–10. Transitions out of employment crucially depend on the type of contract: compared to permanent employees, fixed-term employees and quasi-employees have a probability of job termination that is higher by 11 to 12 percentage points, while being self-employed has no effect on those probabilities. In order to detect which types of people were most hurt in the downturn, in column 2 of Table 5.3, we show the estimates derived after interacting year dummies with type of contract, education, gender, and age. Women have a generally higher probability of losing their job than men, but were less affected by the crisis. Also university graduates suffered less than workers with lower education. During the GR, self-employed workers had a lower probability of exiting employment than permanent employees, and temporary employees experienced a substantial and significant deterioration of their chances of retaining their job (with the partial exception of quasi-employees in 2008–9). Once these compositional effects are taken into account, no significant impact of the crisis on transition probabilities is found for younger workers (those aged 15–34).

We report the results for the probability of transition from non-employment in quarter t–4 to employment in t in columns 3 and 4 of Table 5.3. The model is identical to the one used for the opposite transition, save for the dropping of job-related controls and for the addition of dummies for benefit receipt, length of the non-employment spell, and previous job experience.

Table 5.3. Labour market flows during the Great Recession

Variable	Transition from employment in t–4 to non-employment in t				Transition from non-employment in t–4 to employment in t			
	Coeff.	SE	Coeff.	SE	Coeff.	SE	Coeff.	SE
2008–7	0.003**	(2.00)	0.015***	(5.05)	0.002	(0.86)	0.005	(1.15)
2009–8	0.006***	(4.08)	0.014***	(4.41)	−0.015***	(7.56)	−0.011**	(2.56)
2010–9	0.007***	(4.56)	0.016***	(5.08)	−0.015***	(7.32)	−0.001	(0.20)
Fixed-term employee	0.112***	(38.41)	0.093***	(17.89)	−		−	
Quasi-employee	0.125***	(20.95)	0.119***	(9.81)	−		−	
Self-employed	0.002	(1.49)	0.013***	(4.80)	−		−	
Woman	0.043***	(32.50)	0.054***	(21.83)	−0.040***	(21.58)	−0.046***	(13.79)
High school	−0.020***	(13.51)	−0.017***	(6.99)	0.033***	(18.86)	0.037***	(10.39)
College	−0.030***	(16.01)	−0.021***	(5.92)	0.111***	(24.19)	0.131***	(12.88)
Aged 25–24	−0.057***	(15.30)	−0.057***	(15.32)	0.070***	(19.32)	0.072***	(19.98)
Aged 35–44	−0.072***	(19.71)	−0.071***	(16.89)	0.046***	(12.70)	0.039***	(8.39)
Aged 45–54	−0.069***	(18.40)	−0.068***	(15.76)	0.001	(0.27)	−0.008*	(1.83)
Aged 55–64	0.043***	(9.78)	0.044***	(8.98)	−0.082***	(28.44)	−0.090***	(22.22)
Public sector	−0.032***	(20.11)	−0.032***	(20.08)	−		−	
Manufacturing sector	−0.025***	(7.07)	−0.025***	(7.12)	−		−	
Services	−0.027***	(7.87)	−0.027***	(7.92)	−		−	
Fixed term× (2008–7)	−		0.009	(1.23)	−		−	
Fixed term× (2009–8)	−		0.041***	(5.30)	−		−	
Fixed term× (2010–9)	−		0.025***	(3.10)	−		−	
Quasi-employee× (2008–7)	−		−0.013	(0.84)	−		−	
Quasi-employee× (2009–8)	−		0.011	(0.68)	−		−	
Quasi-employee× (2010–9)	−		0.031*	(1.69)	−		−	
Self-employed× (2008–7)	−		−0.013***	(3.67)	−		−	
Self-employed× (2009–8)	−		−0.013***	(3.64)	−		−	
Self-employed× (2010–9)	−		−0.017***	(4.74)	−		−	
Woman× (2008–7)	−		−0.013***	(3.90)	−		−0.004	(0.95)
Woman× (2009–8)	−		−0.015***	(4.35)	−		0.008*	(1.71)
Woman× (2010–9)	−		−0.016***	(4.62)	−		0	(0.06)
High school× (2008–7)	−		−0.004	(1.10)	−		0.002	(0.45)
High school× (2009–8)	−		−0.004	(1.02)	−		−0.014***	(2.85)
High school× (2010–9)	−		−0.002	(0.42)	−		−0.006	(1.15)
College× (2008–7)	−		−0.012***	(2.80)	−		−0.022*	(1.66)
College× (2009–8)	−		−0.014***	(3.16)	−		−0.018	(1.37)

College× (2010–9)	–		–0.009*	(1.86)	–		–0.047***	(3.64)
Young (15–34)× (2008–7)	–		–0.003	(0.91)	–		0.001	(0.15)
Young (15–34)× (2009–8)	–		0.004	(1.19)	–		–0.012***	(2.69)
Young (15–34)× (2010–9)	–		0.002	(0.55)	–		–0.023***	(5.05)
Constant	0.112***	(21.64)	0.104***	(18.68)	0.350***	(41.32)	0.367***	(41.27)
Observations	396,447		396,447		307,164		307,164	
R-squared	0.06		0.07		0.11		0.10	

Notes: Authors' estimates from LFS data (2006–10), using heteroskedasticity-robust linear probability regression. Robust t-statistics in brackets clustered at the individual level;* significant at 10%;** significant at 5%;*** significant at 1%.

Estimated job-finding probabilities did not change significantly in 2007–08 as compared to previous year, but fell by 1.5 percentage points in subsequent two years. By interacting gender, age, and education with each of the GR years, women do not seem to be particularly affected. Job-finding probabilities decreased for workers with a university degree, but not for those with a high school diploma, except for the youngest.

In short, the fall in employment levels during the GR was due to both an increase in transitions out of employment and a decrease in transitions into employment, but the latter played a quantitatively bigger role (see also D'Amuri 2011). Job separations increased relatively more for men and for workers with lower education, but not for young workers once composition effects are controlled for: the major determinant of changes in job separation probabilities was the type of contract, with flexible contracts being particularly penalized. Conversely, no difference emerged in the variation of job finding probabilities between men and women, while getting a job became relatively harder for young and more educated workers.

5.2.2 Income Support for Job-Losers

The income loss associated with losing a job may be significant in Italy because of the fragmentation and inadequacy of the social safety net. The main income support schemes are the wage supplementation fund ('Cassa integrazione guadagni', CIG), the ordinary unemployment benefit, the unemployment benefit with reduced requirements, and the mobility subsidy (for further details, see Anastasia et al. 2009). CIG is a short-time work subsidy, extensively used during the GR, aimed at preventing lay-offs as a response to temporary demand drops: the subsidy is paid to employees without interrupting the labour relationship. The ordinary unemployment benefit is paid to individuals who are laid off or whose contract expires. It has short duration (up to 12 months for workers aged 50 years or more, eight months for the others) and its replacement rate decreases from 60% to 50% after six months, and to 40% after eight months. Eligibility criteria are rather strict (at least 52 weekly contributions paid in the two years preceding the lay-off). The unemployment benefit with reduced requirements is paid to individuals who do not meet the eligibility criteria for the ordinary benefit but who have paid contributions for at least 78 days in the two years prior to job separation, and replacement rates are lower than those of the ordinary benefit. The mobility subsidy is an income support scheme reserved for permanent employees with a job tenure of at least one year in a firm that is undergoing closure or a major restructuring, and its duration increases with the worker's age up to four years. Both the CIG and the unemployment benefits are capped at relatively low levels.

In 2008, the Italian government extended the coverage of income support schemes to categories of previously-uncovered individuals as part of its anti-crisis measures. A three-month unemployment benefit was introduced, with a 60% replacement rate for individuals whose contract was temporarily suspended, provided that they had paid 52 weekly contributions in the previous three years and were not covered by the CIG scheme. A one-off payment equal to 20% of last year labour income was also introduced for a subgroup of quasi-employees. These interventions constituted an attempt to cushion income losses for individuals who were hardest hit by the crisis and yet among the least protected by welfare schemes, that is workers on flexible contracts who lacked an adequate number of contributions and quasi-employees who were not entitled to any income support before the crisis. Note that no universal basic income support scheme is available in Italy.

In our model, we simulate all these benefits using information available in the LFS to approximate entitlements. For instance, we use job tenure as a proxy of weekly contributions paid. Our simulations show that the variability across types of contract and sectors implies substantially different replacement rates for individuals with similar pre-displacement earnings (see also D'Amuri 2011: 172, figure 2). Benefit caps are binding for most workers, making the system fairly progressive, being funded by a flat rate tax on all earnings. Many workers do not enjoy any income support, either because they are not eligible (most quasi-employees and all the self-employed) or because they have not paid enough weekly contributions. On average, simulated replacement rates decrease from around 25% in the first two quarters of non-employment to less than 20% in the third quarter and 10% in the fourth quarter.

5.2.3 *Imputation of Income from Labour or Pension and the Household Total Income*

Employees' post-tax earnings are available in the LFS only since 2009. To enhance comparability over time, we impute earnings for every year using a set of six standard survey-weighted Mincerian regressions estimated separately for the strata defined by two sexes and three geographical areas. The dependent variable is the post-tax wage earned in 2009, while explanatory variables include age group, education, industry, and firm size. In order to preserve the variance of the actual wage distribution, we add to fitted values a random variable with zero mean and variance equal to the regressions' mean square error. In 2010 the mean and the standard deviation of imputed values (€1,245 and €555, respectively) are very similar to those actually recorded, which is reassuring evidence of the reliability of the imputation.

For self-employed workers and retirees, income is imputed pooling data from the SHIW for 2006 and 2008. The dependent variable is expressed in 2009 Euros and is top- and bottom-coded at percentiles P1 and P99. As before, we run a set of survey-weighted regressions, for each of the previous-mentioned six strata, using as regressors variables that capture the main individual characteristics (age group, education, and sector of activity). The estimated parameters are projected on 2006–10 LFS data. The resulting imputed distributions are then calibrated in order to replicate the percentiles of the donor distribution conditional on the observables. This process ensures that the imputation process preserves the original distribution of self-employed workers' and retirees' incomes conditional on observables. Such a calibration introduces a bias that increases with the changes in the respective income distributions taking place between during the 2006–8 interval (covered by the donor sample) and the end of the period analysed in this chapter (2010). For this reason we multiply income deciles by coefficients that reproduce in these data the same income trends that are observed in tax data covering the 2006–9 period, separately for self-employed workers and pensioners (no adjustment is made for 2010 as the tax data are unavailable).

To obtain the distribution of equivalent household incomes, we sum the incomes from all sources within each household and divide the household income total by the square root of the household size. This procedure provides us with a synthetic database to assess the distributive implications of the GR, but has two important limitations. First, we are unable to account for income changes caused by changes in income earned on real and financial assets, as there is no reliable way to impute them to LFS observations. As discussed above, however, changes in (recorded) property incomes are likely to have been less important than changes in income from labour and transfers. Second, all simulated changes in the income distributions are driven by the flows into and out of employment. While benefit payments are consistently simulated according to existing entitlement rules, it is implicitly assumed that firms' compensation policies, the remuneration of self-employment activities, and pension entitlements, have not changed during the period under examination, except for the adjustment in their real trends derived from tax data.

Available information on national labour contracts, company-level agreements, and pension regulations suggests that this assumption may be an acceptable approximation; less, however, is known about the remuneration structure for people working on their own account.

5.3 Income Distribution Among Working-Age Individuals

How did changes in labour market flows impinge on income distribution during the GR? To what extent did unemployment benefits manage to cushion income losses for displaced workers? As retirees were less affected, we concentrate first in this section on the working-age population, that is people aged between 15 and 64 years.

Employment rates went down from 59.1% in 2007, to 57.5% in 2009, and 57.3% in 2010. Consistent with the flow estimates reported earlier, the drop in employment rates between 2007 and 2010 was more pronounced for men than for women, and was particularly acute for individuals aged 15–39: see Figure 5.3(a). The average post-tax monthly individual income (from labour, unemployment benefits, and pensions) calculated on the whole working age population, that is including those with nil income, equalled €902 in 2007, at 2009 prices. It fell by 0.3% in 2008, 1.3% in 2009, and 0.2% in 2010. Individuals aged 15–39 experienced the strongest drop in income; the impact was weaker for relatively older workers. See Figure 5.3(b).

As explained above, the imputation procedure is based on the actual incomes earned in 2009 for employees and in 2006–8 for pensioners and self-employed. Imputed values for 2006–9 are then adjusted using the trends in pre-tax incomes as measured in tax records (no adjustment is made for 2010 as data are lacking). The comparison between the imputed income distribution before and after this adjustment provides some information about the impact of variables different from changes in the composition of the workforce in terms of observables. The similarity of results before and after this adjustment appears to confirm that the changes in labour market flows dominate the variation in income dynamics.

The Gini inequality index for post-tax individual income among the whole working-age population increased between 2007 to 2010 by 1.6 percentage points to 0.547. This increase reflects changes both in the proportion of individuals who have no income and in income dispersion among individuals with a positive income (from any of the sources considered here). We can try to disentangle these two factors by decomposing the Gini index, G_P, for the whole population as $G_P = (1-e) + eG_E$, where e and G_E are the population share and the Gini index, respectively, for the individuals with positive income. The observed increase in inequality is entirely due to the larger proportion of

(a) Employment rates (percentage points)

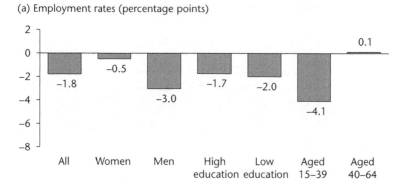

(b) Mean post-tax individual income (%)

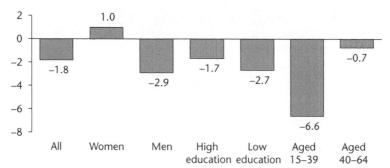

Figure 5.3. Changes in (a) employment rates (percentage points) and in (b) mean post-tax individual income (%), 2007–10, working-age population, by individual characteristics
Source: Authors' estimates.

individuals without any income rather than to a rise in inequality among positive income earners. The stability of the index G_E suggests that composition effects have not played any significant role, as earnings for given observables are assumed to be unchanged by construction.

5.4 Income Distribution Among All Individuals

When we consider the whole population, we estimate that the average monthly equivalent disposable income diminished by 1.8% between 2007 and 2010, from €1,273 to €1,250: see Figure 5.4(a). The median fell more, by 3.0%. The tenth percentile of equivalent incomes (P10) decreased by 14.4%, while P90 increased slightly by 0.6%. As a consequence, the P90/P10 ratio rose from 5.1 in 2007 to 6.0 in 2010: see Figure 5.4(b). The Gini inequality index rose by 1.7 percentage points from 0.326 to 0.343. Focusing on the bottom of the distribution, the share of individuals with an equivalent household

(a) Real income levels

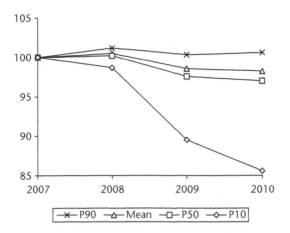

(b) Income inequality

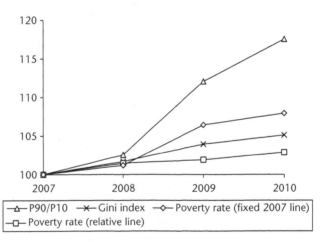

Figure 5.4. The distribution of equivalent disposable income, 2007–10 (2007 = 100): (a) Real income levels, and (b) Income equality

Source: Authors' estimates.

income that is less than 60% of the contemporary median increased from 23.0% in 2007 to 23.7% in 2010. This median-based poverty cut-off decreased, however, by 3% between 2007 and 2010, from €709 to €688 (at constant 2009 prices). Thus, all poverty rates would be higher in 2010 were we to fix the low-income cut-off at its 2007 level in real terms. With this constant threshold, the poverty rate increases by 1.8 points, by contrast with the 0.7 percentage point increase measured with the conventional relative poverty line.

For households with a head aged 15–39, equivalent income fell by 1.4% between 2007 and 2010, but the drop was even more acute for households

(a) Equivalent disposable income

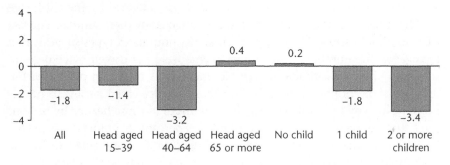

(b) Poverty rates

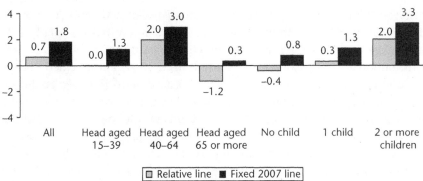

☐ Relative line ■ Fixed 2007 line

Figure 5.5. Changes in equivalent disposable incomes (%) and in poverty rates (percentage points), 2007–10, by household characteristics: (a) Equivalent disposable income and (b) Poverty rates

Source: Authors' estimates.

with a head aged 40–64 years (–3.2%), consistent with the evidence that job losses were high among young people still living with their parents: see Figure 5.5 (a). In contrast, incomes increased slightly for elderly households (head aged 65 or more), as pensions were not hit by the GR. Households with two or more children were far more affected by the crisis than those with a child, while childless households experienced a slight rise in real income. These changes over time in mean equivalent disposable income are reflected in the changes of poverty rates: see Figure 5.5(b). The incidence of relative poverty increases by three-times the average in households with head aged 40–64 or with two or more children, but decreases where the household's head is aged 65 or more. The worsening of poverty rates across household types is qualitatively similar but quantitatively larger when the low-income cut-off is fixed in real terms.

Combining the results of this section with those of the previous section, we conclude that younger individuals were the most affected by the GR in the labour market but, at the same time, were protected by their families. The fact that household size did not vary much across household types suggests that changes in the number of income recipients were not driven by changes in size. But when we estimate the employment rates of young people within different types of households, we find that they decreased far less in households headed by a person aged 16–34 rather than in those headed by persons aged 40–64 or 65 or more (–2.1, –5.0, and –6.9 percentage points respectively). Variations in the employment rates of older workers were small within all household types. Young individuals who left home were relatively less affected by the crisis, while those remaining in their family of origin suffered higher job-related income losses. This is even more evident when we decompose the change in total equivalent income between 2007 and 2010 by age group. The incomes of individuals aged 16–39 accounted for a fall of 3.2 percentage points of total income, which was partly offset by the positive contributions of the incomes of the adults aged 40–64 and of elderly people (0.9 and 0.5 percentage points respectively), leading to the average drop of 1.8%. The negative contribution was relatively larger for young workers living in households with an older head. These results may follow from the fact that young individuals who feel more at risk of unemployment due to low job security tend not to leave the household of origin, given also that access to unemployment benefits is more limited for initial work experiences. Indeed, temporary and quasi-employees, who have the highest probability of moving out of employment and are the least covered by income support schemes, as seen above, in 2007 accounted for 12.8% of all employed workers, but for only 7.2% of household heads.

5.5 Conclusions

Italy suffered a severe fall in aggregate output and household incomes during the GR. The trends in the labour market were the main channel through which the effects of the crisis propagated to household budgets, and in this chapter we have built a microsimulation model to link labour market transitions to income trends at the household level. From our analysis, we can draw two main conclusions.

First, the available information on individual pre-tax income, on household consumption expenditure, on deprivation indicators, and on self-assessed economic conditions consistently suggests that the impact of the GR on inequality and poverty has been fairly limited, despite the considerable fall in mean income. This aggregate outcome may have been associated with substantial differences for different types of individual, associated with the different trends of labour and pension incomes, which may have partly reinforced (for employees and pensioners), or partly reversed (for self-employed workers), the movements that characterized the 15 years before the GR.

Second, simulation of labour-related changes in the distribution of equivalent incomes indicate that inequality and poverty, defined with respect either to a relative line or to a fixed line in real terms, may have slightly risen during the recession, although the distribution of job terminations and the family compensating role may have muted a more substantial increase of summary income distribution indices. The effects of the GR are likely to have been felt more by non-elderly households than elderly households, who appear to have been shielded from the income fall. Thus, the fact that workers more likely to lose their job were not breadwinners, and the fact that a large share of population relies on pension income, both help explain why the short-run distributional impact of the GR has been relatively mild in Italy, even though the drop in output was unprecedented.

These conclusions might be modified were our analysis to incorporate property incomes (about which data are currently lacking), even though our calculations on the allocation of these incomes across the distribution seem to suggest that their impact might be small.

More importantly, these conclusions only concern the immediate, short-term, effects. Italy faces a severe consolidation of public finances in the medium-term, due less to the effects of the GR than to the pre-GR legacy. In the second half of 2011, the Italian parliament approved three packages for the public finances to achieve a balanced budget in 2013. Cumulatively, the reduction in net borrowings due to these measures is valued at €48 billion in 2012, €76 billion in 2013, and €81 billion in 2014, or 3.0%, 4.6%, and 4.8% of GDP, respectively (Visco 2011: Table 8). These packages will influence the standard of living of households both directly, reducing their incomes, and indirectly, through a rise in indirect taxation, a cut in public services, or a rise in fees (Table 5.4). Preliminary estimates for the first package adopted in July 2011, based on microsimulation tax-benefit models, suggest that some of the measures might have a perceptibly regressive effect (Baldini 2011). However, it is difficult to assess the implication for income distribution of the overall adjustment package, as some measures are only sketched and assessed in terms of their aggregate impact on the public budget. None the less, it is fair to conclude that the consequences of the GR for the living standards of Italians might be far more serious in the medium-term than they have been during the crisis itself.

Table 5.4. Adjustment packages adopted in 2011 in response to the tensions in the financial markets

---

Measures with an impact on personal incomes or wealth holdings

- Solidarity contributions on high incomes (3% of income above €300,000) for 2011–13
- Solidarity contributions on high pensions (5% of pension income above €90,000; 10% of pension income above 150,000) for 2011–14
- Tax rate on income from financial assets equalized at 20% (except for government and equivalent securities and supplementary pension plans)
- Increase in stamp tax on securities accounts
- Pension system (freezing of cost-of-living adjustment above certain levels, increase in retirement age)
- Measures against tax evasion and rules on tax collection
- Public employment measures (postponement of payment of severance benefits)

Measures with an impact on expenditure

- Increase in VAT rate from 20% to 21% as of September 2011
- Increase of excise taxes
- Surtax on luxury cars, aircrafts and boats

Measures with an unspecified impact

- Savings from fiscal and welfare reform to be enacted by September 2012 (if not implemented, flat across-the-board cut in tax allowances, increase in VAT)

Measures that may lead to cuts in the provision of public services

- Rationalization of health spending, reduction of ministries' and local government spending

---

Note: Authors' derivations from Banca d'Italia (2011) and Visco (2011).

Acknowledgements

We thank John Micklewright and Stephen Jenkins for very useful comments on a first draft of the chapter, and Giuseppe Grande and Giordano Zevi for helping us with the information on stock market prices and housing prices, respectively. The views expressed here are solely those of the authors; in particular, they do not necessarily reflect those of the Bank of Italy.

6

Country case study—Sweden

Anders Björklund and Markus Jäntti

International comparisons of income inequality suggest that Sweden has one of the most equal distributions of income in the world (OECD 2008; Brandolini and Smeeding 2009; Ward et al. 2009). While inequality has increased in recent years, it is still low by international standards, and there is evidence that the political system is committed to keeping it that way (Björklund and Jäntti 2011).

However, Sweden has experienced two large macroeconomic shocks in the past two decades. Both the recession of the early 1990s and the Great Recession (GR) in the late 2000s took place while most OECD countries, including Sweden's main trading partners, suffered an economic downturn. It is therefore reasonable to ask if the Swedish economic downturns, by many standards quite sizeable, were associated with adverse changes to the distribution of income. The purpose of this chapter is to examine how the Swedish distribution of income changed between 1985 and 2009, and to consider the extent to which the two macroeconomic shocks led to similar changes in the distribution of income.

The large economic downturns in 1992–3¹ and in 2008–9 were quite different in Sweden in their macroeconomic nature, as OECD (2011g) points out. The early 1990s recession was influenced by a downturn in external demand, but was mainly driven by domestic developments—a housing market bubble driven by financial deregulation and weakened aggregate demand driven by capital tax reform. The recent recession, the GR, was very much driven by external factors. We will see below that the magnitude of the downturn was far greater in the GR. This appears to be largely due to a substantial decline in export demand. By contrast, during the early 1990s recession, there was a large increase in real short-term interest rates coupled with a devaluation of Swedish currency in 1992 that further weakened domestic demand but most likely boosted Swedish exports.

To put the macroeconomic developments in perspective, we show in Figure 6.1 growth in quarterly GDP (measured by the first difference in its natural logarithm) and monthly unemployment rates from 1985 to early 2011. While GDP growth has been negative several times across the years, the early 1990s and late 2000s stand out. The unemployment rate, which reached a low of less than 2% of the labour force in 1988–90, increased rapidly during the 1990s crisis, peaked again in the late 1990s and in 2005, and rose again during the late-2000s recession.

In order to compare macroeconomic indicators across the two crises, we plot the evolution of quarterly GDP, the monthly unemployment rate and an index of industrial production relative to a baseline year for each recession: see Figure 6.2, panels (a), (b), and (c). We initialize the three series in the first quarter/January of 1991 and 2007 and track changes for up to four years (48 months and 16 quarters). GDP and industrial production are normalized to a baseline value of 100. Unemployment is expressed as a percentage of the overall labour force. All statistics are derived from the OECD's *Main Economic Indicators* database.

During the 1990s recession, quarterly GDP reached its lowest point in 1993Q1, at which point it was 5% below its value in 1991Q1. Industrial production bottomed out in February in that quarter. Unemployment, by contrast, reached its maximum value of 9.9% in January 1994, a full year after the decline in GDP peaked (although it should be noted that unemployment reached a new high of 10.5% in 1998 after declining between 1994 and 1995: see Figure 6.1(b). In the recession starting in 2007, the decline in GDP was at least as great, reaching a total decline of 5.4% in 2009Q1. The decline in industrial production was much greater than in the 1990s, reaching a minimum in May 2009 of more than 23% below its value in January 1997, compared to a decline of no more than 6% in the 1990s. Unemployment, by contrast, started from a substantially higher level in the GR than in the 1990s, but peaked at a lower level of 9% in April 2010.

Thus, while the decline in GDP and loss in industrial production were larger in the GR, the increase in unemployment was less. There are many dimensions along which the two recessions differed, which in part accounts for the differential change in production and employment. For instance, the recession of the early 1990s was accompanied by dramatic turbulence in financial markets and a substantial banking crisis. While financial market turmoil was very much a feature of the GR, Swedish banks and financial markets were much less subject to such pressures this time around, probably at least in part because of the lessons learnt from the painful adjustments that followed the 1990s recession.

The pattern of change in the unemployment rate in the GR, including the decline from its peak in April 2010, looks remarkably similar to the shape of the change in unemployment round the 1990s recession, when unemployment rates declined after reaching a maximum in January 1994. But in the late 1990s unemployment increased again to a higher level despite there being no dramatic slowdown in aggregate GDP.

(a) Change in quarterly GDP

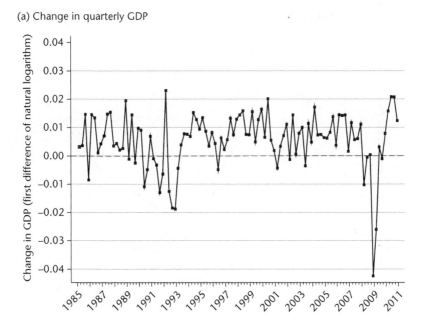

(b) OECD-harmonized unemployment rate (monthly, %)

Figure 6.1. GDP growth and unemployment rates, 1985–2011: (a) Change in quarterly GDP, and (b) OECD-harmonized unemployment rate (monthly, %)
Source: OECD, *Main Economic Indicators*, 2011, series s101 and s501.

(a) Real quarterly GDP₁ index

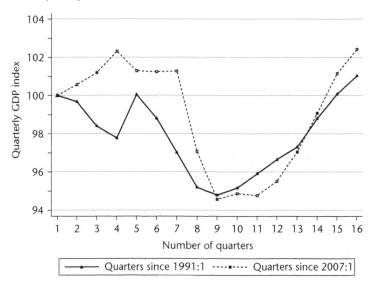

(b) OECD-harmonized unemployment rate (%)

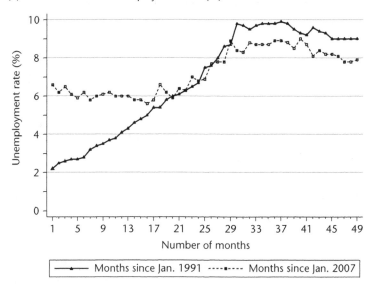

(c) Industrial production index

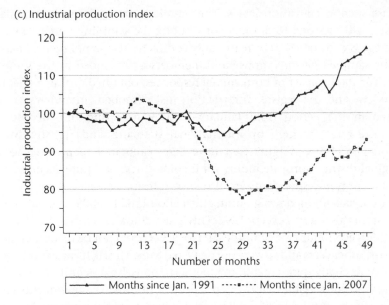

Figure 6.2. Two macroeconomic downturns compared: (a) quarterly GDP, (b) unemployment rate, and (c) industrial production
Source: OECD, *Main Economic Indicators*, 2011, series s101, s201, s501.

To sum up, the two recessions that Sweden experienced in the past two decades had different causes—domestic demand declined more in the 1990s and external demand more in the 2000s—and different consequences—a much steeper increase in unemployment in the 1990s and a greater decline in aggregate production in the 2000s. The 1990s recession was associated with a substantial weakening of the public sector fiscal position, an effect that is largely absent in the 2000s recession. Sweden responded successfully in both recessions with efforts to bolster employment and demand but, in the 2000s, it did so with little need for fiscal consolidation (OECD 1996, 2011*d*).

6.1 Data

Our data are drawn from the Swedish main income distribution survey, Household Finances (HF; Swedish *HEK*), formerly known as Household Incomes (HI; Swedish *HINK*). The HF is an annual sample survey of about 30,000 persons and 15,000 households of the population registered as living in Sweden at any time during the year. This is a different source from the data for Sweden analysed in Chapter 2 (EU-SILC). All income data used in this chapter are derived from various registers, as are many of the other variables we use such as education levels. The sample is drawn from the population register with persons 18 or older constituting the sampling frame. The frame coverage is considered to be reasonably complete. The sampling is of persons; all the sampled persons' household members are included in the sample as well. The data consist of both survey responses, obtained during a telephone interview, and the register information just described. Interviews are conducted in the period from January to May following the income year. Response rates are high by international standards and Statistics Sweden provides sampling weights that have been calibrated to provide accurate marginal distributions, including for income (these are quite accurate as the incomes of non-respondents are also known from registers).

We use data for incomes spanning the period 1985 to 2009. Our data include all years in this interval except 1992. This is unfortunate, as this is the first year of the 1990s economic crisis, but the data for 1992 could not be made comparable with the other years and so were not delivered to us. The HF has also undergone a number of changes in its sampling methods, household definition, and definition of income variables. From our perspective, one main issue concerns a major change in the definition of the household, from essentially the nuclear family prior to 1991 to economic household (Swedish *kosthushåll*) after 1991. The earlier household definition defined persons to be in the same household if they were married (and included any children under the age of 18), and cohabiting couples as the same household if they had common children (under the age of 18). The reason is that this was traditionally the tax-system's definition of a family. This means that children who are 18 or older but live with their parents count as single-person households. It also means that cohabiting couples who do not have common children belong to different households, even if one of them has children of their own. The economic household follows the standard definition of an economic household (see Expert Group on Household Income Statistics 2001). For our analysis, we use the narrower older definition, as this allows us to compare the effect of the GR with the effect of the early 1990s recession (on the impact of the latter, see Aaberge et al. 2000). Comparisons with the shorter time series that is based on the broader household concept suggest the changes in definitions lead to different estimates of real income levels and of inequality levels, but not of their trends (estimates not shown but available from the authors on request).

The income variables have also undergone some changes. One change took place from 1990 to 1991 as part of a major tax reform. Among other changes, the reform involved broadening the tax base by including more benefits in taxable income and a change in capital income taxation so that such income was taxed at source and thus also reported to tax authorities directly from the source. Assessments of these changes suggest that reported inequality measured by the Gini index increased by around 0.02: see Björklund, Palme, and Svensson (1995) for more information. Another change concerns negative transfers, which prior to 2004 only included repayments of student loans and alimony payments, but after 2004 also include deductions for certain pension-related savings. Taxable transfers are measured at the individual level during part of the period and at the household level in other parts. Official income distribution statistics in Sweden include capital gains. We exclude those from our analysis for two reasons. First, measures of disposable income for other countries rarely include capital gains, and they are not included in the definition of national income. Second, the measures of capital gains have undergone several changes across the time period we examine, and we are unable to construct a consistent series. Moreover, while a strong case can be made for including the value of capital gains in the definition of disposable income (see Roine and Waldenström 2012 for a thorough analysis of the issue), we can only observe those capital gains that have been realized, rather than the variable of greater interest, which is the change across the year in net worth, only part of which is realized as either gains or losses during the year.

Our data do not contain good measures of labour market status, unfortunately. In particular, we do not have good information about working time, not even full- or part-time employment status, nor do we have anything like a measure of unemployment according to the ILO's definition. We can only examine joblessness in terms of whether the person (and, for households, the household) does or does not receive labour market income during the year.

We differentiate the following four household income components: earnings (wages and salaries and self-employment income), capital income (all capital income sources excluding capital gains), all taxable and non-taxable public transfers (less negative transfers), and income taxes (recorded as negative income). The sum of the four components across all members of a given household equals that household's disposable income.

The incomes are collected from various linked registers, such as those of the tax authorities, government agencies in charge of different transfer schemes, and so on. All incomes are annual and refer to the calendar year shown in the graphs regardless of income source. All incomes are inflated to 2009 prices using the consumer price index, and all incomes in the household-level analysis (Section 6.4) are equivalized by the square root of household size.

6.2 Inequality in Sweden

The distribution of disposable income in Sweden is among the most equal distributions of OECD countries (OECD 2008; Brandolini and Smeeding 2009; Ward et al. 2009). In Table 6.1 we show estimated Gini inequality indices and poverty rates for selected countries from the Luxembourg Income Study (LIS)

Table 6.1. Income inequality and poverty rates, selected countries, mid-1980s to mid-2000s

Country	Year	Gini coefficient	Poverty rate (%)
Canada	1987	0.283	17.5
	1991	0.281	16.6
	1994	0.284	17.6
	2000	0.315	18.9
	2004	0.318	19.9
Denmark	1987	0.254	17.2
	1992	0.237	14.3
	1995	0.218	12.0
	2000	0.225	13.1
	2004	0.228	13.2
Finland	1987	0.206	10.6
	1991	0.209	10.6
	1995	0.216	9.1
	2000	0.250	12.4
	2004	0.255	13.2
Germany	1989	0.258	11.8
	1994	0.270	13.1
	2000	0.266	12.7
	2004	0.278	14.3
Netherlands	1987	0.243	9.7
	1990	0.266	12.2
	1993	0.257	13.7
	1999	0.231	11.1
	2004	0.266	11.8
Norway	1986	0.234	12.8
	1991	0.231	12.1
	1995	0.227	11.5
	2000	0.250	12.3
	2004	0.256	12.8
Sweden	1987	0.212	11.5
	1992	0.229	12.1
	1995	0.221	10.0
	2000	0.252	12.3
	2005	0.237	12.0
United Kingdom	1986	0.303	17.7
	1991	0.336	22.8
	1995	0.344	22.1
	1999	0.346	21.8
	2004	0.344	19.0
United States	1986	0.316	21.0
	1991	0.313	20.9
	1994	0.355	24.3
	2000	0.342	20.3
	2004	0.337	19.3

Source: LIS Inequality and Poverty Key Figures (2011).

Notes: The poverty line is defined as 60% of the contemporary national median. Data are taken from the LIS Key Figures and refer to equivalent disposable income. The concept of disposable income in LIS differs slightly from that used in the estimates based on HF data in this chapter, as do minor details in estimation, so values are not exactly the same for the years of overlap for the Swedish data. The equivalence scale used in both the LIS Key Figures and this chapter is the square root of household size. LIS uses the old household definition prior to 2000 and the new definition starting at that time. See www.lisdatacenter.org for more information. A closer examination of Sweden in this table requires that two major changes in definitions (mentioned in Section 6.1) are taken into account. First, the tax reform in 1991 raised measured inequality as measured by the Gini coefficient by around 0.02 points from 1990 to 1991. Second, the LIS data from the year 2000 and onward apply the new household definition that lowered the Gini coefficient by some 0.015 points.

database from the mid-1980s to around 2005, the latest time for which comparable data are available. Of the countries we show, only Denmark has a Gini coefficient that in 2004 was as low as that in Sweden in 2005—0.228 compared to Sweden's 0.237. In the mid-2000s, inequality in Finland and Norway, the two other Nordic countries in LIS, was clearly greater than in Sweden, as was the case for the Netherlands and Germany. The Anglophone countries (Canada, the UK, and the USA) have substantially higher levels of inequality.

Sweden also had a low poverty rate in the mid-2000s compared to other LIS countries: 12%. (The poverty line is defined as 60% of contemporary median income.) Only the Netherlands has a (slightly) lower rate at 11.8%. The poverty rates in the other Nordic countries—Denmark, Finland, and Norway—are only slightly higher, while they are of the order of 20% in the Anglophone countries shown in Table 6.1.

Evidence on longitudinal income inequality is less extensive, but it suggests that Sweden has both relatively low intra-generational and inter-generational inequality (Solon 1999; Aaberge et al. 2002; Björklund and Jäntti 2009). Several recent reports (in Swedish), such as Waldenström (2009), Jonsson, Mood, and Bihagen (2010), and Björklund and Jäntti (2011) have highlighted the fact that income inequality in Sweden is on the increase. But, although Swedish inequality is increasing, so too is inequality in many or most developed nations (OECD 2008), and Sweden retains its position among the least unequal developed countries when looking at the overall distribution of income. Moreover, recent work on the concentration of incomes at the very top of the Swedish income distribution suggests that, although concentration has increased in recent years, top-income inequality is lower than in most other developed nations (Roine, Waldenström, and Vlachos 2009; Atkinson, Piketty, and Saez 2010). Sweden also has relatively low rates of income poverty, whether measured using a poverty line that is fixed in relative or in absolute real-income terms (Jäntti and Danziger 2000; Bradbury and Jäntti 2001; Ward et al. 2009).

6.3 Individual-Level Analysis

We start by examining the evolution of real annual earnings among individuals with any positive earnings in the year (persons aged 20–64): see Figure 6.3, panel (a). We plot the change across time in average earnings as well as the 10th, 50th, and 90th percentiles, from 1985 to 2009. (Note that here, as in the remainder of the chapter, we have no data for 1992.) Up to 1991, earnings increased across the board. Between 1991 and 1993, the 10th percentile fell sharply, consistent with a sharp increase in unemployment leading to sharp drops in earned income. While its growth picked up after the low in 1993, it grew at approximately the same pace but on a quite

(a) Real earnings (gross; for workers with positive earnings in the year) (%), persons aged 20–64

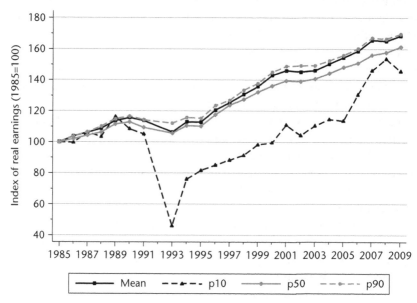

(b) Prevalence of receipt of labour earnings (any during the year) and social transfers (%), persons aged 20–64

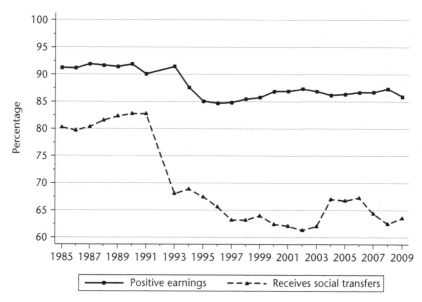

Figure 6.3. Real earnings (gross) and prevalence of receipt of earnings: (a) Real earnings (gross; for workers with positive earnings in the year) (%), persons aged 20–64, and (b) Prevalence of receipt of labour earnings (any during the year) and social transfers (%), persons aged 20–64.

Source: Own calculations from HF data.

Note: The HF data cover the years 1985–2009 annually with the exception of 1992 for which comparable data could not be obtained.

different trajectory than the 50th and 90th percentiles or mean earnings until 2005, after which time it increased rapidly for two years. There is a small downturn in the 10th percentile again between 2008 and 2009, which again sets the bottom of the earnings distribution apart from the remainder of the distribution which continued to grow despite the recession.

In sum, the earnings distribution among the working-age population displayed remarkable stability despite dramatic changes in unemployment rates (Figure 6.1), with the exception of the lowest decile.

Figure 6.3, panel (b), shows the proportion of the working-age population (again persons aged 15–64) that received any labour earnings at all during the relevant calendar year. This is our measure of the jobless rate, and joblessness has increased over time. Until 1991, more than 90% of the working-age population received some labour earnings across the year. This proportion declined to a low of just above 85% in 1995, after which it has hovered between 85% and 88%. There is a small decline between 2008 and 2009.

Figure 6.3(b) also shows the proportion of the working-age population receiving any transfer income during the year. The fraction was as high as 80% or greater until the early 1990s, after which it declined rapidly, reaching a low point in the early 2000s of about 63%. Here we must note, however, that from 1 January 1993 onwards, employers became by law obliged to compensate for the first week of each sickness spell, with a lower prevalence of measured social transfers as a result. In 2009, just under two-thirds of working-age persons received some social transfer income during the year. Recall that transfers do include some private transfers (Section 6.1), and we are not able to distinguish between public and private in our cash transfer variable.

6.4 Household-Level Analysis

We now turn to the distribution of equivalized household disposable income among all persons. We start by showing the evolution of real income in different parts of the distribution (10th, 50th, and 90th percentiles, as well as the mean), from 1985 until 2009, indexed relative to 1985 values: see Figure 6.4, panel (a). Until 1991, the three deciles and the mean increased at roughly the same pace. The 10th percentile increased somewhat less rapidly. All measures of real income fell from 1994 to 1995. After 1995, the distribution of disposable income became more dispersed. The 90th percentile grew substantially more rapidly than either the mean or the median and the 10th percentile lagged behind. Between 2008 and 2009, the 10th percentile fell in real terms, while the mean and especially the 90th percentile increased. The median (the 50th percentile) rose slightly over the 2007–9 period. This is

(a) Real income level (mean, 10th, 50th, and 90th percentiles)

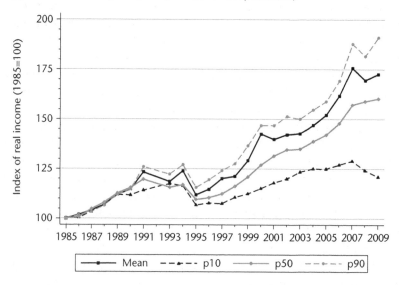

(b) Change in real income across two macroeconomic shocks

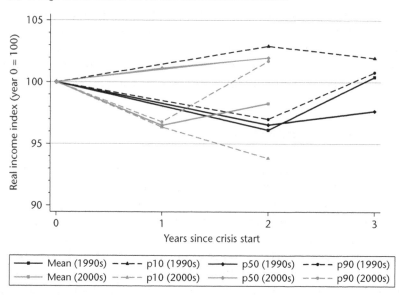

Figure 6.4. Real disposable household income: levels and changes across two macroeconomic shocks: (a) Real income level (mean, 10th, 50th, and 90th percentile), and (b) Change in real income across two macroeconomic shocks

Source: Own calculations from HF data.

Note: The HF data cover the years 1985–2009 annually with the exception of 1992 for which comparable data could not be obtained.

consistent with the direction of change shown for the median in the analysis of EU-SILC data for Sweden in Chapter 2 (Table 2.5).

In Figure 6.4, panel (b), we have reorganized the data from panel (a) so that we can compare the change in real income in different parts of the distribution across the two recessions. Incomes in 1991 and 2007 (both labelled year 0), respectively, are indexed to 100. Real disposable household income fell for all except the 10th percentile in the 1990s crisis. By contrast, in the 2000s recession, initially mean income and both the 10th and 90th percentiles declined, while the median did not. From 2008 to 2009, the 10th percentile continued to decline while median income, and especially the mean and the 90th percentile, recovered.

In Figure 6.5, panel (a), we show the trends in the 10th percentile for all persons, elderly persons (aged 70+), children (aged 0–17), and persons in lone-mother households, expressed relative to their 1985 baseline. Panel (b) shows the corresponding estimates for the 50th percentile. The 10th percentile for the elderly experienced more rapid income growth by a substantial margin than the 10th percentile for all persons and children during the whole period. The 10th percentile for lone-mother households kept up with that for the other groups in most years, but declined from 2007 to 2008 to recover slightly in 2009. The median income for all persons, elderly people, and children, by contrast, increased at about the same pace, even if the elderly median increased during the 1990s and early 2000s more rapidly than the others. But the median for persons in lone-mother households grew more slowly since the early 2000s and, by 2009 (when median income growth for all groups slowed down), it had grown substantially less than that for the other groups.

Changes in inequality, shown in Figure 6.6, are largely as one might expect given the evolution of real income shown in Figure 6.4. The Gini coefficient of disposable household income has been trending upward since 1985, albeit not monotonically. Aside from some year to year variation, inequality appears to have peaked in 2000, declined and remained constant in the early 2000s, and increased thereafter. The percentile ratios reveal that the increase in the Gini coefficient reflects changes in inequality in different parts of the distribution. In the 1990s, inequality in the upper half of the distribution—as measured by the increase in the ratio of the 90th to the 50th percentile ($p90/p50$)—dominated the increase in inequality. After 2004, inequality in the lower half of the distribution—measured by the ratio of the 50th to the 10th percentile ($p50/p10$)—increased more rapidly. The picture of rising inequality between both 2005 and 2007 and between 2007 and 2009 contrasts with that of stability shown in the analysis of EU-SILC data for Sweden in Chapter 2 (Figure 2.18 and Table 2.5).

Now we consider which income sources appear to be driving the inequality changes. We do so by examining the decomposition of the Gini coefficient by

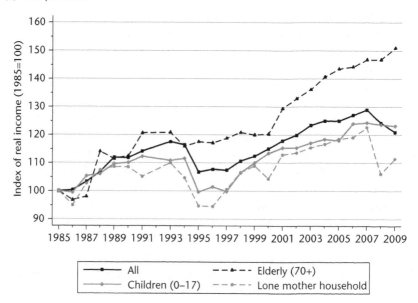

(a) 10th percentile

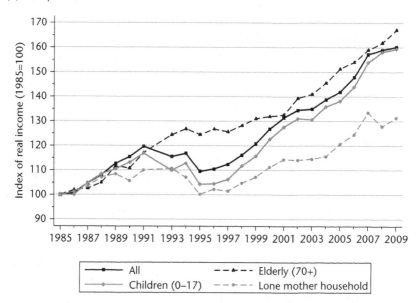

(b) 50th percentile

Figure 6.5. Real household disposable income: 10th and 50th percentiles for all persons and selected subgroups: (a) 10th percentile, (b) 50th percentile.

Source: Own calculations from HF data.

Note: The HF data cover the years 1985–2009 annually with the exception of 1992 for which comparable data could not be obtained.

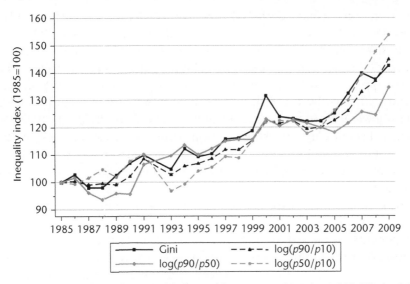

Figure 6.6. Inequality of household disposable income: Gini, log(p90/p10), log(p90/p50), and log(p50/p10)

Source: Own calculations from HF data.

Note: The HF data cover the years 1985–2009 annually with the exception of 1992 for which comparable data could not be obtained. The 2009 values for the Gini coefficient, log(p90/p10), log(p90/p50), and log(p50/p10) are 0.200, 0.576, 0.246. and 0.330, respectively.

factor components: see Figure 6.7. The Gini coefficient can be expressed as the sum over all components of income of the concentration coefficient of a component with respect to disposable income multiplied by the factor share of the component. So, the relative 'importance' of a given source for total inequality depends on both how concentrated the source is, and on how important it is in households' income packages. We look first at the concentration coefficients (panel a), then the income shares (panel b), and finally the product of the two (panel c), which summed across income components equals the Gini coefficient of disposable income.

Consider first the concentration coefficients of earnings, capital income, public transfers, and taxes: see Figure 6.7, panel (a). The concentration coefficients of both earnings and taxes have hovered close to 0.4 over the whole time period. Transfers have moved from more to less negative. Interestingly, the concentration of transfers increased (i.e. became less negative) in both the 1990s and the 2000s recessions, reflecting increased receipt of transfers higher up in the income distribution. The concentration coefficient of capital income shows a substantial secular increase, from about 0.2 in 1985 to about 0.8 in 2009. This increase reflects, in part, changes in measurement associated with the 1991 tax reform, but is notable all the same. Capital income appears to move differently in the 1990s and 2000s recessions. In the 1990s, its concentration fell markedly between 1991 and 1993, while there is a small dip from 2007 to 2008 and a subsequent return to pre-crisis levels in 2009.

Consider next the factor shares of each income component: see Figure 6.7, panel (b). While earnings are overwhelmingly the important source, their share dipped markedly in the 1990s recession but not in the 2000s one. Transfer income, by contrast, increased its share in both recessions, albeit from a lower level in the later one. Taxes increased slightly in the 1990s, but decreased slightly in the 2000s recession. Thus, in the earlier recession, taxation counteracted the income-alleviating impact of the public sector while in the current one, it strengthened it. Capital income, in turn, declines in both recessions.

The product of the factor shares and the concentration coefficients (which equals the Gini coefficient of disposable income when summed across income components), is plotted for each income source in Figure 6.7, panel (c). The contribution of earnings to the Gini coefficient was flat in the 1990s, but increased in the 2000s recession, reflecting the slight increase in its concentration across the two years. Transfer income did relatively little in either recession, as the contribution is very close to zero throughout the period we examine. By contrast, the contribution to overall inequality from capital income is quite negative in both recessions, suggesting that part of the reason why inequality changes so little is that a declining share of capital income does much to mitigate inequality. Changes in the distributional contribution of taxes were flat in the early 1990s but contributed to an increase in inequality in the 2000s.

Thus, we find that inequality did not increase much in either of the two major recessions that Sweden has experienced since 1990. That inequality did not increase by much seems to be accounted for not only by public sector transfers—their role appears quite small, although their absence would probably have resulted in much larger increases in inequality—but also by changes in capital income.

How do these findings compare with earlier work on the 1990s recession? Aaberge et al. (2000) examined income inequality in Sweden before and during 1990s recession (through to 1994) also using the Gini decomposition, but only using data for persons who were aged 30–54 years (see also Chapter 1 of this volume). Their analysis was motivated by the fact that inequality in the early 1990s hardly increased in Sweden, despite a large shock to unemployment. They hypothesized that this might have been due to the generosity of benefits: the replacement rate of earnings-related unemployment insurance was 90% at the outset of the shock but was reduced to 80% in 1993. Other hypotheses considered were that the incidence of unemployment was evenly spread across the distribution of income, possibly because of intra-household adjustments (i.e. that spousal income increased in response to unemployment) or, further, other

(a) Concentration coefficients

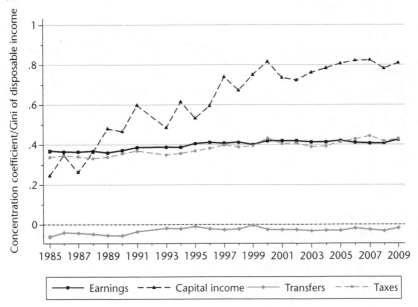

(b) Income shares (%)

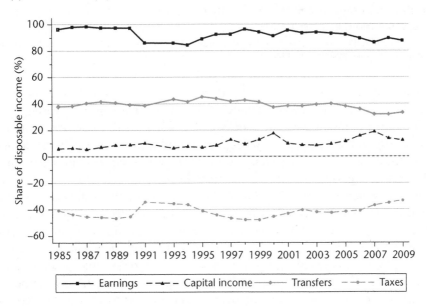

(c) Components of the Gini coefficient: income share times concentration coefficient, by income source

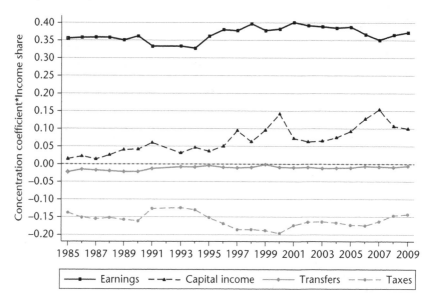

Figure 6.7. Components of inequality: concentration coefficients and income shares: (a) Concentration coefficients, (b) Income shares (%), (c) Components of the Gini coefficient: income share times concentration coefficient, by income source

Source: Own calculations from HF data.

Note: The HF data cover the years 1985–2009 annually with the exception of 1992 for which comparable data could not be obtained.

income sources, possibly transfers other than unemployment benefits, may have counteracted the loss of earnings and kept inequality from increasing.

Examining unemployment shocks and income distribution also in Denmark, Finland, and Norway, Aaberge et al. find quite varied patterns across countries. For Sweden, they compare a year of low unemployment, 1989, with the year unemployment hit its peak, 1993, between which two years the Gini coefficient increased from 0.215 to 0.223, a small and statistically insignificant change. Their decomposition reveals that earnings declined as a share of disposable income, but became more concentrated, so their overall contribution at the height of the crisis was larger than during low unemployment. Unemployment benefits increased as a share of disposable income, and became less concentrated (i.e. more evenly spread across the distribution). While the net changes in unemployment benefits did to some extent counteract the increase from earnings, the magnitude of this counteracting change was much smaller than the increased contribution from earnings. The mitigating effect of taxes declined across these two years, mostly as the result of the 1991 tax reform. However, the inequality-reducing effect of tax-free transfers increased, and capital income contributed less to inequality than before. Thus, the reason why inequality did not change—despite an increase of unemployment (for this age group) from about 1% to 6%—is as a result of several counteracting changes. Although income transfers did counteract the increase in inequality, the effect of a declining contribution from capital income was just as large, at least in the sense measured by the decomposition of the Gini coefficient. Thus, the results from this earlier study on the 1990s recession are largely consistent with what we find in the 2000s recession.

The relatively minor role played by transfers in the Gini coefficient across both of these recessions is, perhaps, surprising. One possibility is that, when looked at across the full distribution of disposable income—as the Gini decomposition does—transfers play a relatively minor role, but when focusing on different income ranges the relative roles of different components of disposable income differ. To examine the sensitivity of our conclusions to the area of income distribution analysed, we show in Table 6.2 the share in disposable income of each of our four components—earnings, capital income, transfers, and taxes—in the lowest, fifth, and top decile groups of disposable income in the recession years 1991–4 and 2006–9. As one might expect, transfers are more important in the lowest decile group, accounting for between 70.0% and 83.3% of disposable income, respectively. The pattern of change in the 1990s is quite different from that in the 2000s, however. The transfer share of disposable income *increased* between 1991 and 1994 from 76.8% to 83.3% but *decreased* between 2006 and 2009 from 77.0% to 72.7%, although in 2008, it was lower still at 70.0%. For the fifth decile group, the development in the early 1990s was similar to that in the bottom tenth but, in the 2000s, the share of transfers declined between 2006 and 2007 only to increase back to 2006 levels in 2009. Capital income is important in the top tenth, with its share declining from 53.7% in 2007 to 37.9% in 2009. Taxes, in turn, declined in importance for all three groups considered here from 2006 to 2009. This decline is consistent with the tax-credits introduced in these years, and at the bottom this decline partly counteracted the fall of the transfer share. We conclude by noting that, while transfer income did seem to increase somewhat as a share of disposable income between 2008 to 2009, our finding from the earlier decomposition of Gini coefficients of complex counteracting changes in the distribution of several income components still holds after looking in detail at changes across decile groups.

Finally, we show the poverty rates for all persons as well as among elderly people, children, and persons living in lone-mother households: see Figure 6.8. The poverty line is set equal to 60% of contemporary median income. The poverty rates for all persons and for children increased throughout most of the

Table 6.2. Factor shares (%) of disposable income in the 1990s and 2000s recessions, by income decile group

Decile group	Year	Earnings	Capital income	Transfers	Taxes
1st (lowest)	1991	33.7	8.7	76.8	−19.1
	1993	35.1	6.3	78.2	−19.5
	1994	31.4	5.2	83.3	−20.2
	2006	37.9	5.0	77.0	−19.9
	2007	35.9	4.3	75.9	−16.1
	2008	40.5	4.4	70.0	−14.9
	2009	36.8	5.4	72.7	−14.9
2nd	1991	81.8	4.5	45.0	−31.1
	1993	75.7	3.4	53.0	−31.9
	1994	81.0	2.8	50.3	−34.2
	2006	88.6	3.2	43.7	−35.5
	2007	90.0	3.4	38.3	−31.7
	2008	88.7	3.7	38.1	−30.5
	2009	83.4	2.7	43.2	−29.2
10th (highest)	1991	105.0	24.1	17.7	−45.6
	1993	111.4	14.1	21.2	−46.8
	1994	93.7	19.7	19.0	−43.6
	2006	88.3	47.8	15.7	−51.8
	2007	78.6	53.7	14.0	−46.2
	2008	89.3	40.9	14.6	−44.8
	2009	90.8	37.9	14.6	−43.3

Source: Authors' calculations from HF data.

2000s, but levelled off between 2008 and 2009. Slight rises for all persons and for children over 2007–9 were also found using the EU-SILC data for Sweden in Chapter 2 (Table 2.5). The poverty rate for elderly persons has fluctuated a lot, most likely because the income of many elderly people is very close to the poverty line of 60% of median income. The poverty rate for persons living in lone-mother households was quite similar to the rate for all persons until the early 1990s (but higher than for all children), but thereafter it increased substantially to reach a high of 33% in 2008, after which it fell by three percentage points in 2009.

6.5 Concluding Remarks

Our results suggest that, while Swedish real incomes at both the individual and household level have grown reasonably steadily since 1985, incomes at the lower end of the distribution have periodically tended to grow less quickly, and incomes at the high end have tended to grow more rapidly than the average. As a result, both inequality and relative poverty rates have increased over time. The incomes of some vulnerable groups, children in particular, show broadly similar trends to those of the population taken as a whole and indicate potentially increasing problems. The increase in poverty among lone

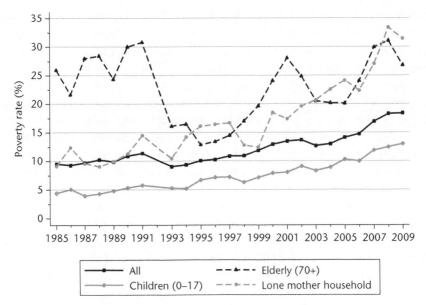

Figure 6.8. Poverty rates (%), all persons and selected subgroups

Source: Own calculations from HF data.

Note: The HF data cover the years 1985–2009 annually with the exception of 1992 for which comparable data could not be obtained.

parent households is particularly pronounced. Other traditionally vulnerable groups, elderly people in particular, do not seem to have been adversely affected. This is unsurprising, because in Sweden the incomes of elderly people are largely determined by historically-set pension agreements and are therefore unlikely to be vulnerable to short-term economic or political shocks.

An examination of income sources does not suggest any clear reasons for increased inequality. Taxes have become less redistributive across time, but the contribution from earnings, the source of the bulk of income inequality, has also become relatively less important. Most likely a multitude of factors, including the evolution of incomes at the very top, as well as declining tax progressivity, are responsible for the observed increase in income inequality.

Our comparison of real income growth and income inequality in the two recessions reveals some interesting differences between the two periods. In particular, in the 1990s recession, there was real income growth throughout the income distribution with incomes at the lower end growing no less rapidly than middle and higher incomes. From 2008 to 2009, the 10th percentile clearly declined more than did either the median or the 90th percentile, so the 2000s recession is associated with more of an increase in inequality than is the 1990s recession.

What about the future prospects in light of what is known about public finances? The Swedish economy was relatively hard hit by the GR of the late

173

2000s—the decline in GDP exceeded that of the OECD average—but its fiscal position is better than that of most OECD countries in many ways. Sweden's estimated fiscal balance in 2011 was several percentage points higher than the average of the OECD countries considered in this book (see Table 2.6 in Chapter 2), and its level of public debt substantially lower than the OECD average. Sweden was estimated in 2011 to need to consolidate its public finances, but the cumulative need for consolidation was considered to be no more than 0.6% of GDP (OECD 2011b). The consolidation was projected to come from temporary infrastructure, labour market and education measures, and stimulus provided to local governments enacted in response to the economic downturn.

The relatively favourable Swedish fiscal position is driven by the fact that, compared to many other countries, Sweden supported its banks with relatively small capital injections, about 1.5% of GDP, compared to 20% in Germany and 60% in the UK (Vis, van Kersbergen, and Hylands 2011). In addition, while Sweden responded to the recession by loosening monetary policy, and selectively lowering taxes to and with various jobs programmes, much of the response came through automatic stabilizers such as unemployment insurance and benefit programmes. Strict fiscal rules implemented in the 1990s in response to the previous recession have ensured fiscal discipline during years of growth.

As Chung and Thewissen (2011) point out, Sweden promoted increased employment and continued to provide income security during the GR. Employees and employers were given increased support through lowered payroll and unemployment contributions. The government further decreased employment taxes for employers that hired long-term unemployed persons, and provided increased student grants to persons aged 25 and over if they entered education. The Swedish government also expanded the in-work tax credit in several stages to increase the incentive to participate in employment.

The expansion of the in-work tax credit is central to the Swedish government's 'work-first' policy, but it is also the key policy to combat low income. The Ministry of Finance estimated in 2009 that, based on both microsimulation and projected labour supply responses, disposable income would increase in the medium-term by between 4.3% and 6.9% if one ignores labour supply responses, and between 5.5% and 12.1% if they are taken into account (Swedish Ministry of Finance 2009: Table 5.10). It is especially low-income women who are expected to experience large gains in disposable income due to the direct effect of taxes (4.4%), and also taking labour supply responses into account (12.9%). Moreover, as the increase in disposable income is projected to be very large for low-income earners, the tax reforms enacted by the current government are expected to lead to (moderately) decreased income inequality. In its spring budget of 2011, the government estimated that as a consequence of both tax- and social-policy reforms enacted in the period 2006–11, the poorest tenth has experienced an increase in disposable income of 4%, or 17% if behavioural responses are taken into account (Government of Sweden 2011: diagram 2.6).

The expansion of in-work tax credits is not primarily a response to the recession. Rather it should be seen as a structural reform aimed at permanently increasing work incentives on both the extensive and intensive margins. All the same, it can be considered, along with the automatic stabilizers built into social insurance programmes, an important mechanism for increasing work incentives and for increasing in-work income during a recession.

Although inequality in Sweden has increased, Sweden continues to have one of the most equal distributions of disposable income in the world. As Björklund and Jäntti (2011) report, all major political parties have mentioned their desire to uphold a reasonably equitable distribution of resources. There is little indication that either fiscal consolidation or other political pressures will change this outlook.

7

Country case study—UK

Robert Joyce and Luke Sibieta

The UK recently experienced its deepest recession since the Second World War, during which GDP fell by over 7% between the first quarter of 2008 and the second quarter of 2009. We would naturally expect these falls in national income to have consequences for UK households' living standards. In this chapter, we examine how earnings, employment and household incomes evolved immediately before, during and after the Great Recession (GR) in the UK. In Section 7.1, we show that employment fell by less than GDP during the GR, and that the largest falls in employment were experienced by young people, men and individuals with little education. In Section 7.2, we show that average incomes surprisingly grew during the recession, but seem likely to have fallen substantially in the financial year immediately afterwards (April 2010 to March 2011): the pain was delayed, but not avoided. We also show that income changes during the GR were relatively progressive, with the bottom slightly catching up with the top and middle. As might thus be expected, relative poverty fell. In Section 7.3, we discuss the likely effects on UK households of the fiscal consolidation currently underway—which comprises tax rises and cuts to welfare spending and public services totalling 6% of national income—as the government attempts to redress the fiscal position that deteriorated so rapidly during the GR. This means that poorer households and families with children will be most affected by tax and benefit reforms, whilst pensioners are relatively protected and will in fact gain from a reform to the basic state pension. More uncertain are the distributional impacts of public service cuts and trends in the macroeconomy.

7.1 Employment and Earnings in the UK During the Great Recession

In the UK, GDP reached its pre-recession peak at the start of 2008, before falling in each quarter up to the second quarter of 2009. From peak to trough,

GDP fell by 7.1%. As we saw in Chapter 2, this was the deepest UK recession since the Second World War. As Figure 7.1 shows, the economy began to expand again from the second half of 2009, but by the start of 2011 was still over 4% below its pre-GR peak.

Figure 7.1 also shows employment rates and hours worked amongst employees relative to their level at the start of the GR. This makes clear that although employment fell during the GR, it did not fall by nearly as much as GDP. Employment fell by around 2.6% during the GR, much less than the 7.1% fall in GDP. This was observed by Gregg and Wadsworth (2010), who show that this was not the case in previous UK recessions. However, as Figure 7.1 makes clear, during 2010 the UK economy expanded while employment remained largely constant. Hence, by the start of 2011, the gap between the two series had narrowed slightly, with employment 2.7% below its pre-GR peak and GDP 4.5% lower. Whilst the economy recovered slightly, employment levels did not.

We also observe those who kept their jobs working shorter hours, on average. Hours worked amongst employees fell by just over 1%, on average, over the course of the GR, and then continued to fall as the economy expanded and employment stagnated during 2010. This left hours worked amongst employees 2.1% lower at the start of 2011 than at the beginning of the recession. Combining this with the fall in employment, we see that total hours worked was 4.7% lower at the start of 2011 than at the beginning of the GR, similar to the 4.5% drop in GDP. This means that that GDP per hour

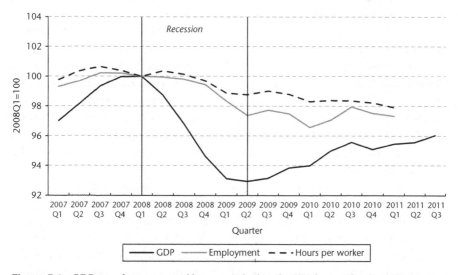

Figure 7.1. GDP, employment, and hours worked in the UK during the Great Recession
Source: Office for National Statistics, series ABMI (GDP) and authors' calculations using the Labour Force Survey (employment and hours worked).

worked (a measure of productivity) was largely unchanged between the start of the GR at the beginning of 2008 and the start of 2011.

Figure 7.1 also shows the evolution of GDP up to the third quarter of 2011, the latest available data at the time of writing. This shows that the recovery continued at a slow pace throughout 2011. In November 2011 the Office for Budget Responsibility significantly downgraded its expectations for economic growth in 2011 (from 1.7% to 0.9%) and even more so in 2012 (from 2.5% to 0.7%). It also revised its expectations for changes in total employment, with falls in employment rate through to late 2013 (Office for Budget Responsibility 2011). The tough times for the macroeconomy are thus far from over and the date by which the economy will return to its pre-GR peak has been pushed further into the future.

Which groups saw the largest drops in employment? Table 7.1 shows average employment levels among men and women of different ages from 2007 through to 2010. The age groups are defined as under-25, 25–44, 45 to state pension age (SPA), and over SPA. (The SPA is currently 60 for women, and 65 for men.) This shows a very stark gradient in employment trends by age. Employment fell by more for young people, with a fall of 6.9 percentage points for men under 25 and 5.1 percentage points for women under 25. Individuals over SPA actually saw an increase in employment over this period, albeit from a relatively low base. Amongst each age group, employment fell by more for men than women.

Table 7.1 also shows employment amongst individuals with different levels of educational qualifications (none, below degree level, degree, or equivalent). This breakdown is only available for working-age individuals. This shows very clearly that, although employment fell across all education groups, it fell most for lower education groups. We can conclude that employment fell by more for young people, men and those with less education. Berthoud (2009) has shown that in past UK recessions individuals from ethnic minorities and those with low levels of education were disproportionately likely to see their employment prospects suffer, but there were not disproportionate effects by gender, ages, or disability. However, Bell and Blanchflower (2011) have shown that young people in other countries also suffered disproportionately from the GR. See also Chapter 2.

Figure 7.2 (a) shows how real weekly earnings amongst full-time workers have evolved during the GR. It shows the 10th percentile (P10), the 50th percentile (P50, the median), and the 90th percentile (P90) between the start of 2007 and the start of 2011. They are each indexed to 100 at the start of the GR in the first quarter of 2008, and adjusted for quarterly inflation based on the all-items RPI index. This is based on the quarterly Labour Force Survey (LFS), the main source of official labour market statistics in the UK, which permits an examination of trends in real earnings across quarters within years.

This shows that real earnings grew during the GR, with the median growing by the most (3.8%), followed by P10 (1.9%) and finally P90 (1.6%). However, earnings fell in real terms during 2010, and by more at lower percentiles. By the first quarter of 2011, P10 was over 6.1% lower in real terms compared with the start of the recession, whereas P90 had fallen by just less than 4.5%. The median fell by 1.4% in real terms over this period. Taken together these results suggest an ambiguous picture for earnings inequality. The bottom of the earnings distribution fell away from the middle, but the middle caught up with the top. However, as Figure 7.2(b) shows, these changes are relatively small and earnings ratios changed little during the GR or afterwards.

The LFS is not the only source of information on earnings in the UK. The Annual Survey of Hours and Earnings (ASHE) also provides detailed information on earnings amongst full-time workers and is collected each April. The ASHE data published by the Office for National Statistics shows that P10, P50, and P90 each grew by a little under 7% in cash terms between April 2007 and April 2009, or by around 3.5% after accounting for inflation over these two years. Cash term growth between April 2009 and April 2010 was outstripped by annual inflation close to 5%, meaning that each percentile fell by close to 3% in real terms during 2010. The ASHE data thus suggest that full-time earnings changed little in real terms between April 2007 and April 2010, and that this was the case for various percentile points across the distribution.

Between April 2010 and April 2011, the latest ASHE survey points to further real term drops in earnings. The median and P10 both fell by more than 4% in real terms, and P90 by just over 3% in real terms. Cumulatively, this suggests

Table 7.1. Employment rates (%) during the Great Recession, by group

Group	2007	2008	2009	2010	Change 2007–10 (percentage points)
Age and sex					
Male (under 25)	68.3	66.7	61.3	61.4	−6.9
Male (25–44)	89.1	88.4	86.3	86.0	−3.0
Male (45–64)	76.8	77.2	76.0	75.4	−1.4
Male (over 64)	9.9	10.5	10.3	11.3	1.4
Female (under 25)	62.2	61.7	58.8	57.1	−5.1
Female (25–44)	73.7	74.0	73.4	73.1	−0.7
Female (45–59)	72.6	73.4	73.5	73.8	1.2
Female (over 59)	11.7	12.4	13.0	13.4	1.7
Educational qualifications					
None	61.5	61.3	58.8	57.7	−3.8
Below degree level	78.1	78.2	76.0	75.0	−3.1
Degree or equivalent	87.0	86.5	85.6	85.4	−1.6
All	61.0	61.0	59.7	59.4	−1.6

Source: Authors' calculations using Labour Force Survey, 2007 Q1 to 2010 Q4.

Note: Employment rates by educational qualifications are only shown for working-age adults. Educational qualifications are unknown or missing for about 1% of working-age adults, who are excluded from this classification.

(a) Percentile points of full-time weekly earnings

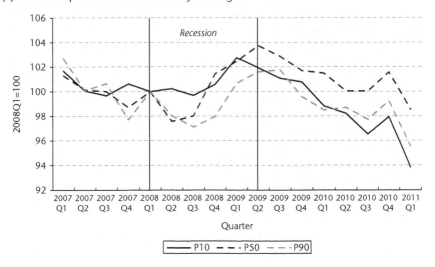

(b) Percentile point ratios

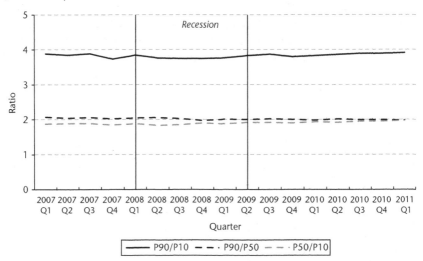

Figure 7.2. Full-time weekly earnings during the Great Recession, percentile points and percentile point ratios: (a) Percentile points of full-time weekly earnings, (b) Percentile point ratios

Source: Office for National Statistics, series CHAW for RPI. Authors calculations using the Labour Force Survey.

Notes: Real-terms index calculated using RPI All-Items quarterly index.

that real earnings have fallen by about 7% between April 2009 and 2011 according to ASHE.

Although there is some disagreement between the two data sources on the precise changes in real earnings during the GR, both suggest that the fall in real earnings was concentrated during 2010 when inflation accelerated and that there was little change in earnings inequality over the period.

7.2 Household Incomes in the UK During the Recession

We now consider the evolution of living standards during the GR explicitly by looking at the distribution of household incomes. The measure of household income used is net of taxes, inclusive of benefits and tax credits, before any housing costs have been deducted, and equivalized using the square root of household size. This is comparable with the measures used in other chapters, but different to UK official statistics, which use the modified OECD equivalence scale (Department for Work and Pensions 2011). Existing analysis of official UK statistics during the recession suggests that using a different equivalence scale does not qualitatively change any conclusions here (Jin et al. 2011). Equivalized income amounts are expressed in terms of the equivalent income for a 2-person household. Incomes are measured at the household level, but the unit of analysis remains the individual: for example, median income refers to the household income of the *individual* in the middle of the household income distribution. All monetary amounts have been converted to 2010–11 prices using the all-items Retail Prices Index (RPI), and all discussion of changes in incomes thus relates to changes in real incomes.

7.2.1 *Data and Simulation Techniques*

The primary source for the analysis presented in this section is the Family Resources Survey (FRS), which includes around 25,000 households each financial year (beginning in April) and underlies the official statistical series used by the UK government to measure trends in the income distribution (Department for Work and Pensions 2011). This is a different source to the one used for the UK in Chapter 2 to compare changes in household incomes during the GR in European countries (Section 2.6). That source, the EU-SILC survey for the UK, differs in a number of respects, including a notably smaller sample size than the FRS.

Data from the FRS for the 2010–11 financial year are not yet available at the time of writing. To gain a fuller picture of what happened to the income distribution during the GR, we therefore simulate household incomes for 2010–11. The basic methodology behind this simulation follows that used (and described in detail) in recent work simulating future poverty rates in the UK (Brewer, Browne, and Joyce 2011). We begin with the 2008–09 FRS data and then adjust these data in various ways to account for changes that we expect to see by 2010–11 on the basis of other data sources. These adjustments are described below. It was not possible to use the 2009–10 FRS in these simulations. However, in previous work we have been able to produce summary statistics based on the 2009–10 FRS data (Jin et al. 2011), which we also include here.

We reweight the data to account for the reduction in employment—reducing the sampling weights, on average, applied to employed individuals—using the Labour Force Survey as the source of employment data. We account for these employment changes within subgroups defined by age and gender (jointly) and by family type (couple or single), part-time/full-time status, and gender (jointly). Accounting for differences in employment trends across different population groups in this way (rather than simply accounting for the aggregate employment change and assuming that the average characteristics of unemployed workers remain the same) is potentially important for capturing changes in the distribution of income, as shown in previous empirical work (Dolls, Fuest, and Peichl 2012) and discussed in Chapter 1. Other expected demographic changes (for example, changes in the number of single-person households) are also incorporated through the reweighting process, using projections from the Office for National Statistics (ONS).

Average nominal gross earnings in the 2008–09 data are increased by the rate of average annual earnings growth to 2010–11 measured by the ONS Average Weekly Earnings (AWE) index; but we allow for differential earnings growth in each quintile of the distribution of jobs by gender and full-time/part-time status (a total of $5 \times 2 \times 2 = 20$ cells), based on official statistics produced by the ASHE data described in Section 7.1.

The impacts of reforms to the tax and benefit system between 2008–9 and 2010–11 are incorporated using TAXBEN, the static tax and benefit microsimulation model of the Institute for Fiscal Studies (IFS). No behavioural responses to such reforms are assumed as reforms over this period had mostly marginal impacts on behavioural incentives. One important exception is at the very top of the earnings distribution where the marginal rate of income tax for those with gross earnings above £150,000 was increased from 40% to 50% in April 2010. This is likely to reduce taxable incomes from 2010–11 as a result of changes to labour supply and increased avoidance behaviour (Brewer and Browne 2009; Brewer, Saez, and Shephard 2009). TAXBEN simulates tax liabilities and benefit and tax credit entitlements. Hence, to account for incomplete take-up of means-tested benefits and tax credits, we subtract simulated benefit or tax credit income from people if they did not report receiving that benefit or tax credit in the 2008–9 FRS but they were (according to our simulation) eligible for it in that year.

Note that the evolution of incomes at the very top of the distribution is highly uncertain. In the UK government's official statistical series based on the FRS, the measured personal incomes of the very richest individuals are replaced with values from the Survey of Personal Incomes (SPI)—a survey of tax returns—because of the lack of sufficient sampling of very rich individuals. However, the SPI data only become available with a long lag. Moreover, the significant changes to top rates of tax in the UK in April 2010 mean that past changes to top incomes are highly unlikely to be a good guide to future changes. We therefore have no credible way of simulating trends at the very top of the household income distribution (which we define as the top five percentile groups) in 2010–11. Key summary statistics which depend on these trends are mean incomes and the Gini coefficient. For these statistics, we present two different simulations designed to capture the possible range of values for income growth at the very top in 2010–11: real income growth of 0% and −10% in the top five percentile groups of the distribution. As we shall see, these scenarios correspond to income growth in the top five percentile groups being approximately five percentage points above or below that at the 90th percentile. Such differences relative to the 90th percentile would be unusual by recent historical standards (the main exception being 2009–10 when there was a change in the way official UK statistics treat top incomes) but changes to top rates of tax in April 2010 would leave one to expect income growth at the very top to be below that seen at the 90th percentile, other things being equal. Due to the uncertainty regarding the evolution of top incomes, these scenarios should be viewed as purely illustrative.

7.2.2 Average Incomes Before and During the Recession

Figure 7.3 shows how average net household incomes in the UK have evolved in recent years. The graph shows that average income growth was very sluggish in the years *before* the UK entered recession. In the four years between 2003–4 and 2007–8, net income growth averaged about 0.5% per year at the median and about 1.2% per year at the mean.

Despite the falls in GDP per head and the increases in unemployment during the GR, average incomes actually seem to have increased. (This contrasts with the picture shown for the UK in the EU-SILC data used in Chapter 2—see Figure 2.16.) Indeed, the average annual growth rate of net household income between 2007–8 and 2009–10 was virtually identical at both the mean (1.2% per year) and median (0.6% per year) to that seen in the previous four years. Jin et al. (2011) further show that average income growth between 2007–8 and 2009–10 is statistically significant.

The dotted lines in Figure 7.3 represent our simulations of the changes in average incomes in 2010–11. We expect there to have been a real fall in median household income of about 3.5%. This would leave median net income around its level in 2003–4, and would be the largest one-year fall since 1981. Nevertheless, this should not come as a surprise. As we saw earlier, employment was lower during 2010–11 than 2009–10, on average; real earnings amongst workers fell quite sharply; and rising inflation eroded the real value of state benefits. Given that Jin et al. (2011) show that earnings are likely to have been overestimated in the FRS in 2008–9, there is good reason to believe that the true one-year fall in 2010–11 is likely to be more than 3.5%. The path of mean income in 2010–11 depends on the highly uncertain trends at the very top of the income distribution (see Section 2.1), but it fell substantially under either scenario for top income growth.

The impact of the GR on average net household incomes in the UK was thus not felt until after the economy had stopped contracting: the pain was delayed, but not avoided. This matches the trends in real earnings we saw in Section 7.1.

Interestingly, falls in household spending were evident significantly earlier than falls in household incomes, coinciding quite closely with the period when the economy contracted, and were particularly sharp relative to falls in spending during previous UK recessions. Between the first quarter of 2008 and the second quarter of 2009, real household spending fell by almost 5%, which compares with falls of about 3% during the recessions of the early 1980s and early 1990s; and the recovery in real household spending was slow, remaining 4.4% below its peak in the first quarter of 2011 (Crossley, Low, and O'Dea 2011). Thus, the evidence to date suggests that the falls in household spending and household income as a result of the GR were of similar severity, but differed in timing.

Muriel and Sibieta (2009) examined changes in average incomes during previous recessions in the UK (specifically, the recessions of the mid-1970s, early 1980s, and early 1990s): see the case study discussion in Chapter 1. Comparing their values with our estimate for the total fall in median income between 2007–8 and 2010–11 (just over 2% in total), we see that median incomes in the UK during the GR seem to have fallen by more than during the early 1990s recession (when they largely stagnated). However, they have fallen by less than they did during the recessions of the early 1980s and mid 1970s, when they fell by more than 5% in total over the course of the recession. This is despite the total drop in UK GDP being smaller than during these two recessions. However, as we shall see later, the effects of the GR on UK households seem likely to persist strongly over time. This stands in contrast to the recessions of the 1970s and 1980s, after which there were strong rebounds in average incomes.

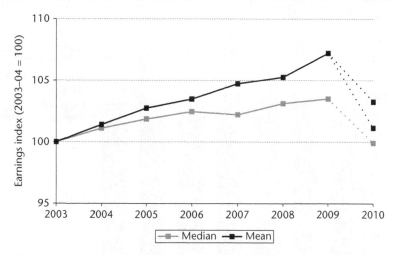

Figure 7.3. Average real equivalized net household incomes in the UK, 2003–4 to 2010–11

Sources: Authors' calculations using Family Resources Survey, various years.

Note: Years refer to financial years. Data points for 2010–11, marked by dashed lines, are the results of simulations. Two scenarios are presented for mean income in 2010–11, to reflect the uncertainty over the evolution of top incomes: the scenarios correspond to real household income growth of 0% and −10% in the top five percentile groups of the distribution (see text).

7.2.3 Composition of Net Household Incomes Before and During the Recession

To start to understand what has driven changes in incomes, we can examine the proportion of net incomes coming from different sources. We continue here to take the individual as the unit of analysis and to refer to household income sources, equivalized using the square root of household size. We consider the following components of net household incomes: gross earnings; gross self-employment profits; gross income from savings, investments, and pensions; state benefits and tax credits, net of any taxes paid on them in the case of taxable benefits; all other income tax payments and social security contributions (subtracted from net income); other payments, such as local taxes (subtracted from net income); and miscellaneous other additions to income (less than 3% of total net income, on average). Figure 7.4 shows these income components as a proportion of total net household incomes from 2003–4 to 2009–10.

Changes in earnings will be crucial for average incomes: gross earnings amount to about 90% of net household incomes, on average (net earnings account for about two thirds of net household income). Furthermore, Muriel and Sibieta (2009) show that family types more dependent on earnings for their total income have seen their average incomes fall by more during

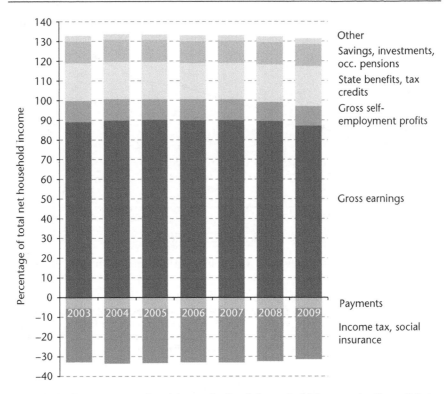

Figure 7.4. Composition of net (unequivalized) household income in Great Britain, 2003–4 to 2009–10

Sources: Authors' calculations using Family Resources Survey, various years.

Note: Years refer to financial years. Payments include deductions from income, e.g. local taxes and pension contributions. High income individuals whose incomes are adjusted under official HBAI methodology are excluded. Income tax payments exclude income tax paid on taxable state benefits. State benefits are net of any such taxes paid.

previous recessions. In the immediate pre-GR years, the share of earnings in total household income remained extremely stable, fluctuating by no more than one percentage point between 2003–4 and 2007–8. But the share of earnings in net income fell notably following the start of the GR: it was about three percentage points lower in 2009–10 (the latest year of FRS data) than in 2007–8. This is not surprising given the combination of stagnant real earnings among those employed and falling numbers of people employed over those two years.

We saw earlier that average net incomes rose slightly between 2007–8 and 2009–10, despite the declining contribution of earnings to household incomes over that period. The next largest component of net income—state benefits and tax credits—seems to have played an important role in making this happen: the share of state benefits in net income rose by almost two percentage points over these two years, from 18.5% to 20.3%. Given the reduction in the numbers of people employed and the corresponding increase in the numbers of people eligible for out-of-work benefits, a shift in the composition of net income away from earnings and towards state benefits is something that we would typically expect during a recession. But there were also factors specific to the GR which contributed to this.

First and foremost, state benefits and tax credits are by default uprated each April in line with the annual inflation rate to the previous September: inflation was particularly high in September 2008, so state benefits and tax credits were by default increased by 5% or 6.3% (depending on the price index used to uprate them), but it subsequently fell sharply and the annual rate of RPI inflation in 2009–10 was less than 0.5%. Hence, real state benefit and tax credit amounts grew substantially in 2009–10. Second, the child element of the child tax credit—a means-tested payment for low-income families with children—was increased by £175 per year above average earnings in April 2008 and a further £75 per year above average earnings in April 2009. Real average earnings were still growing over this period, so this represented a large real rise in state support for many families with children.

The period between 2007–8 and 2009–10 also saw a reduction in income tax payments and social security contributions as a share of net income, from 27.3% to 25.8%. There are two likely reasons. First, reductions in employment are associated with reductions in tax paid on employment income. Second, the Labour government replaced the 10% and 22% marginal income tax rates with a single 20% rate in April 2008, and subsequently compensated the majority of the losers from this reform by substantially increasing the tax-free personal allowance, meaning that the package of reforms as a whole represented a net tax 'giveaway'.

The share of net income accounted for by the other income components—gross self-employment profits, gross income from savings, investments and pensions, payments such as local taxes (subtracted from net income), and miscellaneous other additions to income—remained very stable between 2007–8 and 2009–10.

The shift in the composition of net income away from earnings and towards state benefits clearly has potentially important implications for the pattern of changes in income across the income distribution. We turn to this below.

7.2.4 *The Distribution of Net Household Incomes During the Recession*

We now turn our attention away from average measures of income and look at how the whole distribution changed during the GR. Figure 7.5 plots the percentage change in income at each percentile point of the distribution between 2007–8 and 2010–11, as well as the corresponding changes for each year within that period. Income changes above the 95th percentile are not shown for 2010–11 due to uncertainty regarding changes to top incomes (see earlier). The dotted lines highlight data that is the product of our simulation described earlier, rather than obtained directly from the FRS. It is important to remember that we do not observe the same households over time, but we observe changes in percentile points of the income distribution based on repeated cross-sections. For a study of income dynamics among the same individuals, see Jenkins and Van Kerm (2011).

The first striking aspect of the graph is that, throughout the distribution, real incomes performed much better in 2008–9 and 2009–10 than in 2010–11. Real incomes grew at almost all points of the income distribution in 2008–9 and 2009–10; but, throughout most of the distribution, the fall in real incomes in 2010–11 dwarfs the rise seen over the previous two years. Thus, the impact of the GR on real household incomes is only clearly evident significantly after the economy started contracting. This confirms that what we saw earlier for average incomes is true for the whole distribution.

The second noteworthy feature is that, up to the 95th percentile, income growth since 2007–8 has largely been inequality-reducing, being higher amongst lower income households. This is driven by the growth in incomes that took place between 2007–8 and 2009–10, which was relatively robust in the bottom 35% of the distribution but close to zero for most of the rest (the particularly strong growth at the bottom in 2009–10 can be explained by large real rises in almost all state benefits and tax credits in that year—see earlier).

In contrast, the pattern of income losses in 2010–11 is relatively flat, at between 3.5% and 4.5% for the vast majority of the distribution. This is driven by the fact that, unlike in the previous two years, the real value of most state benefits and tax credits fell substantially in 2010–11. As already stated, the default position is to uprate benefits and tax credits each April in line with inflation to the previous September. Annual RPI inflation in September 2009 was negative, so the then Labour government decided instead to increase those state benefits and tax credits that were normally uprated in line with the RPI by 1.5% in April 2010 (with plans to increase them by RPI inflation minus 1.5% in April 2011). Nevertheless, inflation subsequently rose sharply and averaged around 5% in 2010–11, implying significant real cuts in most state benefits and tax credits in that year. Thus, while losses further up the distribution in 2010–11 are driven by falling real employment income, similar reductions in real benefit and tax credit amounts in that year explain the similar magnitude of losses towards the bottom of the distribution.

Lastly, changes in incomes above the 95th percentile were particularly dramatic during the GR. Real falls in top incomes in 2008–9 were more than offset by large rises in 2009–10. Indeed, Jin et al. (2011) show that the rise in top incomes in 2009–10 was larger than in any year in at least the last decade.

The falls in top incomes in 2008–9 are perhaps unsurprising given the stock market decline and collapse in interest rates, which are likely to have affected the very richest the most as they tend to have more income from savings and investments (note that capital gains are not included in the income definition used here, but dividend income is), as well as the troubles faced by the UK's financial sector in that year (those on top incomes are relatively likely to work in that sector). The rise in top incomes in 2009–10 is more surprising. It could be partly driven by the subsequent recovery in financial markets and forestalling or avoidance behaviour with regard to the introduction of the 50% marginal tax rate in April 2010. In 2010–11, the introduction of the 50% marginal tax rate and withdrawal of the tax free personal allowance for those with earnings over £100,000 are likely to have depressed top incomes, both directly and indirectly via labour supply responses and avoidance behaviour (including the forestalling behaviour that is likely to have resulted in some income being brought forward to 2009–10). It is therefore highly uncertain as to how top incomes will have changed in total over the course of the GR.

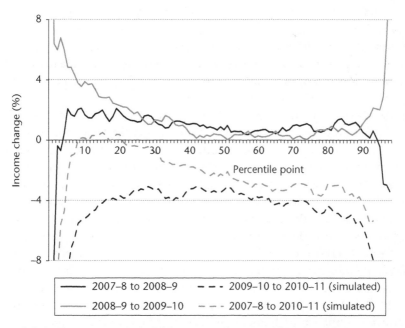

Figure 7.5. Real income growth (%) by percentile point, 2007–8 to 2010–11

Source: Authors' calculations using Family Resources Survey, 2007–8, 2008–9, and 2009–10.

Note: Simulated income growth at points above the 95th percentile is not shown due to uncertainty over the evolution of top incomes.

7.2.5 Inequality in Net Household Incomes Before and During the Recession

Here we document the consequences of the pattern of income changes that we saw earlier for income inequality, and place them in recent historical context. We use three simple ratio measures of inequality, which give the ratio between incomes at two percentile points of the distribution: the P90/P10 ratio for a measure of inequality between the top and bottom of the distribution; the P50/P10 ratio for comparing the middle and bottom; and the P90/P50 ratio for comparing the top and middle. We also present the Gini coefficient, a number bounded between zero and one which summarizes the degree of inequality throughout the distribution. For all measures, higher numbers imply greater inequality.

Figure 7.6 shows the time series of these inequality measures in Great Britain since 2000–1 (for consistency Northern Ireland, which was not included in the FRS until 2002–3, is excluded—Northern Ireland accounts for less than 3% of the UK population so its exclusion will make little difference). The ratio measures of inequality are plotted against the left-hand axis, and the Gini is plotted against the right-hand axis. The graph shows that inequality has been quite stable over the last decade, with small reductions between 2000–1 and 2004–5 and small rises between 2004–5 and 2007–8.

In 2008–9, the first full financial year since the start of the GR, inequality fell slightly. This is what we would expect given the pattern of income growth between 2007–8 and 2008–9 shown in Figure 7.5—changes in income were clearly inequality-reducing except for the poorest 5%, which are irrelevant for the ratio measures of inequality looked at here and are given a relatively low weight in the calculation of the Gini.

In 2009–10, different measures of inequality moved in different directions. This reflects the fact that, whilst income growth in that year was clearly inequality-reducing within the bottom half of the distribution, it was almost uniform between the median and P90, and the top decile group saw faster income growth than the rest of the top half of the distribution (see Figure 7.5). Hence, the relative gaps between the bottom and middle and the bottom and top both fell, but the relative gap between the top and middle widened slightly: the P50/P10 and P90/P10 ratio measures of inequality declined, but the P90/P50 ratio increased. The Gini coefficient increased slightly, which reflects the increase in inequality near to the very top of the distribution.

Jin et al. (2011) show that the rise in the Gini coefficient between 2003–4 and 2007–8 is statistically significant, and the Gini coefficient in 2009–10 was statistically significantly higher than its recent low-point in 2003–4.

According to our simulation for 2010–11, there was little change in the ratio measures of inequality in that year because the percentage income losses were close to uniform across much of the distribution (see Figure 7.5). Nevertheless, taking the three years between 2007–8 and 2010–11 as a whole, inequality narrowed slightly: this is true both for inequality between the bottom and middle, and between the middle and top, as reflected by falling P50/P10, P90/P10, and P90/P50 ratios. The narrowing of inequality in the bottom half of the distribution is very much driven by the pattern of real income growth in 2009–10, which was very robust at the bottom of the distribution as most state benefit and tax credit amounts grew strongly in real terms. It is worth noting that, despite these small reductions during the GR, the ratio measures of inequality in 2010–11 are still at or above their mid-2000 levels.

Figure 7.6 also highlights that the uncertainty over the evolution of top incomes in 2010–11 (see earlier) prevents us from coming to firm conclusions about what happened to the Gini coefficient. Under the two scenarios of real income growth of 0% and −10% in the top five percentile groups of the income distribution in 2010–11, the Gini would have risen and fallen respectively (this is true both for the single year between 2009–10 and 2010–11, and for the three years between 2007–8 and 2010–11 taken together). It is however worth noting that, under either scenario, inequality in 2010–11 as measured by the Gini would still lie above its 2006–7 level.

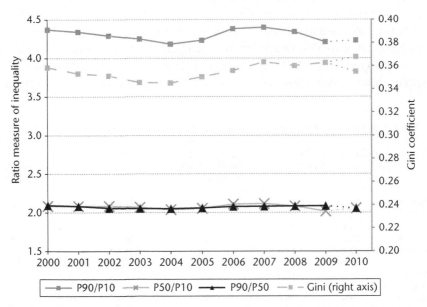

Figure 7.6. Household net income inequality in Great Britain, 2000–1 to 2010–11

Sources: Authors' calculations using Family Resources Survey, various years.

Note: Years refer to financial years. Data points for 2010–11, marked by dotted lines, are the results of simulations. Two scenarios are presented for the Gini coefficient in 2010–11, to reflect the uncertainty over the evolution of top incomes: the scenarios correspond to real household income growth of 0% and –10% in the top five percentile groups of the distribution (see text).

In previous UK recessions inequality has increased, been unchanged, or fallen (Muriel and Sibieta 2009). However, in each of the recessions they examine one observes a pattern of income inequality reducing growth across much of the income distribution. The key differences occur in terms of the changes in top incomes, which have shown vastly different trends in each of the three most recent recessions in the UK. Therefore, the GR is similar to previous recessions in terms of the pattern of income growth across much of the income distribution, and similar to the extent that highly uncertain trends in top incomes will determine the actual change in overall measures of income inequality.

The fact that inequality in the bottom half of the income distribution declined so clearly during the GR strongly suggests that relative poverty is likely to have fallen. In the next subsection, we confirm that this is the case in the aggregate, but show that this was driven by particular demographic groups.

7.2.6 Poverty Before and During the Recession

Table 7.2 shows relative poverty rates in Great Britain since 2000–1 among major demographic groups (as in the previous section, we exclude Northern Ireland for consistency), where the poverty line is the commonly-used 60% of contemporary median income. These poverty rates are different to those used in official UK statistics, which use the same definition of household income but use the modified OECD equivalence scale and are calculated for the UK as whole. This affects the level of poverty observed in any year, but is less likely to

Table 7.2. Relative poverty rates (%) in Great Britain, 2000–1 to 2010–11

Year	Children	Working-age parents	Working-age adults without children	Pensioners	All	Median income growth
2000–1	25.0	19.2	13.0	29.0	19.9	2.6
2001–2	25.8	20.2	12.6	29.8	20.3	5.4
2002–3	24.0	19.0	12.7	28.4	19.4	1.5
2003–4	23.6	18.9	13.0	26.1	19.0	–0.6
2004–5	22.8	17.9	12.8	24.8	18.3	1.2
2005–6	22.9	18.7	13.2	23.7	18.4	0.7
2006–7	23.6	18.8	13.1	26.8	19.1	0.6
2007–8	23.4	18.8	14.0	25.7	19.2	–0.1
2008–9	22.4	18.8	14.4	23.7	18.8	0.8
2009–10	20.4	17.4	14.8	20.9	17.7	0.5
2010–11	20.0	17.1	14.4	23.7	18.0	–3.5

Source: Authors' calculations using Family Resources Survey, 2000–01 to 2009–10. The figures for 2010–11 result from simulations (see main text).

Note: The poverty line for a given year is 60% of the median household income in that year. Incomes have been equivalized using the square root of household size.

affect trends over time. Indeed, existing analysis using the official UK statistics has reached the same qualitative conclusions as we do here regarding changes in poverty among various groups in recent years (Jin et al. 2011).

The table highlights that, despite small rises in the middle of the previous decade, there were overall reductions in poverty among children and pensioners in the years preceding the GR. Interestingly, the reduction in poverty among working-age parents was much less notable than that among children because it is families with larger numbers of children who have seen falls in their poverty rate, as highlighted in Brewer et al. (2010). This contrasts with the trend among working-age adults without children, whose poverty rate rose slightly (and has been rising steadily for most of the past three decades). Tax and benefit policy is an important reason for these trends: overall, the Labour government's tax and benefit reforms heavily favoured low-income families with children and pensioners (Browne and Phillips 2010) and they were a very dominant driver of both the overall reduction in child poverty and the partial reversal of this reduction in the middle of the decade (Brewer et al. 2010).

In both 2008–9 and 2009–10, families with children and pensioners again experienced substantial falls in poverty of similar magnitude to those seen in the early 2000s, more than reversing the small rises in poverty among those groups in the previous few years. Child poverty fell by three percentage points and pensioner poverty fell by almost five percentage points over the two years. Tax and benefit reforms are again key to the explanation. Low-income families with children and pensioners are the major demographic groups most likely to be entitled to state support, and so both benefited disproportionately from the large real increases in most state benefits and tax credits that occurred over these years—see earlier. However, poverty among working-age adults without children continued its gradual rise after the GR hit. This group are less likely to be in receipt of state benefits and tax credits, so would not have benefited to the same extent from the large real increases in most state benefits and tax credits in April 2009; and they were not major beneficiaries of any discretionary state benefit or tax credit changes during the GR.

According to our simulation for 2010–11, overall poverty in that year remained stable, as we would expect given the relatively flat profile of income changes in 2010–11 that we saw in Figure 7.5. Pensioners are the only group whose poverty rate is expected to have changed notably in 2010–11, but the rise in pensioner poverty that we simulate would only return it to its 2008–9 level and would thus still be two percentage points lower than just before the GR in 2007–8.

Relative poverty also fell during the three most recent recessions in the UK, (Muriel and Sibieta 2009). However, this was mainly due to substantial falls in pensioner poverty, with falls of over 15 percentage points, something that did not occur during the GR. The most likely reason for this contrast is the fact that pensioner poverty is now at a much lower base than it was at the time of past recessions when it stood at close to 40%.

Given the substantial fall in median income and hence the relative poverty line in 2010–11, trends in relative poverty are of course not a good guide to the evolution of absolute living standards amongst those on low incomes in that year. In fact, absolute poverty (using the 2010–11 poverty line fixed in real terms) actually rose by about two percentage points under our simulations between 2009–10 and 2010–11; and it rose for pensioners, children, and those of working age without children. Taking the three years since the recession began as a whole (2007–8 to 2010–11), absolute poverty stayed relatively stable overall, as it did for pensioners. It fell by about one percentage point for children and rose for those of working-age without children by about one percentage point. Hence, the overall trends in absolute poverty over time are unsurprising given what we have seen happened to real incomes across the distribution during the recession; but as with relative poverty, there have been clear differences between the fortunes of major demographic groups—in particular, between pensioners and those of working-age, and between families with and without children.

7.3 The Aftermath of the Great Recession: Fiscal Consolidation

We consider, finally, the prospects for living standards in the immediate post-recession years. This is a highly uncertain exercise because of the substantial uncertainty about how the macroeconomy, and in particular the labour market, will evolve. But the Conservative–Liberal Democrat coalition government has already set out its public spending plans for the next few years as part of a total fiscal tightening of £102 billion in 2011–12 terms, or 6.6% of national income, by 2015–16 in an effort to redress the fiscal position which deteriorated so rapidly during the course of the GR (Crawford, Emmerson, and Tetlow 2011). About three quarters will come from public spending cuts and about a quarter from tax rises. According to the IMF, the planned reduction in public spending as a share of national income between 2010 and 2015 is the third largest out of 29 leading industrial countries, behind only Iceland and Ireland (International Monetary Fund 2010). Assuming that these plans are adhered to, the impacts of policy reforms due to be implemented over the next few years on household incomes can already be estimated. In this section we draw on analysis of these reforms conducted by the Treasury and IFS. We do not discuss policy decisions announced by the government in the autumn statement of November 2011, but the impacts of these were very minor relative to the measures that had already been announced. This analysis uses the modified OECD equivalence scale, as is used for official UK statistics, rather than the square root of household size used in the rest of this chapter. As already discussed, this is very unlikely to qualitatively affect any conclusions. Equivalization is irrelevant when calculating the loss or gain from a reform as a percentage of income. Its only impact on the distributional analysis in this section is to affect the grouping of households by income.

The impacts of reforms have been estimated using data on the current population. Hence, to the extent that the impacts of reforms depend upon macroeconomic developments (for example, the impact of cuts to income-related benefits depends upon how people's gross incomes evolve), this is an approximation only. We are abstracting from changes to the macroeconomy, which will clearly also be crucial in determining how the distribution of incomes evolves in the years ahead but which are extremely uncertain.

7.3.1 Reforms to the Tax and Benefit System

At the time of writing, planned tax and benefit reforms in the post-recession period constitute a large net takeaway from households, amounting to about 5% of total net household income by 2014–15. Examples include a rise in the basic rate of value added tax (VAT) from 17.5% to 20% in January 2011 (raising £13.5 billion per year in 2014–15); a change in the price index used to uprate benefit and tax credit amounts annually which will in general result in less generous increases in those amounts (an estimated welfare cut of £6 billion per year by 2014–15); and a series of aggregate cuts to tax credits and housing benefit. The cuts to welfare spending are in total expected to save the government £18 billion per year by 2014–15 (HM Treasury 2010).

Figure 7.7 shows the estimated distributional impact of all modelled tax and benefit reforms to be implemented between January 2011 and April 2014, under the assumptions of no behavioural responses or changes in pre-tax prices as a result of those reforms (as assumed by the UK Treasury in its distributional analysis). The underlying data used are from the 2008–9 Expenditure and Food Survey (not the FRS as in previous sections) because it includes detailed consumer expenditure data (as well as income data) which allows the estimated impacts of consumption tax changes to be included. The combined impact of all reforms on households is presented as a percentage of net household income. (There are good arguments for also looking at losses in relation to household expenditure, particularly when looking at reforms to consumption taxes, but in this instance the distributional pattern is affected little by doing this.)

Taking all family types together, Figure 7.7 shows that within the bottom nine income decile groups those with the lowest incomes are set to lose the most from these reforms as a percentage of income. The loss corresponds to about 6% of net income for the bottom income quintile, on average. Given that the annual welfare budget is being cut by £18 billion, this is perhaps not a surprise. The percentage loss in the tenth decile group is higher than in all but the bottom three decile groups, but this is largely driven by tax rises for the very richest (approximately the top 1%): those households with an individual earning above £100,000 per year had tax relief on pension contributions restricted from April 2011 (the very rich had in fact already been hit by two tax rises under the previous Labour government in April 2010: a rise in the marginal income tax rate from 40% to 50% for those with gross earnings above £150,000 per year, and a gradual withdrawal of the personal income tax allowance for those with gross earnings above £100,000 per year).

Therefore, tax and benefit reforms seem likely to squeeze the living standards of the less well-off by more than those on higher incomes (except for those on the very highest incomes). Using the numbers in Figure 7.7 we can approximate the implied proportionate changes to ratio measures of inequality as a result of these reforms by assuming that households' rankings in the distribution remain the same and that the percentage loss at the midpoint of each quintile is equal to the average loss in that quintile group (for the top quintile group, we exclude families containing someone with gross earnings above £100,000 from this calculation, since we know that their average losses far exceed those in the rest of the quintile). Under these assumptions, all the ratio measures of inequality shown in Figure 7.6 would increase as a result of the reforms: the P90/P10 ratio by about 3.5%, the P50/P10 ratio by about 2.6%, and the P90/P50 ratio by about 0.8%. To put this in context, they compare to the respective falls in these measures of inequality of 3.8%, 2.8%, and 1.1% that we expect to have taken place between 2007–8 and 2010–11 (see Figure 7.6). Hence, the impact of upcoming tax and benefit reforms seems likely to be to reverse a substantial part (if not all) of the reductions in ratio measures of inequality seen during the GR.

Figure 7.7 also explores the impact of these tax and benefit reforms across family types. It shows that families with children are to be hit harder by these reforms than other family types, on average. This is not simply because losses are decreasing in income and having children is negatively correlated with income: within given income decile groups, families with children will on average lose more. There are various cuts to child-contingent state support which help to explain this. Child benefit amounts are to be frozen in cash terms (a real cut) for three years; aggregate child tax credit spending is to be cut (one element of it is to be increased and other elements are to be cut or abolished); the percentage of childcare costs that can be claimed by those receiving the working tax credit was cut from 80% to 70% in April 2011; the minimum weekly working hours requirement for a couple with children to claim working tax credit is to rise from 16 to 24 in April 2012; and child benefit is to be removed from families containing a higher rate income tax-payer from January 2013. Hence, in contrast to recent trends in the UK (see Section 7.1), families with children are not to be favoured by tax and benefit reforms in the near future.

Recent IFS modelling predicted that child poverty would remain stable in 2011–12 before rising in each of the four years between 2011–12 and 2014–15, and that it will be more than one percentage point higher in 2014–15 as a result of the tax and benefit reforms planned by the current government. Poverty among those of working age without children is also expected to continue rising, but the estimated impact of the package of tax and benefit reforms on the poverty rate among that group in 2013–14 is lower, at about 0.5 percentage points (Brewer, Browne, and Joyce 2011). Across almost the whole income distribution, pensioners are the least affected by the reforms as a percentage of net income. A contributing factor is that annual increases in the basic state pension are to become more generous. Hence, unlike for

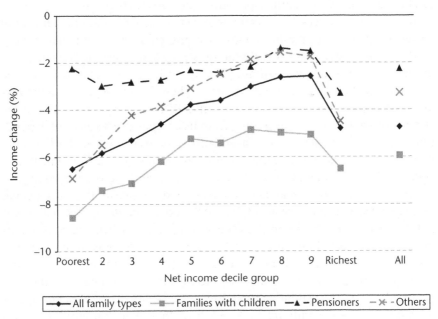

Figure 7.7. Distributional impact of modelled tax and benefit reforms implemented between January 2011 and April 2014 in the UK, by income and family type

Source: Institute for Fiscal Studies analysis based on the 2008–9 Expenditure and Food Survey (see presentation by James Browne after the March 2011 Budget at http://www.ifs.org.uk/publications/5524).

Note: The unit of analysis is families, i.e. it is families rather than individuals who are grouped into decile groups on the basis of net equivalized household income. The equivalence scale used here is the modified OECD equivalence scale, which is used for official measures of poverty and inequality in the UK.

families with children, tax and benefit reforms look set to continue to favour pensioners just as they did under the Labour government in the years before the GR.

7.3.2 Cuts to Expenditure on Public Services

The fiscal consolidation is by no means confined to tax and benefit reforms. Very large real cuts to public service spending are also planned. The average real cut across all departments is currently expected to be around 12%. However, this will not be equally distributed across all areas (Crawford, Emmerson, and Tetlow 2011). Some small areas of spending will be increased (International Development, and Energy and Climate Change), whilst others have been offered some relative protection (health spending will be approximately frozen in real-terms, and defence and schools will receive smaller cuts than most). The largest cuts will be most strongly felt by other areas such as universities, transport, housing, local government, justice, and the home affairs. Further details can be found in Brewer, Emmerson, and Miller (2011: chapter 6).

Since public services are largely received as benefits-in-kind, allocating losses and gains from public service spending changes to particular households is notoriously difficult and requires strong assumptions. The UK Treasury has attempted this by assuming that the value people get from a public service is equal to the cost of providing it to them (which depends on the per-unit cost of provision and the amount that different people actually use the services provided), and by excluding from its analysis cuts to areas of expenditure where it was unable to measure and value usage, for example capital expenditure, central government administration and spending on pure public goods such as national defence, the environment and the Foreign and Commonwealth Office. IFS researchers have explored the sensitivity of the overall estimated distributional impact of the public service spending cuts to different (arbitrary) assumptions about the value of these unmodelled cuts to different households (Brewer, Emmerson, and Miller 2011). Under one assumption, the cash value of unmodelled public services is the same for everyone; under another assumption, that value is proportional to household income. Figure 7.8 shows the estimated total distributional impact of impending cuts to public service expenditure under each of these two (purely illustrative) assumptions about the value of unmodelled services to households. Losses are expressed relative to the counterfactual where all such expenditure had been kept constant at 2010–11 levels in real terms.

Under either assumption about the value of unmodelled public services to different households, the bottom three income quintile groups would lose more in percentage terms from the impending public service spending squeeze than the top two income quintile groups (given the other crucial assumption made about the modelled public service spending: namely, that its value to households is equal to the cost of providing the service to them). Losses as a percentage of net income (plus the value of benefits in kind) are between 5% and 6% at the bottom of the distribution, which is similar to the magnitude of the losses for those on the lowest incomes from tax and benefit reforms shown in Figure 7.7. Of course, this regressive pattern is less stark under the scenario where the value of unmodelled public services is proportional to income.

It is important to remember that these scenarios do not represent upper and lower bounds on the overall progressivity or regressivity of the public service spending squeeze. Although we have some idea of the differential usage of public services by different income groups in the case of modelled public services, we have little idea of the value placed on them by different income groups. In the case of the unmodelled public services, no data exists on the differential usage (where relevant) or valuation of these services across income

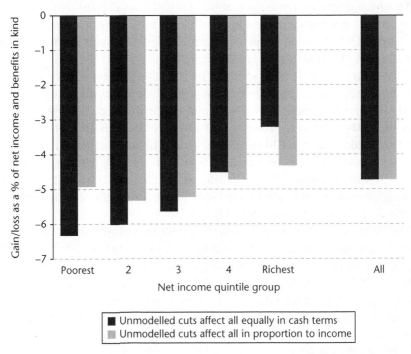

Figure 7.8. Distributional impact of changes to public service spending by 2014–15 in the UK under different assumptions

Source: HM Treasury (2010) and Institute for Fiscal Studies: see presentation by Cormac O'Dea after the October 2010 Comprehensive Spending Review at http://www.ifs.org.uk/publications/5314

Note: The 'unmodelled' cuts to public service spending are cuts to capital expenditure, spending on pure public goods (e.g. national defence, the environment, the Foreign and Commonwealth Office) and central government administration costs. Estimated losses are expressed relative to the scenario where all public spending had remained constant in real terms.

groups. In principle, one could come up with assumptions that changed the regressive impact of public service cuts, for example the rich value national defence very highly. It is left to the reader to judge the plausibility of such assumptions. Therefore, where this can be measured, poorer households are disproportionate users of public services facing cuts, and thus have more to lose in this sense. What we do not know is the relative value placed on public services by different income groups and their relative usage of unmodelled public services. Without this knowledge, it is impossible to be definitive about the distributional impact of the overall fiscal consolidation.

As mentioned above, the evolution of living standards in the near future will also depend heavily on things less directly under the government's immediate control, most notably the labour market recovery (or lack thereof). As of late 2011, the UK government's independent fiscal watchdog expected average real earnings among those employed to continue falling until early 2013. It also expected the unemployment rate to rise in both 2011and 2012, with unemployment remaining above its 2010 level until 2015. General government employment was expected to fall by 600,000 between 2010–11 and 2015–16 (Office for Budget Responsibility 2011). Such macroeconomic forecasts are of course highly uncertain.

If these forecasts were to be accurate, IFS modelling suggests that median net household income in the UK would be more than 5% lower in real terms in 2015–16 than at its peak in 2009–10, and that it would be no higher than it was in 2002–3 (Brewer, Browne, and Joyce 2011). This lack of growth in median income over a 13-year period would be unprecedented in the UK since consistent records began, and would imply that median income in 2015–16 will be about 20% lower than it would have been if its historical average annual growth rate (since 1961, when consistent records began) of 1.7% had continued beyond 2002–3.

The Office for Budget Responsibility also publishes forecasts for real household disposable income. The most recent set of forecasts from November 2011 imply that, in per-capita terms, real household disposable incomes will fall by 3.0% in 2011 and further 1.1% in 2012, with sluggish growth thereafter meaning that it will only return to its 2010 level by 2015.

The signs for the future are thus very clear: the post-recession years will continue to see much greater strains on people's living standards than was the case during the GR itself.

7.4 Conclusions

During the Great Recession, UK GDP fell by over 7%. Employment fell, and it fell by more for the young, male, and less educated. Hours worked amongst employees fell, suggesting a rise in part-time working. It may thus be surprising to learn that average incomes increased in the UK whilst the economy was contracting. However, in 2010–11, earnings, state benefits and tax credits fell in real terms. This is likely to have led to the largest drop in average net household incomes in any single year since 1981, and would leave them at their 2003–4 level. It seems that the impact of the GR on net household incomes in the UK was not felt until after the economy had stopped contracting. The pain was delayed, not avoided.

Between 2007–8 and 2010–11, the bottom half of the distribution caught up with the middle, which led to declines in relative poverty, particularly amongst pensioners and families with children. At the very top of the distribution, top incomes increased up to 2009–10, but seem sure to have been hit by the introduction of the 50 pence tax rate in April 2010. By how much is highly uncertain and will depend on how individuals' behaviour responds. Trends in top incomes will determine the path of overall measures of inequality, but it seems likely to be higher than that seen in the mid-2000s.

Declines in living standards look set to continue until at least 2012–13, with only a relatively slow recovery thereafter. If this happens, this means that average living standards will not have grown in well over a decade, making it the worst period for changes in living standards since at least the Second World War. This partly reflects expectations of continued falls in real earnings, as well as tax and benefit reforms planned as part of the fiscal consolidation. Welfare cuts and tax rises will act to reduce household incomes and those with the lowest incomes are clearly set to lose the most from these reforms as a percentage of income (with the important exception of those with the very highest incomes). This is likely to increase poverty, other things being equal, offsetting some of the falls in poverty over the past decade. Though their distributional impact is harder to quantify, large public service cuts will surely reduce living standards still further. The Great Recession looks set to cast a very long shadow in the UK.

8

Country case study—USA

Jeffrey Thompson and Timothy M. Smeeding

The Great Recession (GR) is the most dramatic economic downturn that the USA has experienced in more than six decades. Tumbling stock and housing markets erased more than $15 trillion in national wealth in 2008, or nearly 10% of real total national financial assets, the largest drop on record since 1945. As financial markets and the rest of the economy slowed to a halt, real GDP did not grow in 2008 and fell by 2.6% in 2009, the largest decline in six decades. In addition house prices dropped 30% since their 2005 peak (Kowalski 2011). Overall, the GR resulted in over $7,300 in foregone consumption per person by 2011, or about $175 per person per month (Lansing 2011).

With the nation's economic growth abruptly halted, millions of workers lost their jobs. Between July of 2008 and 2009 the US economy shed 6.8 million jobs. Total non-farm employment fell by 5%, more than at any point since the nation returned to a peace-time economy following the Second World War. The employment–population ratio (number of adults 16 and over with jobs relative to same population) fell to its lowest level since 1990, 58.2%, even as older workers increased their employment. A full 20% of 25–54 year old male workers were not in work in April 2011, the lowest fraction since 1948 and 5 points below the trough of any previous recession (Leonhardt 2011*a*; US Department of Labor 2011). And the unemployment rate climbed to over 10% at its highest, but at the time of writing remains at 9.2% 24 months after the 'recession' was declared ended in summer 2009 (US Department of Labor 2011).

All of these powerful economic shocks have also resulted in stagnant wages and declining incomes for most households (Levy and Kochan 2011). In this chapter we explore the distributional impacts of those changes. Inequality had steadily risen in the decades leading up to the Great Recession. This chapter addresses the question: Has the impact of the GR halted or hastened those trends, or not had any impact whatsoever?

This chapter covers the impacts of the GR on inequality of wages and family incomes, and poverty, comparing these impacts to those in the previous three recessions, primarily using data from the Current Population Survey and secondarily from the Congressional Budget Office post-tax income series (CBO 2010). We also explore the degree to which the tax and transfer system mitigated these impacts in the GR and several other recent recessions.

The main findings are as follows. Inequality growth has been mixed during the GR. Some measures of inequality rose, others remained flat, and others declined. The choice of measure matters, as does the inclusion of taxes and transfer programmes and the age groups analysed. Most measures of inequality, however, remain at or near historic high levels, and inequality has increased for everyone except elderly people.

Flat and falling real hourly wages at the bottom and the middle of the distribution, alongside marked growth at the top of the distribution, have produced a surge in wage inequality in the USA, with the Gini index and the P90/P10 and P90/P50 ratios reaching 30-year highs. After adjusting for taxes, transfers, and household size, the P90/P10 ratio for equivalized net income for all households declined between 2007 and 2009, while the Gini index and P90/P50 ratio were flat. But among non-elderly households each of these inequality measures climbed sharply. Inequality measures using 'top incomes' data sources indicate that, at least through 2008 and 2009, the long-term trends toward rising top income shares were halted. The income share of the top 1% of households, though, has fallen only slightly below modern peak levels reached in 2007. But history and recent evidence suggests that the rich recover incomes and shares much more rapidly than do the middle class. Indeed the very best US data source, unfortunately running only through 2007, suggests that the income share of the entire bottom 80% of Americans is lower now than in 2002, and far less than the peak value in 1993.

Poverty increased during the GR, but by 2009 the official poverty rate for all households remained below levels reached during the economic downturns of the early 1980s and early 1990s. For households with younger heads (under 34), and childless households (with heads under 55), though, the official poverty rate reached a 30-year high.

Public transfers have risen, and taxes have declined, as a share of income across the distribution since 2007, indicating that public sector policy action has softened the impact of the GR on household well-being.

Average household size has increased across the income distribution since 2007, but particularly among the lowest-income groups, suggesting households are opting to live together—or stay together—as a coping mechanism. Even with this movement, poverty and inequality rose amongst the non-elderly during and now just after the GR.

With the lag in availability of data on household incomes (see Chapter 1) and labour markets still a long way from fully recovering, the final chapters of the story about the distributional and poverty impacts of the GR in the USA are yet to come. Events unfolding between 2009 and 2011 suggest the full picture will likely be even worse than we describe in this chapter. Unemployment remains high in late 2011 and the value of the primary assets of middle-income households—their homes—will take years to recover the value lost since 2007. Stock markets, though, have rebounded. Indeed, the share of post-recession income growth since the trough that is accruing to capital (businesses, corporation, stockholders) has been over 85%. And, the public sector actions—both increased transfers and decreased taxes—that softened the impact on poverty and even more than offset trends in some inequality measures, are phasing out. Temporary transfer increases in the federal stimulus package phased out in mid-2011. Further reductions in transfer programmes are a likely outcome as policy-makers in the USA have turned their attention away from the recession and toward the deficit.

8.1 Methods

8.1.1 *Household Income and Poverty*

In the analysis we use the Annual Social and Economic (ASEC) Supplement to the Current Population Survey (CPS). The ASEC, or 'March CPS' as it is conducted in March of each year, is a survey of approximately 50,000 households that has been conducted annually in the USA for more than 50 years. The ASEC asks respondents to provide detailed income, family, and demographic detail for the previous calendar year.

Our analysis uses data from the surveys conducted between 1980 and 2010, covering household income for the calendar years between 1979 and 2009. (Chapter 2 contains some limited analysis of figures published by the Census Bureau for incomes in 2010 as well, drawing on the March CPS for 2011—see Section 2.6.) Our baseline figures use the Census Bureau's 'money income'. Money income is a broad income concept, and includes earnings, social insurance benefits, public assistance transfers, pensions and other retirement income, capital income, and other forms of income. Money income does not include capital gains income or reflect personal income taxes, social security taxes, union dues, or Medicare deductions. Money income also does not include non-cash benefits, such as food stamps, employer-subsidized health benefits, rent-free housing, and goods produced and consumed on the farm. In addition, money income does not reflect the fact that non-cash benefits are also received by some non-farm residents which often take the form of the use of business transportation and facilities, full or partial payments by business for retirement programmes, medical and educational expenses, and so on. In order to capture these elements of income as well as all taxes and benefits, we also use the Congressional Budget Office (CBO) income data, the most complete US source, but with the proviso that it does not include data beyond 2007.

In addition to calculating measures of inequality using money income, we also calculate equivalized disposable income by netting out taxes, adding some transfer payments that are not included in 'money income' and dividing by a standard equivalence scale to account for household economies of scale (the square root of household size). Taxes are estimated using the National Bureau of Economic Research TAXSIM model (Feenberg and Coutts 1993). Using the household income and demographic data from the March CPS, TAXSIM produces state and federal income taxes, including the earned income tax credit (EITC), as well as FICA social insurance taxes. We further supplement the baseline Census 'money income' definition by adding estimated food stamp benefits, now known as the supplemental nutrition assistance programme (SNAP). This estimate combines the CPS variables for food stamps receipt status, number of beneficiaries, and months of receipt with average monthly benefit amounts from the USDA. When considering long-term trends in any income measure, we include adjustments for top-coding in the March CPS, using the consistent cell mean series made available by Larrimore et al. (2008), and also account for the 1994 (survey year) series break by smoothing the relevant series at the break-point, similarly to the approach used by Atkinson, Piketty, and Saez (2011).

We calculate several measures of inequality, including the Gini index and ratios of key income percentiles, such as the P90/P50 and P90/P10 ratios, and also describe the composition of income (earnings, transfers, and capital income) and how these have changed in the GR. We calculate poverty rates, based on both the official poverty thresholds determined by the US Census Bureau, and also the relative measure of poverty (60% of median household income) used by the European Union. We calculate measures of poverty and inequality for the overall population, and also for different age groups and educational attainment levels.

8.1.2 Top Incomes

One important limitation of the March CPS is that it does not adequately capture income received by those at the very top of the distribution. The CPS income data are not only 'top-coded', but the survey itself does not include sufficient numbers of high-income households to make reliable estimates of incomes at the very top of the distribution, the top 1% or the top one-tenth of 1%, for example. For a thorough discussion of top-coding in the CPS and how it impacts measuring inequality at the top of the distribution, see Burkhauser et al. (2011).

A number of data sources do exist that can be used to assess inequality levels at the top of the distribution, including the CBO's 'comprehensive household income', Internal Revenue Service (IRS) income tax records, and the Survey of Consumer Finances. We supplement the findings from our analysis of data from the March CPS by reporting some key findings from research that has analysed inequality trends using these top-income data sources (Atkinson, Piketty, and Saez 2011; Smeeding and Thompson 2011). Each of the income sources we use are more fully described in the Appendix on income definitions.

8.1.3 *Wages, Unemployment, and Labour Force Participation*

We use the Outgoing Rotation Group files of the Current Population Survey (CPS ORG), with data covering the period from 1979 to 2010, to examine how the GR and other recent recessions have impacted workers' wages and the extent of inequality in wages. As with income inequality, we calculate the Gini index, and ratios of wage percentiles.

We also calculate unemployment rates across the total workforce, and labour force participation rates for the total working-age population. We look at wage inequality measures for all employed workers, as well as for different age groups and educational attainment levels.

8.2 Labour Market Impacts of the Great Recession

The labour market fallout from the GR has proven to be both dramatic and persistent. With output shrinking throughout 2008, unemployment accelerated, with millions of workers losing their jobs. Overall unemployment averaged 9.6% in 2010, which is slightly lower than the 9.7% unemployment from 1982. In mid-2011, it was still over 9%. Compared to the earlier downturn, long-term unemployment is considerably greater, and the general rate of unemployment among most labour market groups is actually higher than in the early 1980s.

8.2.1 *Rising Unemployment and Falling Labour Force Participation*

In 2010 the unemployment rates for all major educational-attainment and age groups hit 30-year highs. Among college graduates, the unemployment rate jumped from 2.4% in 2006 to 5.6% in 2010, and among those with advanced degrees it rose from 1.5% to 3.5% in the same period (see Figure 8.1 and

Appendix Table 8.A1). But the largest increases—in absolute terms—were felt by younger workers with the lowest levels of education. Unemployment among workers with only a high school degree jumped from 5.3% to 12.2% between 2006 and 2010, and among those lacking a diploma it climbed from 8.6% to 17.4%. Highly-educated workers continue to have lower unemployment rates, but the increases experienced since 2006 are proportionally as large as for less educated workers. All age groups also saw dramatic increases in their unemployment rates, with rates roughly doubling between 2007 and 2010. Workers aged 35–64 saw their unemployment rates go from around 3% to nearly 8%. The youngest workers (aged 18–24) saw their unemployment rate quickly shoot up from 9% to 17%, and the unemployment rate for somewhat more experienced workers (those aged 25–35) went from 4.3% to 9.7%.

The official unemployment rate excludes 'discouraged' workers who have ceased looking for work. In fact, 35% of men aged 25–54 without a high school diploma are out of the labour force (and they are clearly also not in school), compared with less than 10% of those with a college degree (US Bureau of Labor Statistics 2011a). Labour force participation also declined for most age and education groups, although less dramatically than the rise in unemployment. The decline in labour force participation was most prominent among younger and less educated workers. Participation fell by 0.7%

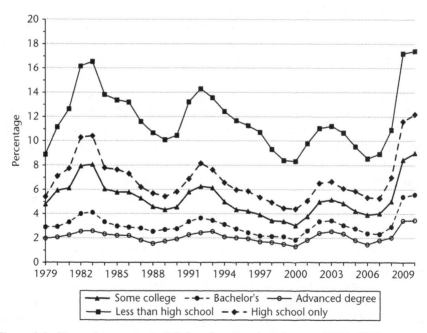

Figure 8.1. Unemployment rate (%), by educational attainment, 1979–2010
Source: Authors' analysis of CPS ORG Files (various years), CEPR extracts.

among college graduates and 0.2% among those with advanced degrees, but it dropped by roughly 2% for all workers with education below BA-level (Table 8.A2). For workers with less than a high school degree, the rate of labour force participation slid from 61.6% in 2007 to just 59.4% in 2010.

Persons of most age groups also decreased their participation in the labour force. Among more experienced workers, including those aged 36–45 and 46–54, the declines were relatively minor, dipping by 0.4% and 0.9%, respectively, between 2006 and 2009. Among workers aged 18–24, however, the labour force drop off has been sizeable, falling nearly 4.5% from 69.5% in 2006 to 65% in 2010. This recent labour force decline among young workers continues a trend present since the early 1990s. In each of the last three recessions, labour force participation has declined among young workers, and not recovered in the ensuing recovery, with the decline in the GR being the greatest. Between 1979 and 2009, the labour force participation rate of 18–24 year olds declined 10%, while the share enrolled full-time in post-secondary education rose by 10% (Snyder and Dillow 2011). The opposite trend has held for older workers, who have steadily raised their participation rates since the late 1980s, through good and bad economic times. The participation rate in the 55–64 year old population climbed from 63.7% to 65.1% between 2006 and 2010, continuing a trend where participation rose in 21 of the last 24 years. And the over-65 group has also increased both its labour force participation and employment (US Department of Labor 2011).

In sum, the picture is one of continuing mass labour market devastation as of mid-2011. Both Farber (2011) and Sum et al. (2011*b*, *c*) suggest that the numbers of displaced workers—those losing their jobs—and the numbers of long term unemployed were at an all-time high in 2010. Howell and Azizoglu (2011) show that new hires and job openings were at a decade-long low in 2010, while permanent job losers were at an all-time high over this same period. And the full effect of the GR on employment is not known with certainty. According to one popular estimate (Greenstone and Looney 2011), it might take eight to ten years to get back to the number of jobs there were before the GR. Both of the main routes to the middle class for those with only a high school education, manufacturing and construction, are closed (Glaeser 2010; Smeeding et al. 2011). In fact, the two major forces driving job opportunity polarization are technological change, with workers being replaced by machines, creating demand for fewer, more-skilled workers to run and repair the machines (Goldin and Katz 2008). The second is trade, the staggering magnitude of growth in imports from China of goods that have been produced in the United States by US workers. While Autor, Dorn, and Hanson (2011) refute the assertion that such findings suggest a need for trade restrictions, this trend deserves more analysis and suggests a need for more-skilled US workers in non-manufacturing jobs.

While many argue that job losses are cyclical, there are therefore good reasons to note they are secular as well. But even a cyclical job loss that extends for three to five years becomes a secular issue almost by definition. Long-term joblessness is damaging to the career and life chances of all workers, especially younger workers, and also negatively impacts family stability and the future of children in these households (Von Wachter 2010). These issues are especially damaging to young men with a high school degree or less, 72% of whom are fathers by age 30, and only 38% of whom earned more than $20,000 in 2002 when the economy was in far better shape than it is today (Smeeding, Garfinkel, and Mincy 2011).

8.2.2 Record High Levels of Wage Inequality

In the face of a deep and sustained labour market downturn, real hourly wages can be expected to decline. Because so many workers have lost their jobs, however, the accompanying composition shifts in the employed workforce may potentially obscure falling wages. Trends in average real hourly wages, in fact, suggest modest wage growth in the GR. Between 2007 and 2010, mean hourly wages rose from $20.26 to $20.57, although they did fall back 0.6% after 2009 (Appendix Table 8.A2, panel A). These wage trends, however, were not shared across the distribution: between 2007 and 2010 real hourly wages fell roughly 1.5% at the 10th percentile (P10) and at the median (P50), but rose by nearly 5% at the 90th percentile (P90).

These divergent wage trends—rising at the top and falling in the middle and at the bottom of the distribution—drove several measures of wage inequality to 30-year highs in 2010: see Figure 8.2. The graph indicates that over the 15 years preceding the GR, there were only relatively modest changes in these measures. (The impact of the series break, which is the result of a general redesign in the CPS—including a move to computer-assisted interviewing and expanded use of internal censoring for top-coded values—on measures of wage inequality in the CPS ORG is discussed by Mishel, Bernstein, and Schmitt 1998.) The P90/P50 ratio fluctuated from year-to-year, but by 2006 remained at the same levels as in the late 1980s. After falling during most of the 1990s, the P90/P10 ratio exhibited modest increases starting in 2001, so that it had returned to 1994 levels by 2006. Starting in 2008, though, each of these inequality measures increased sharply. The P90/P10 ratio of real hourly wages, however, rose in each year since 2007, climbing from 4.4 to 4.8 (see Appendix Table 8.A2, panel B).

Downward wage pressures over this period have been most evident among younger and less educated workers, while older and more highly educated workers have registered wage increases (Appendix Table 8.A2, panel C). Obtaining a bachelor's degree, however, did not make workers immune from wage pressures in the GR. Young workers aged 25–34 years old with a BA saw their wages fall 0.5% per

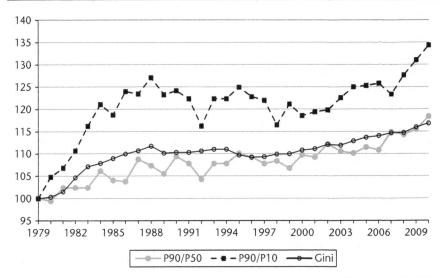

Figure 8.2. Hourly wage inequality, percentile ratios, and Gini coefficient, 1979–2010 (indexed 1979 = 100)

Source: Authors' analysis of CPS ORG Files (various years), CEPR extracts.

Notes: Estimates adjusted to smooth over the effects of the 1993 change in CPS data collection methods (see main text).

year between 2007 and 2010: see Table 8.1. Even older workers (aged 55–64 years old) with a bachelor's degree experienced falling wages of a similar magnitude. The only workers to experience rising wages during this period were workers with postgraduate degrees and training (limited to those under age 55) and 45–54 year old experienced workers with a bachelor's degree.

8.3 Income Impacts of the Great Recession

Because workers are typically part of a household unit that shares resources among its members, several of whom may be earners, and because households

Table 8.1. Annual real wage growth (%), by age and education group, 2007–10

Education	Age (years)			
	25–34	35–44	45–54	55–64
High school degree only	–0.6	–0.7	–0.2	0.1
Bachelor's degree only	–0.5	0.1	1.2	–0.6
Postgraduate education or degree	0.5	1.3	1.4	–0.1

Source: Authors' analysis of CPS ORG files, CEPR extracts.

Notes: Average annual percentage change in real hourly wages (2010 prices, adjusted for inflation using US CPI-U). Hourly wages for non-union workers.

are able to draw upon non-labour sources of income, it is important to go beyond wages or earnings and explore the impacts of the GR on household income. Inflation-adjusted average household income (Census 'money income') fell in both 2008 and 2009, the most recent years of data in the March CPS. (Inflation adjustments are made using the US CPI-U, and in all cases years are referred to according to the year in which the income was received, not the survey year.) In 2009, average real household income was 2.9% lower than it had been in 2007, hitting the lowest level in 12 years: see Figure 8.3, panel (a). While average money income fell for all households, and for non-elderly households, it actually rose somewhat for households headed by someone age 65 and older, reflecting a long term trend in elder incomes. Median income for all households fell 3.7% over the same period, and increases in the Gini index and the P90/P10 and P90/P50 ratios all indicate modest increases in income inequality during the GR using this income definition (Appendix Table 8.A3, panel A).

8.3.1 Adjusting for Taxes, Transfers, and Household Size: Net Equivalized Income (NEI)

In addition to the market factors driving employment losses and depressing wages, a host of actions by the public sector and households as well, combined to influence household well-being during the GR. Automatic 'stabilizers' (including unemployment insurance (UI), SNAP, and the temporary assistance to needy families programme (TANF)) and discretionary fiscal policy all injected hundreds of billions of dollars into household incomes between 2008 and 2010. Total SNAP benefits rose from $37 billion in 2008 to $54 billion 2009, with 2.5 million new households getting 'food stamps'. Although it was only signed into law in February 2009, hundreds of billions of the tax cuts and increased benefits in the Obama Administration's 'American Recovery and Reinvestment Act' (ARRA) impacted on household incomes during that year (CBO 2009).

The baseline Census 'money income' definition does include some sources of transfer income (UI, TANF, and Social Security), but it does not include others (such as the Earned Income Tax Credit (EITC) and SNAP) and it also excludes taxes. To reflect the influence of these transfers and taxes, we calculate a measure of net income which subtracts taxes (including federal and state income taxes and the employee share of social insurance FICA taxes) and additional transfer payments (including the EITC and SNAP benefits) from money income. To reflect household economies of scale, we then divide real net household income by the square root of the household size. The resulting measure, 'net equivalized income' (NEI) is a superior measure of household

(a) Census 'money income'

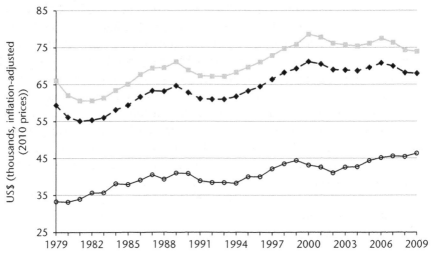

(b) Equivalized net income

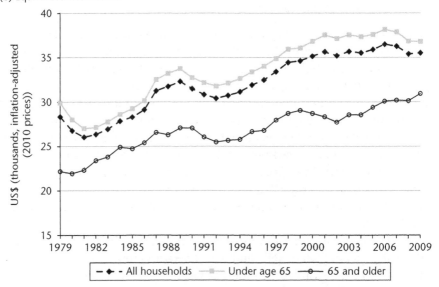

Figure 8.3. Mean real household income, by age and income definition, 1979–2009: (a) Census 'money income', (b) Equivalized net income

Source: Authors' analysis of March CPS (various years), CEPR extracts. Adjusted for inflation using US CPI-U.

Notes: Top-coded income values adjusted using consistent cell means (Burkhauser et al. 2011), and series adjusted to smooth over the effects of the 1993 change in CPS data collection methods.

well-being, since an equivalent amount of gross money income results in a lower standard of living if family size is larger or applicable taxes are higher.

Accounting for taxes, transfers, and household size, average household income declined by only two-thirds as much—falling just 2% between 2007 and 2009, and actually rising slightly after 2008: see Figure 8.3, panel (b). Non-elderly households follow a similar trend, except income is flat after 2008, but elderly households saw their incomes rise over this period. The rise in inequality is also muted once these factors are included (Appendix Table 8.A3, panel B). Instead of rising, the P90/P10 ratio is shown to decline modestly between 2007 and 2009 once taxes, transfers, and household size are incorporated into the measure: see Figure 8.4, panel (a). Figure 8.4 suggests, as Burkhauser and Larrimore (2011) have argued, that taxes and transfers have an impact on the income distribution in a different way than during previous recessions. In the 1980s, policy changes exacerbated inequality trends measured by the P90/P10 ratio for all households but, during the GR, taxes and transfers have reduced this measure of inequality.

The difference between the two series using the P90/P50 ratio is less pronounced, as inequality continues to rise, however faintly, using NEI (Figure 8.4, panel (b)). The longer-term trends in both the P90/P10 and P90/P50 ratios, however, indicate that inequality is indeed different in the Great Recession than in previous downturns. In the deep recession of the early 1980s, and during and immediately following the mild recession of the 2001, inequality increased sharply. Inequality also appears to have increased somewhat during the early 1990s recession, although the pattern is more difficult to discern given the 1993 series break in the March CPS—the result of a general redesign of the survey, including switching to automated coding and expanded use of top-code censoring of income values (Ryscavage 1995). Trends in the Gini index, a measure that is calculated from incomes throughout the income range, also suggest that any change in inequality between 2007 and 2009 was very slight, rising just one-half of 1%, owing most likely to the rising real incomes of the elderly as we see below (Appendix Table 8.A3, panel B).

When we restrict the focus to include only non-elderly households, a very different pattern emerges for inequality measures in the GR. Among non-elderly households, the Gini index and the P90/P50 and P90/P10 ratios all increased substantially between 2007 and 2009, and more generally since 2000: see Figure 8.5. Figure 8.5 is limited to the most recent decade, a period with consistent treatment of top-coded incomes, including assignment of cell means by income source to top-coded observations. For non-elderly households, net equivalized incomes fell less at the top of the distribution than for the non-rich, causing the P90/P10 ratio to climb 3%, and the P90/P50 ratio and the Gini index to rise approximately 2% (Appendix Table 8.A3, panel C). See also Smeeding et al. (2011).

(a) P90/P10

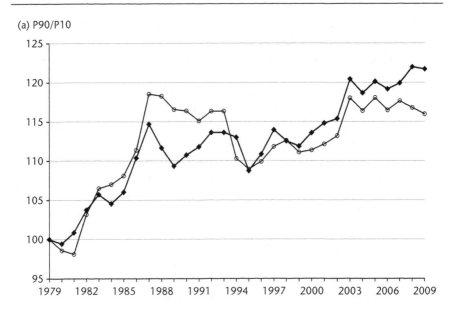

(b) P90/P50

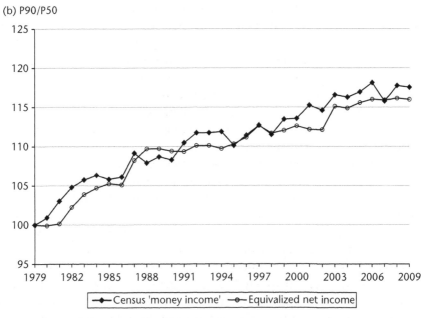

Figure 8.4. Selected household income inequality indices, Census 'money income' and equivalized household net income, 1979–2009 (indexed 1979 = 100): (a) P90/P10, (b) P90/P50

Source. Authors' analysis of March CPS (various years), CEPR extracts, and NBER Taxsim.

Note: Top-coded income values adjusted using consistent cell means (Burkhauser, Feng, and Jenkins 2009), and series adjusted to smooth over the effects of the 1993 change in CPS data collection methods.

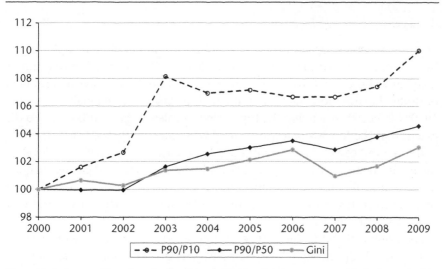

Figure 8.5. Inequality of equivalized household net income, non-elderly households, 2000–9 (indexed 2000 = 100)

Source: Authors' analysis of March CPS (various years), CEPR extracts, and NBER TAXSIM.

These comparisons suggest that households headed by the elderly and non-elderly have experienced different income paths though the GR. Why did the elderly do better than the non-elderly? The elderly depend much more on income transfers (social security) and sources of investment income and far less on the labour market than do the non-elderly. The elderly who were already retired in 2008 lost some home value along with most other owners, but were generally invested in relatively safe portfolios, which protected their assets and income flows (Gustman, Steinmeier, and Tabatabai 2010). Older workers take up social security benefits at high rates once they pass age 62. The 46% of elders who take up benefits between ages 52 and 65 are subject to an earnings test which discourages work in these age ranges (Smeeding et al. 2011). But those who wait until they are at least 65 not only receive higher benefits than at age 62, but are allowed to receive these social pensions without any penalty for earnings. Amongst the higher skilled elderly, employment has increased throughout the recession, owing in part to reluctance to retire (in terms of not working) and increased work after retirement (likely reflecting falling home prices). The success of the tax and transfer system in sustaining the incomes of, and mitigating inequality among, older households, and its failure to do so for non-elderly households is consistent with Ben-Shalom et al.'s (2011) assessment of US anti-poverty programmes increasingly directed toward the elderly (and the disabled) and away from the young.

8.3.2 *Growth in Top Incomes*

Because of income top-coding and the presence of few extremely high income households in the sample, it is not possible to use the March CPS to estimate inequality at the very top of the income distribution. In recent years a number of studies have demonstrated that much of the growth in inequality since the 1970s has been restricted to the top few percentiles of the distribution. To the extent that the top few percentiles are driving inequality, the P90/P10 ratios, and Gini indices calculated with the March CPS, understate the level of inequality at any point in time and possibly the trends toward greater inequality over time. Because of differences in the income composition, it is possible that the Great Recession is having different impacts of inequality at the very top of the distribution.

The Congressional Budget Office's 'comprehensive income' measure, while only available up through 2007, demonstrates the importance of accounting for trends at the very top of the distribution (CBO 2010). CBO 'comprehensive income' is much more extensive than Census 'money income,' and by statistically matching the Census data to IRS tax return data, it includes much more in realized property income. Moreover, comprehensive income shows an even larger rise in inequality up to 2007, especially driven by changes in incomes at the very top of the distribution: see Figure 8.6. These data show that inequality contracted in the 1990–3 and 2001–2 recessions, but rose dramatically after 2002. The top quintile group's share is 52.5% of after-tax net income in 2007 according to the CBO series compared to 48.5% in the census money income inequality series (DeNavas-Walt et al. 2010: table A.5). The trend toward inequality is driven here by the top 1% share (which rises by 228%, from 7.5% in 1979 to 17.1% in 2007), but also by a 15.2% increase in the share of the next 4% of household units, with no change in the share of the next 10% to 15%. Hence, inequality in the CBO data since 1993 and through 2007 is driven almost exclusively by gains in the income of the 95th percentile and higher percentiles of households. We also note that the CBO share of net income in the bottom quintile group is 4.9% by their measure in 2007, compared to 3.7% in the 2007 census income data (DeNavas-Walt et al. 2010). But the trends in both series are the same, with the CBO showing declining shares for all of the bottom four quintile groups since 2002, though especially for the bottom two quintile groups. We now turn to the high income group.

While comprehensive income is only available through 2007, several other top income data sources can be used to estimate inequality trends during the GR. These include income tax records from the IRS, analysed by Piketty and Saez (2007) and Atkinson, Piketty, and Saez (2011) and the Federal Reserve Board's Survey of Consumer Finances (SCF). (See the Appendix for more about income definitions.) Analysis using these data sources suggests that income inequality has risen dramatically at the very top of the distribution: see Figure 8.7. The analysis by Saez (2010) of the IRS data finds that share of federal Adjusted Gross Income held by the richest 1% of households more than doubled between 1979 and 2007, rising from 10% to 23.5% (including capital gains).

The CBO 'comprehensive income' measure (not adjusted for taxes) shows that the top 1% share of total income increased from 9.3% to 19.4% over the same period: see Figure 8.7. However, even these enriched CBO data exclude the vast majority of capital income that is not realized in a given year, including imputed rent on owner-occupied homes as well as accumulated financial and business wealth and changes in such incomes over the 2007–9 recession and earlier recessions. Smeeding and Thompson (2011) use the SCF data to

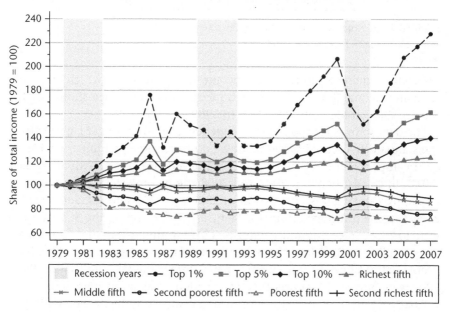

Figure 8.6. Shares of CBO household after-tax 'comprehensive income', quintile and top income groups, 1979–2007 (indexed 1979 = 100)

Source: CBO (2010), 'Average Federal Tax Rates and Income, by Income Category (1979–2007): Shares of After-Tax Income'. http://www.cbo.gov/publications/collections/collections.cfm?collect=13

Notes: The CBO's household 'comprehensive income' equals pre-tax cash income plus income from other sources. Pre-tax cash income is the sum of wages, salaries, self-employment income, rents, taxable and non-taxable interest, dividends, realized capital gains, cash transfer payments, and retirement benefits plus taxes paid by businesses (corporate income taxes and the employer's share of social security, medicare, and federal unemployment insurance payroll taxes) and employees' contributions to 401(k) retirement plans. Other sources of income include all in-kind benefits (medicare, medicaid, employer-paid health insurance premiums, food stamps, school lunches and breakfasts, housing assistance, and energy assistance).

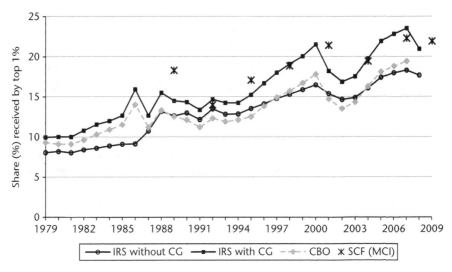

Figure 8.7. Income share of top 1%, by data source, 1979–2009
Source: Smeeding and Thompson (2011).

calculate a 'more comprehensive income (MCI)' measure which combines standard income flows with imputed income to assets. They show that the top 1% share of MCI rose from 18% in 1989 to 22% in 2007.

The data sources for top incomes experience an even longer lag-time than the standard household surveys, but we do have some preliminary evidence on the impact of the GR on inequality at the very top of the distribution. Saez (2010) finds that between 2007 and 2008 the income share of the top 1%, including capital gains, dropped from 23.5% to 21%, and excluding capital gains income it dropped from 18.3% to 17.7%. Projecting the SCF data forward to 2009, Smeeding and Thompson (2011) estimate that the top 1% share of MCI fell from 22.3% to 21.9%. Both sets of results suggest that there have been small declines in top income shares during the GR, but that levels in 2009 were only slightly lower than the previous peak levels from 2007.

Finally we must mention the most recent evidence at the time of writing on incomes from capital compared to labour over the recession. Sum et al. (2011a) show that since the beginning of the recovery in June 2009, 88% of the growth in US national incomes (through to March 2011) accrued to owners of capital (mainly business owners and corporations, but also pensions, rental property owners and stockholders) and less than 12% to workers in the form of wages or benefits, with wage declines almost the same as employer benefit increases. The drop in aggregate wages and salaries is almost surely because of the lack of job growth over this period. The failure of real wages and salaries to grow over the first seven quarters of recovery is unprecedented in any post Second World War recovery. These data suggest that the working class and prime age employees are not gaining from the recovery at this point, and that any increases in aggregate personal incomes since the trough of the recession are accruing to the owners of capital other than owned homes—the top percentiles of the income distribution, stock-holders and retirees.

8.4 Poverty Impacts of the Great Recession

As income has declined, dramatically so for young and less educated families, poverty rates have risen. According to the official US government definition of poverty, 13.4% of households (using the census 'money income' definition) were poor in 2009 (see Appendix Table 8.A3, panel D). Poverty rose sharply in 2008 and 2009, but overall household poverty rates remained below levels reached during the economic downturns in the early 1980s and early 1990s: see Figure 8.8. (See also Figure 2.21 in Chapter 2 for poverty rate estimates to 2010 published by the Census Bureau and also based on 'money incomes' and the official definition of poverty.) The broader definition of poverty adopted by the European Union—set at 60% of median household income—is considerably higher than the official US definition and fluctuates less over time. Over most of the last 30 years this poverty measure has hovered at 30% in good and bad economic times. Between 2007 and 2009, this measure of poverty rose from 30.2% to 30.5%.

These figures suggest that, despite large-scale job losses, the Great Recession's impact on poverty is unremarkable relative to previous recessions. The impact on poverty, though, differs markedly for different demographic groups. Amongst younger households, including those headed by individuals under age 35, poverty rates hit 30-year highs in 2009: see Figure 8.9. Between 2007 and 2009, the official poverty rate rose from 28.1% to 33.7% for households headed by individuals under age 25, and for households with heads between 25 and 34, poverty rose from 14.3% to 16.9%. Indeed poverty rates ticked up for all types of units, except for those headed by a person 65 or over. Consistent with the other data reviewed above, poverty among elderly households fell during the GR, from 11.6% in 2007 to 10.3% in 2009, hitting a new 30-year low.

The official poverty rate for households with children is typically several percentage points higher than it is for households without children. This remains true during the GR, but over the last decade the gap has narrowed: see Figure 8.10. Poverty rates fell dramatically for households (with heads aged less than 55) with children during the 1990s, while they declined only slightly among those without children. For those households with children, the poverty rate rose 2.5 points between 2007 and 2009, returning to levels near, but still below, previous high-points from the early 1980s and early 1990s. Among

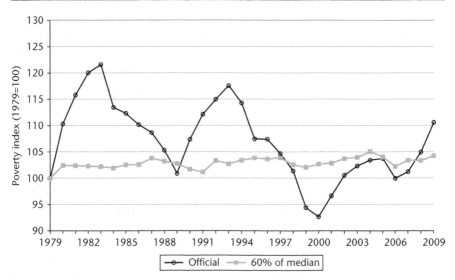

Figure 8.8. Household poverty rates, US Official and 60% of median, Census 'money income', 1979–2009 (indexed 1979 = 100)

Source: Authors' analysis of March CPS (various years).

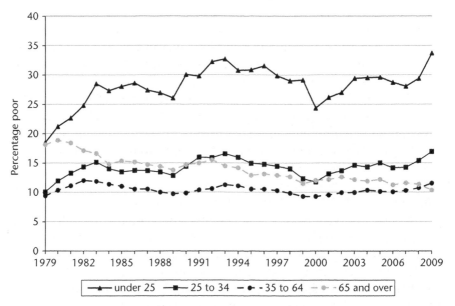

Figure 8.9. Official poverty rate (%), by age of household head

Source: Authors' analysis of March CPS (various years).

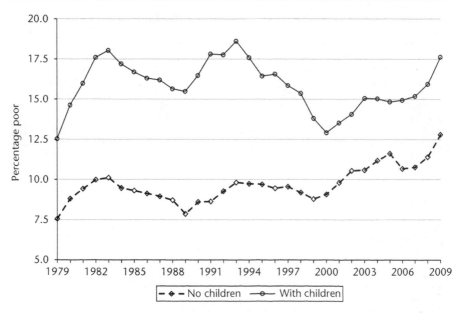

Figure 8.10. Official poverty rate (%), by presence of children, households with head aged less than 55

Source: Authors' analysis of March CPS (various years).

households without children, poverty rose by similar levels, but now exceeds high-points from those previous recessions by more than 25%.

8.5 Shifting Income Composition

The dramatic changes in labour market conditions, as well as government tax and transfer policies, have resulted in substantial shifts in the sources of total household income. For most households, the earnings share of total gross household income ('money income' plus SNAP benefits and the refundable portions of federal and state EITC benefits) declined between 2007 and 2009: see Table 8.2, panel A. For the middle quintile group of all households and the bottom quintile group of non-elderly households, the drop was approximately five percentage points. In the top fifth, though (for both elderly and non-elderly households) the wage share of total income increased between 2007 and 2009, partially offsetting a declining capital income share experienced by both groups.

The impact of public policy was relatively broad-based, with the transfer share of income rising and the tax share declining for nearly every quintile group: see Table 8.2, panels B and D. The distribution of transfer income

221

Table 8.2. Shares of income components in total household income (%), by quintile group and age, 2007–9

	All households			Non-elderly households			Elderly households		
	Bottom fifth	Middle fifth	Top fifth	Bottom fifth	Middle fifth	Top fifth	Bottom fifth	Middle fifth	Top fifth
A. Earnings									
2007	27.9	79.8	86.6	43.5	89.9	91.0	2.7	27.7	46.1
2009	26.8	74.5	87.1	39.3	87.0	91.4	3.3	23.0	48.6
Change	–1.1	–5.2	0.5	–4.2	–2.9	0.4	0.6	–4.8	2.5
B. Transfers									
2007	66.5	12.2	3.2	52.5	6.3	1.8	89.3	42.4	15.6
2009	68.2	17.2	4.1	57.2	9.6	2.4	89.0	48.6	18.8
Change	1.7	5.1	0.9	4.7	3.4	0.6	–0.3	6.2	3.1
C. Capital income									
2007	5.5	8.1	10.2	4.0	3.9	7.1	8.0	29.8	38.3
2009	5.0	8.3	8.8	3.5	3.4	6.2	7.7	28.4	32.6
Change	–0.6	0.2	–1.4	–0.5	–0.5	–1.0	–0.3	–1.4	–5.7
D. Taxes									
2007	2.1	13.2	24.9	3.4	14.5	25.2	0.0	6.2	21.8
2009	2.0	11.9	24.5	3.0	13.6	24.9	0.1	5.1	21.1
Change	–0.2	–1.3	–0.3	–0.5	–1.0	–0.3	0.0	–1.1	–0.7

Source: Authors' analysis of March CPS (various years), NBER TAXSIM.

Notes: Total household income is equal to Census 'money income' plus the refundable portion of federal and state EITC and child tax credit benefits and estimated SNAP benefits. Transfer share includes estimated SNAP benefits and refundable portion of state and federal EITC and child tax credit benefits, as well as the transfer income included in census 'money income'. Tax share excludes the state and federal EITC as well as the refundable child tax credit. Quintile groups refer to the distribution of total household income for all households.

beneficiaries is very different for elderly and non-elderly households. (Transfer income here includes social security, supplemental security income, survivor's benefits, disability payments, public assistance, workers compensation, veteran payments, child support, alimony, unemployment compensation, SNAP benefits and the refundable portions of the federal and state EITC benefits and the child tax credit.) The transfer share of income rose 4.7% for non-elderly households in the bottom quintile group and 3.4% of those in the middle quintile group, but less than 1% for those in the top quintile group. Among elderly households in the bottom quintile group, though, there was no change in the transfer share of income. The transfer share of elderly households in the middle fifth rose more than 6%, but it also rose more than 3% among elderly households in the top fifth.

The capital income share of household income also declined in the GR across most of the distribution, for elderly and non-elderly households: see Table 8.2, panel C. Capital income in the Census Bureau's Money Income definition includes only interest, rental income, dividends, rent, trust, and retirement savings income. It does not include capital gains income. The decline in the capital income share was most notable for the top quintile group, where the capital share fell from 7.1% to 6.2% for non-elderly households and from 38.3% to 32.6% for elderly households.

8.6 Increasing Household Size as a Coping Mechanism

Measures of net equivalized income divide by (a function of) household size to reflect the economies of scale associated with sharing a household. Because of these economies of scale, some people opt to combine households as a coping mechanism during difficult economic times. In fact, the economic stresses from the GR seem to have inspired an increase of 'doubling up' or other forms of shared housing and sharp decline in household formation (Painter 2010; Mykyta and Macartney 2011). Figure 8.11 traces the trends in average household size (indexed to 1979 = 100) by income quintile group, and suggests that the long-term trend toward falling household size has been reversed, or at least halted during the GR. The average household size of the bottom quintile group rose by nearly 5% between 2007 and 2009, climbing from 1.8 to 1.9 persons per household. Average household size in the highest income quintile group rose a little more than 1%, going from 3.09 to 3.13 people per household.

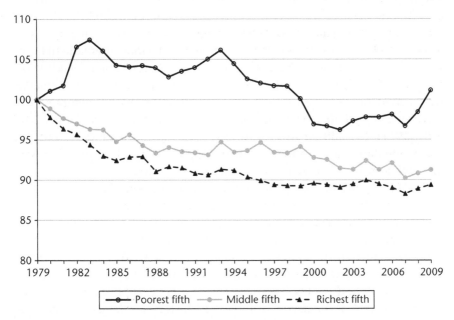

Figure 8.11. Average household size by income quintile group, 1979–2009 (indexed 1979 = 100)

Source: Authors' analysis of March CPS (various years).

The extent to which young adults delay home-leaving, join households, or families combine into households in response to economic stress, suggests that younger adults and those who were not in the labour force were more likely to be doubled-up in 2010 than in 2008. Moreover, doubled-up house-holders and adults were more disadvantaged and experienced a larger increase in poverty rates during the recession than their counterparts who were not doubled-up (Mykyta and Macartney 2011).

But this is only part of the story. The official poverty increases noted above took place despite the fact that there was an increase of 8.4% in young adults (aged 24–35) living with their parents; as well as an 11.6% increase in families who moved in with relatives in large part to avoid poverty. If these two groups instead lived alone, their poverty rates based on their own income would be 43% (Sherman 2011). And so, while doubled-up households had poverty rates higher than those who did not experience this change, the situation would have been far worse had the units who were forced to double up not been able to do so.

8.7 Fiscal Consolidation in the USA

The impacts of the GR on the distribution of household income and on poverty described in this chapter only extend through 2009. In the final accounting, when data are available through 2010 and 2011, the impacts on income levels and poverty are likely to turn out to be more dramatic than the situation described here. (On 2010, see Section 2.6 in Chapter 2.) While the recession officially ended in the USA in the summer of 2009, the job market remained depressed up through the end of 2011, with unemployment remaining higher than 9%, and forecast to remain above 8% until 2014 (CBO 2011). In addition to a continued high level of unemployment, the policy orientation at both the federal and the state levels has shifted in ways that will decrease incomes at the bottom of the distribution.

The 2009 figures in this chapter reflect a large infusion of transfers and tax cuts to households through the American Recovery and Reinvestment Act (ARRA). ARRA included billions of dollars in increases in supplemental nutrition assistance program (SNAP, formerly food stamp) benefits ($20 billion), temporary assistance for needy families (TANF) benefits, unemployment insurance ($40 billion), earned income tax credit (EITC) benefits, as well as tax cuts for all households. These benefits and tax cuts bolstered household incomes in 2009, as is reflected in Table 8.2. The transfer share of income rose 4.7 percentage points for non-elderly households in the bottom fifth of the distribution, and the tax share fell by 1.3 percentage points for the middle fifth of all households. The Center on Budget and Policy Priorities has estimated that in 2009 these provisions of ARRA helped 6 million Americans keep their incomes above the US poverty threshold, and reduced the severity of poverty for 33 million others (Sherman 2011).

The poverty-reducing components of ARRA, however, were primarily concentrated in the last half of 2009 and the first half of 2010. In 2011, most of the provisions of ARRA were being phased out and eliminated. Three-quarters of the $780 billion in ARRA spending was completed by the end of FY 2010, and 91% was completed by the end of 2011 (CBO 2009). The Tax Relief, Unemployment Insurance Reauthorization, and Job Creation Act of 2010 (TRUJCA) continued many programmes into 2011, including extended unemployment insurance and a temporary two percentage point cut in the payroll tax for all earners. None of these provisions have been extended to 2012.

Not only are the temporary components of ARRA and TRUJCA being phased out, but the general discussion over fiscal policy matters has shifted away from economic stimulus efforts toward ways to reduce the federal deficit and debts. The set of policies that will be ultimately adopted are not known at the time of writing, but a unified Republican Party opposition to increased tax revenue or cuts to defence spending, suggests that much of federal deficit reduction will centre on non-military discretionary domestic spending. Budget proposals by new leaders in US House of Representatives (the 'Ryan Budget Plan') include, for example, cuts in SNAP funding of $127 billion over ten years, a reduction of nearly 20% (Rosenbaum 2011).

Preliminary steps toward deficit reduction have already begun to affect spending on the transfer programmes that support the incomes of many non-elderly low-income households. In 2010, President Obama announced a three-year freeze in discretionary spending. The CBO projects that non-defence discretionary spending fell by 1.2% between 2010 and 2011, compared to a 5.7% increase in 'mandatory' (Social Security, Medicare, Medicaid) spending and a 2% increase in defence spending (CBO 2011). The Budget Control Act of 2011 also implements budget caps on discretionary spending, which will reduce those programmes by 5% between 2012 and 2021 (CBO 2011).

Total Federal debt in the USA hit modern highs in the GR, projected to rise above 70% of GDP—levels not seen since the Second World War—by 2012 (CBO 2011). If the political solution to bringing down the debt (it was less than 40% of GDP as recently as 2006) does not include major tax increases and leaves defence spending protected, there is no way to avoid deep cuts in non-defence discretionary spending. These programmes, which include TANF, SNAP, and the federal contributions to Unemployment Insurance benefits, amount to just 19% of all federal spending. If the debt is decreased solely by driving down spending on these programmes, incomes of low-income households, particularly the non-elderly will fall as well. Government transfers accounted for nearly 60% of the income of the poorest fifth of non-elderly households in 2009 (Table 8.2).

8.8 Conclusions and Discussion

This chapter suggests that income inequality and poverty in the USA rose with high and continuing joblessness, but primarily among non-elderly households. When all households are included, we can see that—until 2009 at least—some of the increases in poverty were not as severe as in past recessions and standard measures of inequality were unchanged or even declined (in the case of the P90/P10 ratio). Public transfer and tax policy played an important role in limiting the rise in inequality. When we focus on non-elderly households, however, the GR is shown to have a dramatic effect on inequality and poverty, producing 30-year record high levels of wage inequality and household poverty, despite the lower poverty rates experienced due to doubling up.

The elderly, owners of capital, and most high income households are also doing quite well as we recover from the recession, and as capital markets and executive pay have recovered faster than wages or jobs. Middle and lower-income households—those relying on earning to provide essentially all of their income, those whose primary asset is their home, and those with something less than an advanced degree—are faring much worse. The very steep decline in housing values (about 30% from 2005 to early 2011) has reduced mobility, led to higher rates of default and foreclosure, and negatively affected aggregate consumption (Leonhardt 2011b; Smeeding and Thompson 2011). Discretionary service spending (including non-housing, energy, food, transportation, education, entertainment, restaurant meals, and insurance spending) fell by 6.9% in the current recession, after never falling below 2.9% in any previous post-war recession. Without a revival in consumer spending, employment growth will remain weak, and the incomes of those relying on earnings will continue to suffer. The large overhang of household debt from before the GR, though, continues to put considerable pressure on households. Indeed Greenspan and Kennedy (2007, updated to 2011), suggest that, at the peak of the housing bubble in 2004–6, US households were annually withdrawing about 9% of home equity for spending. By the end of the first quarter of 2011, that fraction had fallen to –4%.

An extended period of high unemployment also threatens to have long-term consequences. Rising poverty, especially among young jobless adults and families, is permanently scarring the futures of millions of unemployed younger (under age 30) unskilled adults. Unless short-term action is taken to improve employment prospects for these particular workers, and to support the incomes of their children as we come out of the recession, poverty will remain high among this group. Over the longer term, traditional upward routes to the middle class, in manufacturing and construction jobs, will continue to disappear as wages and employment fall for those with only high school education or less. It is estimated that it will take eight years or longer for employment to rise to levels where low-skill workers can find good jobs. These individuals need more productive skills than they have at this time, given their current levels of education and human capital.

Two other forces deserve mention, one short-term and the other longer-term. The first is the political push to right the deficit in the US by reducing outlays, not by raising taxes, while at the same time attempting to protect the elderly from income loss. Based on our findings, elderly people are the one demographic group that has fared relatively well during the GR and the feeble expansion that preceded it, and they should not be singled-out for protection in policies to close long-term deficits. Tax increases on upper- and middle-income families are not being seriously considered at the time of writing. If outlays are cut, they will be reduced most for non-elderly discretionary programmes and entitlements such as SNAP, UI, and the EITC. Making these changes will surely increase poverty and inequality over the coming years.

The other longer-term force involves the weakness of labour as a political force in the USA. Labour parties are a force in Europe and have shown their ability to more equally share the burden of the recession: see for example OECD (2011d) and, for Germany, Burda and Hunt (2011). But organized labour is a relatively weak political and economic actor in the political economy of the United States. Unionization is at all-time low levels and, even the public sector, among the most heavily unionized sectors in the USA, has lost 600,000 jobs since the beginning of the recession. The reasons for the long-term decline of labour are complex (Levy and Temin 2009; Levy and Kochan 2011), but any reckoning of the US labour market and the GR's effects on employment, wages, and incomes must recognize this reality.

Policy pundits and applied economists of all types and background recommend that the USA increases its stock of human capital (as suggested by Goldin and Katz 2008). But the country has not yet been very effective at reaching this goal (consistent with the polarization in wages seen above). Graduation rates from high school are now below 1980s rates, unless GED degrees are included and then they become flat since 1980. College completion rates by males, especially those from the most disadvantaged backgrounds, are abysmally low and may in fact be falling (Haveman and Smeeding 2006). The 2010 education bill will help increase US post-secondary enrolment and completion (including two-year technical colleges) but not for a few years, if then. Larger future increases in human capital are therefore anticipated and will be necessary to increase employment and incomes for more Americans. Income transfers can alleviate poverty, but the solution to permanent poverty reduction is a steady well-paying job for otherwise-poor people. Unfortunately these jobs are not currently on the horizon for low-skilled workers, and especially not for low-skilled men.

Income definitions

Census 'money income' is income received on a regular basis (exclusive of certain money receipts such as capital gains) before payments for personal income taxes, social security, union dues, Medicare deductions, and other items.

We calculated *'net equivalized income'* (NEI) by starting with 'money income' and then: (1) adding transfer income not included in 'money income' (food stamps benefits, and refundable tax credits, including the EITC and the child tax credit; (2) subtracting taxes (state and federal income taxes the employee share of social insurance (FICA) taxes (with taxes and refundable credits estimated using the NBER TAXSIM programme); and (3) adjusting for differences in household size by dividing net income by the square root of household size.

SCF Income is defined by the Federal Reserve Board as household income for the previous calendar year as the following: wages, self-employment and business income, taxable and tax-exempt interest, dividends, realized capital gains, food stamps and other support programmes provided by the government, pension income and withdrawals from retirement accounts, Social Security income, alimony and other support payments, and miscellaneous sources of income. See Smeeding and Thompson (2011) for more about this measure.

MCI Income is SCF income as defined above, less income from wealth (interest, dividends, rent, royalties, and income from trusts and non-taxable investments, including bonds, as well as some self-employment income) + imputed flows to stocks, bonds, annuities, and trusts + imputed flows to quasi-liquid retirement accounts (401(k), IRA, etc.) + imputed flow to primary residence + imputed flow to other residences and investment real estate, transaction accounts, CDs, and whole life insurance + imputed flow to other assets and businesses + imputed flow to vehicle wealth – imputed interest flow for remaining debt (after adjusting for negative incomes). See Smeeding and Thompson (2011) for more about this measure.

CBO *'Comprehensive Household Income'* equals pre-tax cash income plus income from other sources. Pre-tax cash income is the sum of wages, salaries, self-employment income, rents, taxable and non-taxable interest, dividends, realized capital gains, cash transfer payments, and retirement benefits plus taxes paid by businesses (corporate income taxes and the employer's share of social security, medicare, and federal unemployment insurance payroll taxes), and employees' contributions to 401(k) retirement plans. Other sources of income include all in-kind benefits (medicare, medicaid, employer-paid health insurance premiums, food stamps, school lunches and breakfasts, housing assistance, and energy assistance).

Individual income taxes are attributed directly to households paying those taxes. Social insurance, or payroll, taxes are attributed to households paying those taxes directly or paying them indirectly through their employers. Corporate income taxes are attributed to households according to their share of capital income. Federal excise taxes are attributed to households according to their consumption of the taxed good or service. For more information on CBO comprehensive income, see www.cbo.gov/publications/collections/collections.cfm?collect=13.

Table 8.A1. Unemployment and labour force participation rates (%), 18–64 year olds

	1979	1983	1989	1992	2000	2003	2006	2007	2008	2009	2010
A. Unemployment rate											
Total labour force	5.5	9.5	5.1	7.2	3.6	5.6	4.2	4.3	5.4	9.0	9.3
By educational attainment:											
Less than high school	8.9	16.6	10.1	14.3	8.3	11.2	8.6	8.9	10.9	17.2	17.4
High school only	5.4	10.4	5.4	8.2	4.4	6.7	5.3	5.3	7.0	11.6	12.2
Some college, no degree	4.8	8.1	4.3	6.3	3.0	5.2	3.9	4.0	5.0	8.5	9.0
Bachelor's	2.9	4.1	2.7	3.7	1.9	3.4	2.4	2.3	2.9	5.4	5.6
Advanced degree	2.0	2.6	1.8	2.4	1.3	2.6	1.5	1.8	2.0	3.4	3.5
By age:											
18–24 years	10.7	16.5	10.0	12.7	8.0	11.2	9.1	9.0	11.4	16.1	17.0
25–35 years	5.1	9.6	5.1	7.4	3.5	5.8	4.3	4.3	5.6	9.6	9.7
36–45 years	3.5	6.9	3.6	5.6	3.0	4.6	3.4	3.3	4.4	7.7	8.0
46–54 years	3.2	6.3	3.4	5.4	2.4	4.0	3.0	3.1	3.9	7.2	7.4
55–64 years	3.0	5.8	3.2	5.2	2.4	4.2	2.8	3.2	3.6	6.5	7.2
B. Labour force participation rate											
All 18–64 year olds	73.9	75.0	78.1	78.4	78.8	77.7	77.5	77.5	77.5	76.9	76.2
By educational attainment:											
Less than high school	63.0	61.2	62.5	60.0	62.4	61.4	61.6	61.6	60.7	60.3	59.4
High school only	75.3	76.1	78.7	78.0	77.3	76.1	75.3	75.2	75.1	74.2	73.5
Some college, no degree	75.6	77.2	80.3	80.9	80.8	79.3	78.6	78.3	78.3	77.5	76.4
Bachelor's	83.9	85.7	87.4	87.3	85.9	84.9	85.1	84.8	84.8	84.9	84.4
Advanced degree	90.2	90.0	90.5	91.2	88.7	87.3	87.1	87.4	87.5	87.2	86.9
By age:											
18–24 years	74.9	74.0	75.1	73.1	73.2	70.3	69.5	68.9	68.4	66.7	65.1
25–35 years	79.3	81.5	83.9	84.0	84.4	82.7	83.0	83.1	83.0	82.5	81.9
36–45 years	79.1	81.7	85.3	85.3	84.8	83.9	83.7	84.0	84.0	83.9	83.2
46–54 years	74.1	75.7	80.1	81.0	82.3	81.7	81.7	81.7	81.7	81.2	80.7
55–64 years	56.9	54.7	55.7	56.4	59.1	62.5	63.7	63.9	64.6	64.9	65.1

Source: Authors' analysis of CPS ORG (various years), CEPR Extracts.

Table 8.A2. The distribution of real hourly wages (2010$), by education and age

	1979	1983	1989	1992	2000	2003	2006	2007	2008	2009	2010
A. Mean, median, and selected percentiles											
Mean	17.51	17.07	17.57	17.63	19.47	20.18	20.06	20.26	20.24	20.70	20.57
P10	8.40	7.28	7.21	7.61	8.17	8.30	8.11	8.34	8.10	8.13	8.00
P50	14.79	14.56	14.85	14.95	15.55	16.21	16.22	15.77	15.95	16.26	16.00
P90	28.90	29.12	30.60	30.45	34.62	36.38	36.50	36.80	37.00	38.12	38.45
P95	34.98	36.41	37.94	38.06	44.12	45.59	46.77	47.79	47.71	48.87	48.56
B. Inequality indices											
P90/P50	1.95	2.00	2.06	2.04	2.23	2.24	2.25	2.33	2.32	2.34	2.40
P90/P10	3.44	4.00	4.24	4.00	4.24	4.38	4.50	4.41	4.57	4.69	4.81
Gini	0.289	0.309	0.318	0.319	0.333	0.337	0.343	0.345	0.345	0.349	0.351
C. Mean by education and age groups											
By education:											
Less than high school	14.45	13.12	12.36	11.73	11.52	11.90	11.58	11.77	11.69	11.85	11.49
High school only	16.16	15.23	15.00	14.67	15.44	15.94	15.69	15.65	15.52	15.87	15.54
Some college, no degree	17.28	16.54	16.81	16.63	17.63	18.00	17.62	17.70	17.44	17.72	17.46
Bachelor's	22.68	22.57	23.63	23.81	26.93	27.48	27.22	27.40	27.19	27.29	27.33
Advanced degree	26.69	26.82	29.40	30.12	33.75	34.31	34.27	34.29	34.22	35.29	35.07
By age:											
18–24 years	12.46	11.00	10.75	10.31	11.40	11.34	11.16	11.34	11.21	11.29	11.04
25–35 years	18.07	17.25	17.14	16.92	18.67	18.96	18.56	18.59	18.63	18.86	18.74
36–45 years	19.75	19.75	20.37	20.13	21.65	22.57	22.48	22.74	22.81	23.24	23.18
46–54 years	19.93	19.83	20.59	20.96	22.83	23.17	23.14	23.18	23.15	23.69	23.56
55–64 years	18.85	19.06	19.35	19.28	21.29	22.99	22.93	23.40	23.02	23.66	23.47
By selected age-education groups:											
Aged 25–34 years											
High school only	16.39	15.24	14.68	14.17	14.84	15.22	14.78	14.62	14.45	14.55	14.36
Bachelor's only	20.95	20.55	21.90	21.99	24.72	24.52	23.95	23.87	23.59	23.82	23.53
Advanced	23.68	23.31	25.41	25.99	29.20	29.15	28.77	28.92	29.32	29.19	29.38
Aged 35–44 years											
High school only	17.71	16.90	16.40	15.97	16.94	17.34	17.08	17.16	16.87	17.23	16.80
Bachelor's only	26.15	25.99	26.07	26.12	29.63	30.75	30.28	30.46	30.58	30.48	30.59
Advanced	29.70	29.26	30.86	31.06	35.21	36.54	36.12	36.16	36.25	37.56	37.52

Continued

Table 8.A2. *Continued*

	1979	1983	1989	1992	2000	2003	2006	2007	2008	2009	2010
Aged 45–54 years											
High school only	18.07	17.57	17.26	16.98	17.20	17.82	17.78	17.59	17.55	17.93	17.51
Bachelor's only	28.63	27.94	27.81	28.13	29.91	30.09	30.49	30.61	30.83	31.02	31.69
Advanced	30.01	31.14	32.45	33.18	35.64	35.81	36.65	36.86	36.66	38.58	38.46
Aged 55–64 years											
High school only	17.99	17.31	16.74	16.50	16.69	17.46	17.14	17.25	17.02	17.58	17.30
Bachelor's only	27.55	28.47	28.23	27.87	28.77	30.85	29.81	30.38	29.32	29.38	29.86
Advanced	29.95	30.09	33.29	32.16	35.64	36.20	36.25	36.16	35.49	36.82	36.07

Source: Authors' analysis of CPS ORG (various years), CEPR Extracts.

Table 8.A3. Income and poverty

	1979	1983	1989	1992	2000	2003	2006	2007	2008	2009
A. Inflation-adjusted household income										
Mean	57,923	54,640	63,055	59,502	71,186	68,888	70,840	69,985	68,183	67,964
P10	12,181	11,201	12,457	11,484	13,181	12,285	12,770	12,584	12,118	12,120
P50	48,617	44,728	50,042	46,638	52,326	50,370	51,125	51,735	49,822	49,806
P90	111,332	108,238	124,490	119,272	140,060	138,421	142,382	141,189	138,300	138,000
P90/P10	9.14	9.66	9.99	10.39	10.63	11.27	11.15	11.22	11.41	11.39
P90/P50	2.29	2.42	2.49	2.56	2.68	2.75	2.78	2.73	2.78	2.77
Gini	0.399	0.409	0.427	0.429	0.456	0.457	0.462	0.455	0.458	0.459
B. Inflation-adjusted equivalized household net income (all households)										
Mean	28,032	26,657	31,984	30,420	35,500	35,692	36,507	36,280	35,430	35,539
P10	9,596	8,766	9,694	9,288	11,049	10,666	11,012	10,944	10,735	10,790
P50	25,518	23,903	27,381	26,122	29,193	29,215	29,525	29,681	28,831	28,824
P90	48,288	47,228	57,093	54,593	63,714	65,193	66,393	66,666	64,950	64,858
P90/P10	5.03	5.39	5.89	5.88	5.77	6.11	6.03	6.09	6.05	6.01
P90/P50	1.89	1.98	2.09	2.09	2.18	2.23	2.25	2.25	2.25	2.25
Gini	0.315	0.331	0.359	0.355	0.369	0.374	0.378	0.373	0.373	0.375
C. Inflation-adjusted, equivalized household net income (non-elderly households)										
Mean	29,573	27,454	33,388	31,785	37,336	37,538	38,156	37,861	36,851	36,797
P10	10,824	8,904	10,205	9,759	12,082	11,402	11,774	11,765	11,400	11,114
P50	27,406	24,991	29,087	27,886	31,189	31,321	31,321	31,491	30,455	30,181
P90	49,361	47,879	58,403	56,029	65,545	66,896	68,133	68,088	66,429	66,337
P90/P10	4.56	5.38	5.72	5.74	5.43	5.87	5.79	5.79	5.83	5.97
P90/P50	1.80	1.92	2.01	2.01	2.10	2.14	2.18	2.16	2.18	2.20
Gini	0.296	0.322	0.348	0.345	0.361	0.366	0.371	0.364	0.367	0.372
D. Household poverty rates (%, using Census 'money income')										
Official	12.1	14.7	12.2	13.9	11.2	12.4	12.1	12.2	12.7	13.4
60% of median	29.3	29.9	30.1	30.2	30.0	30.4	29.9	30.2	30.2	30.5
By age:										
Under 25 years	18.5	28.5	26.1	32.2	24.4	29.4	28.7	28.1	29.4	33.7
25–34 years	10.1	15.1	12.9	15.9	11.8	14.6	14.2	14.3	15.4	16.9
35–64 years	9.4	11.9	9.7	10.6	9.3	10.0	10.1	10.3	10.8	11.6
65+ years	18.1	16.6	13.8	15.5	12.0	12.1	11.3	11.6	11.4	10.3
By child status (head aged under 55 years):										
No child	7.6	10.1	7.9	9.3	9.1	10.6	10.7	10.8	11.4	12.8
Any child	12.5	18.0	15.5	17.8	12.9	15.1	15.0	15.2	15.9	17.6

Source: Authors' analysis of CPS ORG (various years), CEPR Extracts.

9

Summary and conclusions

Stephen P. Jenkins, Andrea Brandolini, John Micklewright, and Brian Nolan

In this book we have analysed the distributional impact of the Great Recession. Core features of our research are that we have focused on household income, we have considered all persons in the population, and we have taken a cross-national perspective though one that is limited to consideration of rich countries.

Our main conclusion is that the changes between 2007 and 2009 in household incomes in total and on average, in income inequality, and in poverty rates, were modest in most of the countries that we study, in spite of the macroeconomic heterogeneity—in nature and size—of the GR across countries. This outcome is remarkably different from the far more dramatic experience of the Great Depression (to the extent that evidence of the same type is available), although not so different from some recent recessions such as the Nordic crisis of the early 1990s.

In this chapter we summarize our findings and draw out some implications for policy. We review the evidence from the past that was highlighted in Chapter 1, and bring out what the 21 OECD countries analysed in Chapter 2 and the six in-depth case studies presented in Chapters 3–8 suggest about the distributional impact of the GR. At the end of the chapter, we consider the lessons that arise for policy-makers.

9.1 Lessons from the Past

Chapter 1 shows that neither existing analytical frameworks nor empirical studies of previous recessions provide clear cut conclusions about the distributional impacts of major recessions. Recessions typically reduce incomes and so raise poverty rates when these are measured using a poverty line that is fixed in real terms. However, the impact on relative poverty rates (as commonly calculated, using a threshold equal to a fraction of contemporary median income) is likely to be smaller, because recessions also reduce median income. Moreover, income inequality may increase or decrease in a recession, depending on precisely who are affected by it and where they are located in the distribution in the first place. The impact of a recession on household incomes works through a wide variety of channels, changing the prevalence of receipt of particular types of income, and the distribution of that income among recipients. (The role of unemployment and changes in labour incomes are the factors that receive the greatest attention in this book.) The effect of a fall in a person's income from a particular source also depends on whom the person lives with and how the incomes of those other people are affected (because we assume incomes are pooled within households).

Cross-national differences in labour markets and socioeconomic institutions have the potential to produce significant variation in distributional impacts between nations, even if they experience the same macroeconomic shock. Moreover, relationships between the income distribution and macroeconomic aggregates, such as the unemployment rate, that are estimated from time series data are not robust and, in any case, the GR might be viewed as an exceptional episode so that extrapolation from models fitted to past data may not be a reliable guide to the present.

9.2 Findings from 21 Rich Countries

To provide information about baseline distributional outcomes round the time of GR onset, we use data on household incomes from the EU-SILC and US Current Population Survey (Chapter 2). When the GR began, inequality and relative poverty rates were generally neither trending upwards or downwards, according to evidence for the immediately preceding years. (The USA is a distinct exception with a long-lasting trend upwards in income inequality.) Decompositions by income source underscored the importance of employment income in households' income packages, and its large contribution to inequality in every country considered. This was true even for people in the poorest fifth, although of course cash transfers were also important for this group. This justifies our concentration on labour income in much of Chapter 2. At the same time, the decomposition analysis also drew attention to a relatively large contribution to the inequality of income from savings and investments in the Nordic countries in particular, which suggests that the GR's impact may be heterogeneous.

Our examination of macroeconomic changes in 21 OECD countries (Chapter 2) reveals that the nature of the GR itself varied substantially across countries. In some countries, there were major declines in economic activity and sharply rising unemployment; in others, there were more modest changes in growth and employment. Almost everywhere, the peak-to-trough fall in quarterly GDP was substantially larger than the average fall during recessions over the previous 50 years, but ranged nonetheless from zero in Australia to nearly 13% in Ireland.

Although GDP fell during the GR, the real disposable income of households, as measured in national accounts by Gross Household Disposable Income (GHDI), actually rose between 2007 and 2009 in 12 countries of the 18 for which we have data (there was no change for Ireland, despite the large fall in GDP). The household sector was protected from the impact of the downturn by both automatic stabilizers and additional support of governments through the tax and benefit system.

In many of the 21 countries, the response of employment to the fall in GDP was smaller than in previous recessions, though job losses were unusually large relative to the fall in output in countries such as Ireland, Spain, and the USA where a boom–bust pattern in the housing market played an important role in the recession. The concentration during the GR of employment loss among men has differed from earlier recessions (and probably reflects the sectoral composition of the aggregate demand shock), while the greater impact on the young followed the pattern of earlier recessions. Large falls in individual employment were accompanied by significant rises in household worklessness in countries such as Ireland, Spain, and the USA, whereas in Denmark and Finland the workless household rate fell despite relatively large increases in the individual non-employment rate, hence muting the impact on the household income distribution. Across the 21 countries, real average earnings typically rose between 2007 and 2009 (though not in the USA), largely because lower-paid workers were more likely to be laid off. Taken with the falls in employment, this is likely to have had a disequalizing impact on the distribution of household incomes. However, earnings inequality among the employed did not change much in the initial part of the GR, relative to trend, nor by 2009 for the few countries for which we have data for this year.

The level of capital income in GHDI, especially distributed income from corporations, generally declined and, since this source is concentrated among richer households, this decline would be expected to have an equalizing impact on the household income distribution. (That impact would be amplified further were we to have included in our household income measure the realized values of large capital losses on risky assets caused by the GR, as discussed in the case of Italy, for example.) The large increases in state support to the household sector through the tax and benefit system, especially the support coming through unemployment benefits, will have been concentrated on households in the bottom half of the income distribution. This will have lessened the disequalizing impacts of the changes in labour incomes.

The predictions of Chapter 2's analysis of different elements of household income packages are that the overall short-term distributional impact of the GR was likely to have been relatively modest in most of the countries considered. For 15 European countries and, to a lesser extent, for the USA, we are able to use published summary statistics derived from household survey and administrative record data to document changes in average real income levels, income inequality, and poverty rates between 2005 and 2009. The data on average income, as measured by the median, give a picture for the European countries that is broadly similar to that shown for total income in national accounts data—average incomes typically rose across the main period of the GR, 2007 to 2009, or changed very little. Women did somewhat better than men as did the elderly compared to other age groups. Income inequality in general fell slightly in the European countries between 2007 and 2009, while rising modestly in the USA. Absolute poverty rates tended to fall slightly in Europe while rising modestly in the USA (as measured with the US official poverty line) but, in both cases, rates fell for the elderly. Relative poverty rates typically fell in the European countries.

The post-2009 distributional impacts of the GR are likely to have been considerably larger however, with greater differences across countries emerging. We return to this point below.

9.3 Findings from Six Country Case Studies

To investigate in more detail how the GR affected distributions of household income, we study six countries in detail: Germany, Ireland, Italy, Sweden, the UK, and the USA (Chapters 3–8). They include the largest economy in the world and the origin of the financial crisis that became the GR, and three of the largest economies in Europe. The six countries differ in economic performance in the decade prior to the GR, with Italy and Germany having relatively poor growth rates and Ireland a boom. The six countries also vary in labour market flexibility and institutions and belong to different welfare state regimes. Income inequality at the onset of the GR ranged from relatively equal in Sweden through to the USA with the highest degree of inequality and poverty. They experienced a wide range of macroeconomic changes and some marked differences in the nature of the initial shock and subsequent evolution of economic and labour market activity, as highlighted in Table 9.1. The top half of the table summarizes changes in these macroeconomic aggregates while the bottom half focuses on the accompanying changes in distributions

Table 9.1. Changes in key indicators for case study countries, 2007–9

Changes in:	Germany	Ireland	Italy	Sweden	UK	USA
Macroeconomic indicators						
Gross Domestic Product (GDP) (%)	−4.1	−9.8	−6.1	−5.8	−5.4	−3.9
Gross Household Disposable Income (GHDI) (%)	0.4	0.0	−4.0	5.1	1.9	0.5
Employment rate (ppt)	1.4	−6.7	−1.2	−3.5	−1.7	−4.2
Government balance as % of GDP (ppt)	−3.3	−15.3	−6.8	−4.5	−8.0	−8.4
Equivalized household net income						
Median (%)	1.8	−1.2	−2.5	2.0	1.2	−2.9
Inequality index (Gini coefficient) (ppt)	−0.1	−2.0	1.0	0.5	0.0	0.2
Percentage below 60% of the median (ppt)	−0.5	−2.8	1.0	1.5	−1.3	−0.5
Percentage below 60% of the 2007 median (ppt)	−0.9	0.3	1.5	0.5	−1.9	0.7

Sources: GDP (Gross Domestic Product) and GHDI (Gross Household Disposable Income) from Chapter 2: Figure 2.4. Employment rate changes from Chapter 2, Table 2.2. Government balance from Chapter 2: Table 2.6. Statistics on the household income distributions for each country are from: SOEP survey (current monthly income) for Germany; SILC survey for Ireland; Bank of Italy survey for Italy; HF survey for Sweden; FRS for the UK; and the CPS for the USA. (See Chapters 3–8 for more details.) The distributions refer to distributions among individuals; household income is equivalized by the square root of household size.

Notes: 'ppt': percentage point. GDP, GHDI, and equivalized household net income are all in real terms.

of household income. Throughout the table, the changes shown refer to changes between 2007 and 2009.

9.3.1 *Changes at the National Level*

In all six countries, the GR's onset took the form of a large decrease in output. Even in Germany, the country in which the GR has had the most modest effect, real GDP fell by 4% over 2007–9, the largest decline since the Second World War. It then recovered rapidly, however, so that by the second half of 2011, GDP was 3% higher than at the start of 2007. The GR was the deepest recession since the Second World War in Italy, the UK, and also in Ireland, which experienced the largest GDP decline among OECD countries. In Sweden the macroeconomic downturn was also large, although this was very similar in size (if different in nature) to what occurred there in the early 1990s and was followed by relatively rapid recovery; by late 2011, GDP was over 5% higher than at the start of 2007. There was a marked contraction in the USA in 2008–9, also followed by some recovery, with GDP returning to its pre-crisis peak during 2011.

In other respects, there were marked divergences across the six countries—in the GR's nature, its immediate impact on household sector incomes and the labour market, and its fiscal consequences. Despite declining real GDP, the aggregate income of the household sector as measured in the national accounts grew or was unchanged from 2007 to 2009 in five of the six case-study countries, the exception being Italy. As already noted, the company sector may bear the brunt of the initial impact of an output decline, and household incomes may be insulated from the immediate impact of the output shock due to the effects of falling taxes and increasing cash transfers as incomes from employment fall and unemployment rises. Issues of timing and measurement may also be particularly important, however, and the scale of the divergence between changes in GDP and GHDI for some of the case study countries highlight the need for in-depth analysis of this relationship over a longer period as the aftermath of the GR unfolds.

Case study countries also differed markedly in the labour market effects of the GR, as summarized in Table 9.1. In the case of Germany, there was little change in levels of employment as output declined and, since the economic slump was short-lived, the overall level of employment was higher in 2009 than two years previously. In Ireland and the USA, at the other extreme, the GR was accompanied by a severe slump in the housing market and construction sector, and unemployment rose rapidly, with the employment rate falling by four percentage points over 2007–9 in the USA and by over 6.5 percentage points in Ireland. Young men suffered particularly in Ireland (unemployment rates for those aged 20–24 rose from 8% in 2007 to 32% in 2010—see Chapter 4). In the UK, employment fell by less than GDP but large falls were experienced by the young, by men, and by less-educated people. In Italy there was no housing market bust, and low shares of more risky assets in household portfolios, high wealth holdings, low indebtedness, and a high proportion of young people living with parents, all of which served to cushion the impact of falling incomes on living standards; yet unemployment rates rose to 1 in 4 among individuals aged 20–24 and to 1 in 7 among those aged 25–29. In Sweden, the downturn resulted in a much smaller fall in industrial production and rise in unemployment than did the recession of the early 1990s and, by early 2010, total employment levels were higher than before the recession.

The short-run impact of the GR on the distribution of household income was relatively modest in the majority of the six countries, but with varying implications for average incomes, income inequality, and poverty, as summarized in the bottom half of Table 9.1. These statistics are based on the same sources of data on household incomes as are used in Chapters 3–8. It is important to note that only in the cases of Ireland and the USA are the sources the same as the ones used to produce published statistics that we drew on towards the end of Chapter 2 to trace changes in the income distribution over 2005–9 (EU-SILC data in the case of the European countries). Different data sources for the same country can give different results in the same way as differences may arise between aggregate and survey figures. This is notably the case for the UK, for which EU-SILC survey data show a fall in median income over 2007–9, in contrast to the rise indicated by data from the larger household survey used in Chapter 7 and drawn on in Table 9.1, which is also the source underlying the UK's official income distribution statistics.

In Germany, median income rose between 2007 and 2009, while income inequality was virtually unchanged. The proportion of persons with a household income less than 60% of contemporary median income declined marginally, with a slightly larger fall (almost one percentage point) in the proportion in households below such an income threshold held fixed in purchasing power at its 2007 level. Chapter 3 shows that median income, inequality, and relative poverty all rose slightly in 2010. In the UK, average household incomes also grew marginally in real terms during 2008 and 2009, with the bottom catching up slightly on the middle and the top because income from state benefits and tax credits grew in real terms. Income inequality was stable from 2007 to 2009, while the number falling below 60% of median income fell by more than 1 percentage point and a fixed real threshold shows a larger decline. However, real individual earnings fell back in 2010, and average household incomes also seem likely to have fallen. In Sweden, median income and the Gini coefficient both rose between 2007 and 2009; the proportion falling below the 60% income threshold increased, although when a threshold fixed in purchasing power terms is employed the increase is a good deal smaller. In Ireland, where the macroeconomic shock was largest, median income declined a little but so did inequality and relative poverty between 2007 and 2009, with the proportion of persons with a household income less than a fixed real income threshold remaining broadly stable. This appears to have reflected the progressive nature of the initial response of social transfers and taxes in particular, although it is highly significant that headline survey results for 2010 show a very sharp increase in inequality and income poverty compared with 2009. Thus the initial impact of the GR may not be a reliable indicator of its medium and longer-terms effects, a point of more general relevance to which we return.

Italy is the case study country exhibiting the largest increase in inequality between 2007 and 2009, with the relative income poverty rate also increasing. Average household income from labour, pensions, and transfers fell by 1.5% between 2007 and 2010, and income losses due to increased non-employment were only partly cushioned by income support. The cushioning effect of social transfers was relatively limited, although the consequent increase in inequality and poverty might perhaps be considered relatively modest given the scale of the initial macroeconomic shock. Finally, in the USA, the GR resulted in falling earnings and income across the range from bottom to top among people in working-age households, and the official poverty rate (calculated using an low-income cut-off held fixed in real terms) increased for this group. (The USA is the only country in Table 9.1 for which the change in median income measured using survey data is of the opposite sign to the change in the total disposable income of the household sector measured in national accounts.) Overall income inequality was virtually unchanged and, although the relative poverty rate declined modestly, this partly reflected a decline in real median income.

9.3.2 Changes for Different Population Subgroups

Not everybody is affected by a recession in the same way; it is important to consider variations in the impact of the GR for different groups within a population. Table 9.2 contrasts the experience of children, people of working age, and elderly people for the period 2007–9. It shows that, in all six case study countries, elderly people were relatively well protected, as we also showed using published statistics for a broader set of countries in Chapter 2. Relative poverty rates for elderly people fell between 2007 and 2009 in all these countries, albeit only marginally in Germany. The proportion of the group with a household income less than 60% of 2007 median income (i.e. a cut-off held fixed in purchasing power terms) also fell, though only very slightly in Italy. In some countries, average real income levels rose for elderly people between 2007 and 2009, most notably in Ireland and the UK where there were substantial changes. Children and individuals of working age also experienced declines in relative poverty rates in some countries, but increases in Italy, Sweden and the USA, while the proportion with incomes less than the 'anchored' 2007 low-income threshold increased between 2007 and 2009 in Ireland, Italy, Sweden, and the USA.

Whether the incomes of elderly people continue to be insulated after 2009 depends not only on explicit policy measures such as those announced as part of consolidation packages, but also on less visible but none the less important parameters such as the formulae used to up-rate cash transfers and pensions

Table 9.2. Changes in mean income and in poverty rates for case study countries, 2007–9, by age group

Changes, by age group, in:	Germany	Ireland	Italy	Sweden	UK	USA
Mean household net income (%)						
Children	–1.1	–3.5	–3.8	–1.4	4.8	–5.8
Working age	–1.4	–5.0	–2.2	–1.7	0.4	–3.1
Elderly	0.2	13.8	0.5	–2.5	7.6	1.3
Percentage below 60% of median (ppt)						
Children	–1.4	–1.3	2.4	2.5	–2.2	2.1
Working age	–0.3	–1.8	1.2	2.5	0.1	0.9
Elderly	–0.2	–10.1	–1.3	–1.0	–4.4	–4.3
Percentage below 60% of 2007 median (ppt)						
Children	–1.9	1.7	3.4	1.7	–3.0	5.2
Working age	–0.6	0.9	2.2	1.7	–0.3	1.9
Elderly	–0.5	–5.1	–0.1	–2.9	–5.2	–3.0

Sources: As for Table 9.1.

Notes: 'ppt': percentage point. Children: aged 0–19 years. Working age: aged 20–59 years. Elderly: aged 60+ years. Household income is equivalized by the square root of household size and is in real terms.

with respect to inflation. On this, see especially Chapter 4 for Ireland and Chapter 7 for the UK as well as our discussion of inflation and up-rating in Chapter 2.

The variation in the distributional impact of the GR to date across the six countries reflects not only differences in the nature of the macroeconomic downturn but also differences in how cash transfers and direct taxes cushioned household net incomes from the full effects of what was happening to market incomes. To some extent, these are differences in automatic stabilization and so vary with the generosity and comprehensiveness of social safety-nets and the structure and levels of direct taxes and social insurance contributions. But policy responses and choices as the recession impacted have also been important. In all six countries, the combined effect of automatic stabilizers and discretionary policies offset the potentially large negative impact of the GR on household incomes in the short run. As we have emphasized throughout this book, the medium- and longer-term impacts of the GR might look very different to the immediate effects.

9.4 Caveats

Several qualifications are important to keep our findings in the right perspective. First, there is a need to broaden the focus of analysis beyond cash income. Second, the distributional impact of the GR may be expected to work through over many years, potentially long after economic activity picks up—these are the medium- and long-term impacts of the GR. Third, our range of countries is limited to selected rich nations. Fourth, we should recognize that the GR may have affected household formation. Finally, our analysis has focused on cross-sectional differences, but the consequences of the GR may turn out to be important from a longitudinal perspective.

9.4.1 *Measuring Living Standards*

The measure of living standards that we have adopted throughout this book is needs-adjusted household net income. It is a measure of money income that does not take account of 'non-cash' income from government services; nor does it take account of reductions in purchasing power arising from increases in indirect taxation. At the aggregate level, we have mentioned in Chapter 2 that in the Euro area the trends in household disposable income were even better after including the value of social transfers in-kind, but we have not pursued this line of inquiry further for lack of suitable data. It would be important to disaggregate this result across households as well as to monitor the evolution in the coming years. Indeed, the effects of fiscal consolidation will manifest themselves not only in net household incomes but also in the services provided or funded by the state and in the indirect taxes that help to finance them. A comprehensive assessment of the distributional impact of the GR therefore needs to go beyond measures of household cash income. Some of the issues are discussed at the end of Chapter 2 and in subsequent chapters reporting on the country case studies, for example in Chapter 7 on the UK.

9.4.2 *The Time Dimension*

Our analysis has focused on the short-term, the main years of the GR itself (2007–9), and the distributional picture is likely to look different after 2009. One reason for this is the impact of stabilization policies on governments' fiscal positions, and there is heterogeneity across the six case study countries here too: see the top half of Table 9.1, which shows changes between 2007 and 2009 in government balance as a percentage of GDP. Germany, towards one end of the spectrum, emerged rapidly from recession with a relatively strong fiscal position. Sweden's growth since 2009 has been even stronger than Germany's and is judged by the OECD to have little need of fiscal consolidation. At the other end of the spectrum are the countries that must grapple with fiscal deficits that ballooned during the GR, notably Ireland, the UK, and the USA, and those which needed to consolidate public finances beforehand, in particular Italy and (outside the case study countries) Greece. The UK case is one of pain delayed rather than pain avoided, with gloomy prospects for household incomes as fiscal consolidation sets in, and household incomes likely to decline to 2013–14, at which point they would be no higher than they were ten years earlier. In the Irish case, the scale of the fiscal adjustment required and the overhang of debt associated with the banking crisis make for an even gloomier picture. In those countries the financial crisis and GR look set to cast a very long shadow. In Greece and Italy the GR has worsened a situation that was already critical. The central role of fiscal adjustment in the prospects for these countries is a crucial reason why distributional effects can take many years to work their way through, long after GDP growth has resumed and the recession is considered to have ended from a purely macro-economic perspective.

The longer-term consequences are difficult to assess more generally. They may emerge over generations, for instance if the young people entering the labour force during the GR experience a permanent weakening of their earnings capacity, as seems to have been the case during the Great Depression in the USA (Ruggles and Ruggles 1977). Using a large longitudinal dataset for Canadian men, Oreopoulos, von Wachter, and Heisz (2012: 26) find that 'the average worker graduating from college in a recession faces earnings losses that are very persistent but not permanent', but more importantly they show that 'the present discounted value of losses in annual earnings could be three to four times larger for the least advantaged as compared to the most advantaged workers—indicating that even within the group of college graduates, there is a large degree of heterogeneity in the costs of recessions'. This evidence suggests that recessions may have long-lasting effects on the distribution of labour earnings, and hence household incomes, *across* as well as *within* cohorts.

Longer-term distributional consequences depend on many other factors outside the labour market. One critically important aspect of the GR is the extent to which it originated in the financial sector, involving a property crash and banking crises and bail-outs in some countries but not in others. This is not only a significant factor in cross-country variation in the short-term, but may also be critical in the longer-term effects of the GR on asset-holdings and debt, and on the relative financial situation—encompassing income and wealth—of one type of household versus another. Long-term consequences also depend on the mix of policies that governments adopt to rebalance public budgets, as well as other factors such as the speed of adjustment. While measures to stimulate the economy and support personal incomes were implemented with relatively wide support from across the political spectrum at the time of GR onset, medium-term measures are more likely to reflect the different ideologies of ruling political parties (Vis, van Kersbergen, and Hylands 2011).

9.4.3 *Country Heterogeneity*

We already emphasized in Chapter 2 that our country coverage is limited to 21 rich countries (each of which is a member of the OECD) and to a subset of 6 of these nations in the country case studies. There is no analysis of middle- or low-income countries, and our case studies exclude Greece, Portugal, and Spain—countries that, together with Ireland and Italy, continue to face severe pressures for fiscal adjustment.

The scale of the austerity measures proposed for Greece, for instance, is substantially larger than that for any of the measures that we have described in this book for other countries, and the consequences for household incomes can only be larger. (For an early assessment of the distributional impact of the crisis in Greece, see Matsaganis and Leventi 2011.) Apart from the size of the adjustment, austerity packages differ greatly also in their design, and so do their distributive implications. In a microsimulation-based study, Callan et al. (2011) estimate the effects of measures implemented in 2009–11 in six EU countries and find that they are regressive in Portugal, substantially neutral in Estonia and Spain, mildly progressive in the UK and Ireland, and strongly progressive in Greece; incorporating also the estimated impact of VAT increases make the overall effect regressive in the UK, Spain, and especially Greece. (See also the analysis using microsimulation of Ireland in Chapter 4 and the UK in Chapter 7.) As we have seen for the direct effects of the GR, the indirect effects generated by economic policies adopted in response to the GR also vary across countries: it is a warning against mechanical generalizations of country-specific results.

The impact of the GR, including the indirect effects of policies, is not distributed evenly across the population, but will hit some groups particularly hard while others will escape relatively lightly. These 'horizontal inequities' are not obvious from analysis of aggregate measures of inequality and poverty, and breakdowns of these indicators by age or other characteristics of the sort presented in this book provide limited information about them. For example, the nature of the employment 'shock' in some countries meant that unemployment rose much more rapidly for men than for women because the construction sector was so badly affected. More generally, the impact of falls in household income on different individuals within the household may depend on whose income is hit. The nature of such variation may well differ across countries, and it will be important to complement the cross-national analysis which has been a core feature of this study with in-depth single-country studies that examine such nuances in much greater detail.

9.4.4 Household Formation

We noted in Chapter 1 that income loss (or its threat) during a recession may lead people to alter their living arrangements, thereby changing both their own equivalized household income and that of the persons they live with. Young people may remain with their parents or may move back in with them, an example of what has been called 'doubling-up' in the USA. We noted some evidence for this in Chapter 2 and in the US case study in Chapter 8, but this has not been a feature of the impact of the GR to which we have devoted much attention, especially for countries other than the USA. Other aspects of household formation that have affected household incomes in the GR and which would be worthy of attention are migration and homelessness. Ireland, for example, has once more become a country of net emigration, following sustained immigration during the boom years that preceded the crisis. There is anecdotal evidence of increased homelessness for a number of countries and yet, by design, the incomes of homeless persons are not measured in household surveys.

9.4.5 The Longitudinal Perspective

The (short-term) distributional stability over the GR period described in this book has been based on an entirely cross-sectional perspective. A lack of change in a country's inequality or poverty rate between one year and the next is consistent with greater (or lower) volatility in the incomes of the individuals within that country. To investigate this aspect of the GR would require up-to-date longitudinal data and they were not available for our analysis.

The importance of the type of perspective taken has already been mentioned in the discussion of the long-term consequences of people entering the labour market in recessions. The GR may have major implications for intergenerational equity, especially if it continues to be the case that elderly people are relatively well-cushioned from its effects compared to younger people. The relative fortunes of the two groups, and hence intergenerational mobility, may be affected by the dramatic swings in the value of property and other assets in some countries, and sustained high unemployment may well result in long-term 'scarring' of those affected, with the risk that their disadvantage is transmitted to the next generation. The intergenerational implications of the GR will play out over a long period and, while difficult to predict at this relatively early stage, they merit serious consideration in future research.

9.5 Policy Lessons

With regard to policy in the macroeconomic domain or concerning the stabilization of the household income distribution, a general lesson of our work is that 'one size does not fit all'. Policy makers in one country should be careful in drawing on the experience and policies of other countries when designing their own policy measures. Taking a cross-national perspective as we have done brings out clearly the heterogeneity across countries in the size and nature of economic downturns, their distributional consequences, and policy constraints such as fiscal position.

The findings of this book indicate, none the less, that stabilization of the household income distribution in the face of macroeconomic turbulence is an achievable goal, at least in the short term. That policy can be effective is an important lesson. And yet, at the same time, the degree of distributional stabilization may be associated with already having a relatively strong welfare state in general and social safety net in particular. (On the path-dependent nature of social policy reactions to the GR, see Chung and Thewissen 2011.) Of the six countries we study in detail, the ones with the 'hardest landings' in the short term in terms of distributional outcomes are Italy and the USA, where a fall in the median income was accompanied by some deterioration of other distributional measures. At the other extreme, Germany and the UK performed well on both accounts. Sweden is an interesting case as income grew on average, but its distribution tended to widen. While the results for Italy and the USA are consistent with their relatively less generous welfare state, the overall picture suggests that the buffering capacity of social safety nets may arise in the context of more than one type of welfare state regime in the Esping-Andersen (1990) sense. Moreover, the countries with stronger welfare states are those with greater 'automatic stabilization': see for example Dolls, Fuest, and Peichl (2011, 2012) for within-Europe and transatlantic comparisons. Of course, welfare state strength is not the only relevant factor, and its specific role is difficult to identify conclusively since it is correlated with other factors such as fiscal balance. (Relative to Italy, for example, Germany and Sweden have both stronger welfare states and healthier fiscal balances.) Countries have taken rather different approaches to the discretionary stabilizers available to them, as the six detailed case studies bring out. Enhancing welfare effort beyond what would occur automatically as unemployment rises can help to lessen the distributional impact of recession. (For more discussion of EU governments' initial responses, see Marchal, Marx, and Van Mechelen 2011.) However, if utilization of such measures also leads to a more severe fiscal correction, the gains may be short term. In such a context, the pressure to increase the targeting of cash transfers is likely to intensify, although that can run the risk of worsening poverty and unemployment 'traps' and undermining the bases for social solidarity and political support for relatively generous provision. These are policy challenges of the kind cited by the OECD's (2011*f*) *Divided We Stand* study discussed in Chapter 1.

Statements during the Great Moderation era of the decade starting in the mid-1990s, that macroeconomic policy had in effect conquered the business cycle, turn out to have been over-optimistic and a safer conclusion is that there is an inherent cyclicality in the economies of rich countries. Welfare states provide important income insurance in this scenario. Put another way, if substantial cutbacks are made to welfare states as part of fiscal consolidation packages, then greater instability in household income distributional outcomes are a likely consequence in recession times. Whether this is seen to matter depends, of course, on the extent to which poverty reduction and prevention of rising inequality are given priority and public support. We are entering an era in which 'the question of who pays what, when, and how will likely give rise to sharp distributional conflicts' (Vis, van Kersbergen, and Hylands 2011: 338). The popular reactions in Greece to the proposed austerity measures are a ready reminder of this point.

There are also lessons for policy-makers regarding measurement and monitoring of income distribution. International agencies such as the OECD and Eurostat with their extensive databases play an important role in facilitating cross-national comparisons. Without such data, a project like ours would have been impossible. The maintenance and further development of cross-national data sources is vital.

Evidence-based policy requires timely data, but information about the distribution of household incomes provided by household surveys and administrative records only appear with a lag of several years, and also data-bases containing summary data of the type provided by the OECD and Euro-stat are not fully up to date. In this book, we have shown how national accounts data about Gross Household Disposable Income and its components, which are available more quickly, can be usefully employed to investigate the distributional impacts of recessions. None the less, the data refer to household sector aggregates and are limited in effect to description of changes in average incomes—they cannot tell us about poverty rates and income inequality. We have also shown that other economic data such as unemployment rates or individual earnings inequality, which are made available more quickly than conventional household income survey data, can also be employed to investigate distributional outcomes. But they too are limited: although labour income forms a major component of household incomes for many households, it is not the only income source that matters, especially for non-working house-holds reliant on other sources such as cash benefits and pensions. Given these data problems, one way to derive timely predictions of distributional outcomes is to make more systematic use of microsimulation modelling in the manner that has been discussed in this book: see especially Chapter 1's review and the case studies for Italy and the UK.

9.6 Envoi

Our analysis shows that the Great Recession, although meriting the 'Great' label from a post-Second World War perspective, was smaller in size in rich countries on average than was the Great Depression. This, together with the pronounced changes in welfare states, household structures, and patterns of labour force participation since the 1930s, explains the generally rather modest distribu-tional effects of the GR in the short term. From this perspective, it seems that advanced economies have learned some lessons from the past about how to deal with the social consequences of major contractions of economic activity.

The longer-term picture for household income is less clear, and depends on when economies return to steady growth, on the ways in which countries deal with the GR's legacy of fiscal deficits, and on how debt and financial market uncertainty work their way through to household incomes and broader living standards. The relatively modest distributional effects seen between 2007 and 2009 provide little reassurance about the medium- and long-term effects of prolonged recession or stagnation accompanied by sustained high unemploy-ment. Whether governments in the rich countries live up to their responsibilities to successfully address the macroeconomic challenges facing the world economy is critical in determining the long-term consequences of the Great Recession.

References

Aaberge, R., Andersen, A. S., and Wennemo, T. (2000). 'Extent, Level and Distribution of Low Income in Norway: 1979–1995', in B. Gustafsson and P. J. Pedersen (eds), *Poverty and Low Income in the Nordic Countries*. Aldershot: Ashgate, 131–68.

Aaberge, R., Björklund, A., Jäntti, M., et al. (2000). 'Unemployment Shocks and Income Distribution: How did the Nordic Countries Fare during their Crises?', *Scandinavian Journal of Economics*, 102: 77–99.

Aaberge, R., Björklund, A., Jäntti, M., et al. (2002). 'Income Inequality and Income Mobility in the Scandinavian Countries Compared to the United States', *Review of Income and Wealth*, 48: 443–69.

Adema, W., Fron, P., and Ladaique M. (2011). 'Is the European Welfare State Really More Expensive? Indicators on Social Spending, 1980–2012; and a Manual to the OECD Social Expenditure Database (SOCX)'. Social, Employment and Migration Working Papers 124. Paris: OECD.

Alvaredo, F., and Pisano, E. (2010). 'Top Incomes in Italy 1974–2004', in A. B. Atkinson and T. Piketty (eds), *Top Incomes. A Global Perspective*. Oxford: Oxford University Press, 625–63.

Anastasia, B., Mancini, M., and Trivellato, U. (2009). 'Il Sostegno del reddito dei disoccupati. Note sullo stato dell'arte. Tra Riformismo strisciante, inerzie dell'impianto categoriale e incerti orizzonti di flexicurity'. ISAE Working Paper no. 112. Rome: ISAE.

Antonczyk, D., DeLeire, T., and Fitzenberger, B. (2010). 'Polarization and Rising Wage Inequality: Comparing the U.S. and Germany'. IZA Discussion Paper 4842. Bonn: IZA. http://ftp.iza.org/dp4842.pdf [accessed 26 July 2012].

Aricò, F. R. and Stein, U. (2011). 'Employment and Economic Recession in Germany, Italy, and UK: Different Remedies for the Same Illness?'. Paper prepared for the 8th EUROFRAME Conference on Economic Policy Issues in the EU, 10 June 2011, Helsinki, Finland.

Atkinson, A. B. (2010). 'Poverty and the EU: The New Decade (Macerata Lectures on European Economic Policy)'. Working paper 24. Marcerata IT: Dipartimento di Studi sullo Sviluppo Economico, Università degli Studi di Macerata. http://www.unimc.it/sviluppoeconomico/wpaper/wpaper00024/filePaper [accessed 26 July 2012].

Atkinson, A. B. and Bourguignon, F. (eds) (2000). *Handbook of Income Distribution*, Vol. 1. Amsterdam: Elsevier.

Atkinson, A. B. and Brandolini, A. (2006). 'From Earnings Dispersion to Income Inequality', chapter 2 in F. Farina and E. Savaglio (eds), *Inequality and Economic Integration*. London: Routledge, 35–62.

References

Atkinson, A. B. and Marlier, E. (eds) (2010). *Income and Living Conditions in Europe.* Luxembourg: Eurostat. epp.eurostat.ec.europa.eu/cache/ITY_OFFPUB/KS-31-10-555/EN/KS-31-10-555-EN.PDF/ [accessed 26 July 2012].

Atkinson, A. B. and Micklewright, J. (1983). 'On the Reliability of Income Data in the Family Expenditure Survey', *Journal of the Royal Statistical Society, Series A*, 146: 33–61.

Atkinson, A. B. and Morelli, S. (2010). 'Inequality and Banking Crises: a First Look', Paper prepared for the Global Labour Forum, Turin. http://isites.harvard.edu/fs/docs/icb.topic457678.files/ATKINSON%20paper.pdf [accessed 26 July 2012].

Atkinson, A. B. and Morelli, S. (2011). 'Economic Crises and Inequality', Human Development Research Paper 2011/06. New York: United Nations Development Programme. http://hdr.undp.org/en/reports/global/hdr2011/papers/HDRP_2011_06.pdf [accessed 26 July 2012].

Atkinson, A. B. and Piketty, T. (eds) (2007). *Top Incomes Over the Twentieth Century: A Contrast Between European and English Speaking Countries.* Oxford: Oxford University Press.

Atkinson, A. B., Piketty, T., and Saez, E. (2010). 'Top Incomes in the Long Run of History', chapter 13 in A. B. Atkinson and T. Piketty (eds), *Top Incomes: A Global Perspective.* Oxford: Oxford University Press, 664–759.

Atkinson, A. B., Piketty, T., and Saez, E. (2011). 'Top Incomes in the Long Run of History', *Journal of Economic Literature*, 49: 3–71.

Autor, D., Dorn, D., and Hanson, G. (2011). 'The China Syndrome: Local Labor Market Effects of Import Competition in the United States', MIT Working Paper. Cambridge MA: MIT. http://econ-www.mit.edu/files/6613 [accessed 26 July 2012].

Bach, S., Corneo, G., and Steiner, V. (2009). 'From Bottom to Top: The Entire Income Distribution in Germany, 1992–2003', *Review of Income and Wealth*, 55: 331–59.

Banca d'Italia (2011). 'The Public Finance Adjustments Approved during the Summer', *Economic Bulletin*, 62: 36–8.

Baldini, M. (2011). 'Chi Paga il Taglio delle Agevolazioni Fiscali'. *www.lavoce.info*, 15.07.2011. http://www.lavoce.info/articoli/pagina1002433.html [accessed 26 July 2012].

Bargain, O., Immervoll, H., Peichl, A., and Siegloch, S. (2011). 'Distributional Consequences of Labour-Demand Shocks: The 2008–09 Recession in Germany', CESifo Working Paper 3403. Munich: CESifo. http://ideas.repec.org/p/ces/ceswps/_3403.html [accessed 26 July 2012].

Barlevy, G. and Tsiddon, D. (2006). 'Earnings Inequality and the Business Cycle', *European Economic Review*, 50: 55–89.

Barrett, A., FitzGerald, J., and Nolan, B. (2002). 'Earnings Inequality, Returns to Education and Immigration into Ireland', *Labour Economics*, 9: 665–80.

Bassanetti, A. and Zollino, F. (2008). 'The Effects of Housing and Financial Wealth on Personal Consumption: Aggregate Evidence for Italian Households', in Banca d'Italia (ed.), *Household Wealth in Italy.* Papers presented at the Conference held in Perugia, 16–17 October 2007. Roma: Banca d'Italia, 219–49.

Beach, C. M. (1977). 'Cyclical Sensitivity of Aggregate Income Inequality', *Review of Economics and Statistics*, 59: 56–66.

Bell, D. and Blanchflower, D. (2011). 'Young People and the Great Recession'. IZA Discussion Paper 5674. Bonn: IZA. http://ftp.iza.org/dp5674.pdf [accessed 26 July 2012].

Ben-Shalom, Y., Moffitt, R., and Scholz, J. K. (2011). 'An Assessment of the Effectiveness of Anti-Poverty Programmes in the United States', NBER Working Paper 17042. Cambridge MA: National Bureau of Economic Research. http://www.nber.org/papers/w17042.pdf [accessed 26 July 2012].

Berthoud, R. (2009). 'Patterns of Non-Employment, and of Disadvantage, in a Recession', *Economic and Labour Market Review*, 3: 62–73.

Biewen, M. and Juhasz, A. (2010). 'Understanding Rising Income Inequality in Germany'. IZA Discussion Paper 5062. Bonn: IZA. http://ftp.iza.org/dp5062.pdf [accessed 26 July 2012].

Bispinck, R. (2006). 'Germany: Working Time and its Negotiation', in M. Keune and B. Galgoczi (eds), *Collective Bargaining on Working Time: Recent European Experiences*. Brussels: European Trade Union Institute for Research, Education and Health and Safety, 111–29.

Bitler, M. and Hoynes, H. W. (2010). 'The State of the Safety Net in the Post-Welfare Reform Era', *Brookings Papers on Economic Activity*, 41 (Fall): 71–127.

Björklund, A. (1991). 'Unemployment and Income Distribution: Time-Series Evidence from Sweden', *Scandinavian Journal of Economics*, 93: 457–65.

Björklund, A., Palme, M., and Svensson, I. (1995). 'Tax Reforms and Income Distribution: An Assessment Using Different Income Concepts', *Swedish Economic Policy Review*, 2: 229–65.

Björklund, A. and Jäntti, M. (2009). 'Intergenerational Income Mobility and the Role of Family Background', Chapter 20 in W. Salverda, B. Nolan, and T. M. Smeeding (eds), *The Oxford Handbook of Economic Inequality*. Oxford: Oxford University Press, 491–521.

Björklund, A. and Jäntti, M. (2011). 'Inkomstfördelningen i Sverige' (Income Distribution in Sweden). Technical Report. Välfärdspolitiska rådets rapport. Stockholm: SNS.

Blank, R. M. (2000). 'Fighting Poverty: Lessons from Recent U.S. History', *Journal of Economic Perspectives*, 14: 3–19.

Blank, R. M. (2009). 'Economic Change and the Structure of Opportunity for Less-Skilled Workers', in M. Cancian and S. Danziger (eds), *Changing Poverty, Changing Policy*. New York: Russell Sage Foundation Press, 63–91.

Blank, R. M. and Blinder, A. (1986). 'Macroeconomics, Income Distribution and Poverty', chapter 8 in S. H. Danziger and D. H. Weinberger (eds), *Fighting Poverty. What Works and What Doesn't*. Cambridge, MA: Harvard University Press, 180–208.

Blinder, A. and Esaki, H. (1978). 'Macroeconomic Activity and Income Distribution in the Postwar United States', *Review of Economics and Statistics*, 60: 604–9.

Blundell, R., Pistaferri, L., and Preston, I. (2008). 'Consumption Inequality and Partial Insurance', *American Economic Review*, 98: 1887–921.

Böheim, R. and Jenkins, S. P. (2006). 'A Comparison of Current and Annual Measures of Income in the British Household Panel Survey', *Journal of Official Statistics*, 22: 733–58.

Boeri, T. and Brandolini, A. (2004). 'The Age of Discontent: Italian Households at the Beginning of the Decade', *Giornale degli economisti e annali di economia*, 63: 449–87.

References

Boeri, T. and Bruecker, H. (2011). 'Short-Time Work Benefits Revisited: Some Lessons from the Great Recession', *Economic Policy*, 26: 697–765.

Bowers, N. and Horvath, F. W. (1984). 'Keeping Time: an Analysis of Errors in the Measurement of Unemployment Duration', *Journal of Business & Economic Statistics*, 2, 140–9.

Bradbury, B. and Jäntti, M. (2001). 'Child Poverty across Twenty-Five Countries', chapter 3 in B. Bradbury, S. P. Jenkins, and J. Micklewright (eds), *The Dynamics of Child Poverty in Industrialised Countries*. Cambridge: Cambridge University Press, 62–91.

Brandolini, A. (1999). 'The Distribution of Personal Income in Post-War Italy: Source Description, Data Quality, and the Time Pattern of Income Inequality', *Giornale degli economisti e annali di economia*, 58: 183–239.

Brandolini, A. (2009). 'L'evoluzione recente della distribuzione del reddito in Italia', in A. Brandolini, C. Saraceno, and A. Schizzerotto (eds), *Dimensioni della disuguaglianza in Italia. Povertà, salute, abitazione*. Bologna: il Mulino, 39–67.

Brandolini, A. and Bugamelli, M. (eds) (2009). 'Reports on Trends in the Italian Productive System', Questioni di economia e finanza (Occasional Papers) 45. Roma: Banca d'Italia.

Brandolini, A., Casadio, P., Cipollone, P., et al. (2007). 'Employment Growth in Italy in the 1990s: Institutional Arrangements and Market Forces', in N. Acocella and R. Leoni (eds), *Social Pacts, Employment and Growth: A Reappraisal of Ezio Tarantelli's Thought*. Heidelberg: Physica Verlag, 31–68.

Brandolini, A. and Smeeding, T. M. (2009). 'Income Inequality in Richer and OECD Countries', chapter 4 in W. Salverda, B. Nolan, and T. M. Smeeding (eds), *The Oxford Handbook of Economic Inequality*. Oxford: Oxford University Press, 71–100.

Brenke, K. (2011). 'Einkommensumverteilung Schwächt Privaten Verbrauch', *DIW Wochenbericht*, 8: 2–15.

Brenke, K. and Grabka, M. M. (2011). 'Schwache Lohnentwicklung im letzten Jahrzehnt', *DIW Wochenbericht*, 45: 3–15.

Brenke, K., Rinne, U., and Zimmermann, K. F. (2011). 'Short-Time Work: The German Answer to the Great Recession', IZA Discussion Paper 5780. Bonn: IZA. http://ftp.iza.org/dp5780.pdf [accessed 26 July 2012].

Brewer, M. and Browne, J. (2009). 'Can More Revenue be Raised by Increasing Income Tax Rates for the Very Rich?' Briefing Note 84. London: Institute for Fiscal Studies. http://www.ifs.org.uk/bns/bn84.pdf [accessed 26 July 2012].

Brewer, M., Saez, E., and Shephard, A. (2009). 'Means Testing and Tax Rates on Earnings', chapter 2 in J. Mirrlees, S. Adam, T. Besley, et al. (eds), *Reforming the Tax System for the 21st Century: The Mirrlees Review*, Vol. II: *Dimensions of Tax Design*. London: Institute for Fiscal Studies, 90–173.

Brewer, M., Browne, J., Joyce, R., and Sibieta, L. (2010). 'Child Poverty in the UK since 1998–99: Lessons from the Past Decade'. Working Paper 10/23. London: Institute for Fiscal Studies. http://www.ifs.org.uk/wps/wp1023.pdf [accessed 26 July 2012].

Brewer, M., Browne, J., and Joyce, R. (2011). 'Child and Working-Age Poverty from 2010 to 2020', *Commentary 121*. London: Institute for Fiscal Studies. http://www.ifs.org.uk/comms/comm121.pdf [accessed 26 July 2012].

Brewer, M., Emmerson, C., and Miller, H. (eds) (2011). *The IFS Green Budget: February 2011. Commentary 117*. London: Institute for Fiscal Studies. http://www.ifs.org.uk/budgets/gb2011/gb2011.pdf [accessed 26 July 2012].

Browne, J. and Phillips, D. (2010). 'Tax and Benefit Reforms under Labour', Briefing Note 88. London: Institute for Fiscal Studies. http://www.ifs.org.uk/bns/bn88.pdf [accessed 26 July 2012].

Buiter, W. H. (2007). 'Lessons from the 2007 Financial Crisis'. CEPR Policy Insight No. 18. http://www.cepr.org/pubs/policyinsights/PolicyInsight18.pdf [accessed 26 July 2012].

Bugamelli, M., Cristadoro, R., and Zevi, G. (2010). 'International Crisis and the Italian Productive System: An Analysis of Firm-Level Data', *Giornale degli economisti e annali di economia*, 69: 155–88.

Burda, M. and Hunt, J. (2011). 'What Explains the German Labor Market Miracle in the Great Recession?' NBER Working Paper No. 17187. Cambridge, MA: National Bureau of Economic Research. http://www.nber.org/papers/w17187 [accessed 26 July 2012].

Bureau of Labor Statistics (2011*a*). *Employment Characteristics of Families—2010*, News Release. Washington, DC: US Department of Labor Bureau of Labor Statistics.

Bureau of Labor Statistics (2011*b*). *Table Containing History of CPI-U U.S. All Items Indexes and Annual Percent Changes From 1913 to Present*. Washington, DC: US Department of Labor, Bureau of Labor Statistics. ftp://ftp.bls.gov/pub/special.requests/cpi/cpiai.txt [accessed 26 July 2012].

Burkhauser, R. and Larrimore, J. (2011). 'Median Income and Income Inequality during Economic Declines: Why the First Two Years of the Great Recession (2007–2009) are Different', Unpublished paper. Ithaca NY: Cornell University.

Burkhauser, R., Feng, S., and Jenkins, S. P. (2009). 'Using the P90/P10 Index to Measure U.S. Inequality Trends with Current Population Survey Data: A View from Inside the Census Bureau Vaults', *The Review of Income and Wealth*, 55: 166–85.

Burkhauser, R., Feng, S., Jenkins, S. P., and Larrimore, J. (2011). 'Estimating Trends in US Income Inequality Using the Current Population Survey: The Importance of Controlling for Censoring', *Journal of Economic Inequality*, 9: 393–415.

Caballero, R. J. (2010). 'Macroeconomics after the Crisis: Time to Deal with the Pretense-of-Knowledge Syndrome', *Journal of Economic Perspectives*, 24: 85–102.

Caivano, M., Rodano, L., and Siviero, S. (2010). 'La trasmissione della crisi finanziaria Globale all'economia italiana. Un'indagine controfattuale, 2008–2010', *Questioni di economia e finanza* (Occasional Papers) no. 64. Rome: Banca d'Italia.

Callan, T., Nolan, B., and Walsh, J. (2011). 'The Economic Crisis, Public Sector Pay, and the Income Distribution', in H. Immervoll, A. Peichl, and K. Tatsiramos (eds), *Who Loses in the Downturn? Economic Crisis, Employment and Income Distribution (Research in Labor Economics*, Vol. 32*)*. Bingley: Emerald Group Publishing Limited, 207–25.

Callan, T., Leventi, C., Levy, H., et al. (2011). 'The Distributional Effects of Austerity Measures: A Comparison of Six EU Countries'. Research Note 2/2011. Brussels: Social Situation Observatory—Income Distribution and Living Conditions. http://www.socialsituation.eu/research-notes [accessed 26 July 2012].

Cantillon, B. (2011). 'The Paradox of the Social Investment State. Growth, Employment and Poverty in the Lisbon Era', *Journal of European Social Policy*, 21: 432–49.

References

Cantillon, B., Marx, I., and Van Den Bosch, K. (2003). 'The Puzzle of Egalitarianism, the Relationship between Employment, Wage Inequality, Social Expenditure and Poverty', *European Journal of Social Security*, 5: 108–27.

Capgemini and Merrill Lynch Global Wealth Management (2011). *2011 World Wealth Report.* http://www.capgemini.com/insights-and-resources/by-publication/world-wealth-report-2011/ [accessed 26 July 2012].

Castañeda, A., Díaz-Giménez, J., and Ríos-Rull, J.-V. (1998). 'Exploring the Income Distribution Business Cycle Dynamics', *Journal of Monetary Economics*, 42: 93–130.

Ceccarelli, C., Discenza, A. R., and Loriga, S. (2006). 'The Impact of the New Labour Force Survey on the Employed Classification', in S. Zani, A. Cerioli, M. Riani, and M. Vichi (eds), *Data Analysis, Classification and the Forward Search*. Heidelberg: Physica Verlag, 359–67.

Central Statistics Office (2011). *Survey on Income and Living Conditions (SILC) Preliminary Results 2010.* Dublin: Central Statistics Office.

Chung, H. and Thewissen, S. (2011). 'Falling Back on Old Habits? A Comparison of the Social and Unemployment Crisis Reactive Policy Strategies in Germany, the UK and Sweden', *Social Policy and Administration*, 45: 354–70.

Cingano, F., Torrini, R., and Viviano, E. (2010). 'Il mercato del lavoro italiano durante la crisi', *Questioni di economia e finanza* (Occasional Papers) no. 68. Rome: Banca d'Italia.

Ciocca, P. (2003). 'The Italian Economy: A Problem of Growth', *Economic Bulletin*, 37: 145–58.

Crafts, N. and Fearon, P. (2010). 'Lessons from the 1930s Great Depression', *Oxford Review of Economic Policy*, 26: 285–317.

Congressional Budget Office (2009). 'Macro Effects of ARRA, Letter to Senator Charles Grassley', 2 March.

Congressional Budget Office (2010). *Average Federal Tax Rates and Income, by Income Category (1979–2007): Shares of After-Tax Income.* Washington, DC: Congressional Budget Office. http://www.cbo.gov/publications/collections/collections.cfm?collect=13

Congressional Budget Office (2011). *Trends in the Distribution of Household Income Between 1979 and 2007. October.* Washington, DC: Congressional Budget Office. http://www.cbo.gov/publication/42729

Crawford, R., Emmerson, C., and Tetlow, G. (2011). 'Disease and Cure in the UK: The Fiscal Impact of the Crisis and the Policy Response', chapter 9 in G. Giudice, R. Kuenzel, and T. Springbett (eds), *UK Economy: The Crisis in Perspective*. London: Routledge.

Crossley, T. F., Low, H., and O'Dea, C. (2011). 'Household Consumption through Recent Recessions'. Working Paper W11/18. London: Institute for Fiscal Studies. http://www.ifs.org.uk/wps/wp1118.pdf [accessed 26 July 2012].

Cutler, D. and Katz, L. (1991). 'Macroeconomic Performance and the Disadvantaged', *Brookings Papers on Economic Activity*, 2: 1–74.

D'Amuri, F. (2011). 'The Impact of the Great Recession on the Italian Labour Market', in H. Immervoll, A. Peichl, and K. Tatsiramos (eds), *Who Loses in the Downturn? Economic Crisis, Employment and Income Distribution (Research in Labor Economics*, Vol. 32). Bingley: Emerald Group Publishing Limited, 155–79.

de Beer, P. (2007). 'The Impact of the Crisis on Earnings and Income Distribution in the EU', Working Paper 2012.01. Brussels: European Trade Union Institute. http://www.etui.org/Publications2/Working-Papers/The-impact-of-the-crisis-on-earnings-and-income-distribution-in-the-EU [accessed 26 July 2012]

DeNavas-Walt, C., Proctor, B. D., and Smith, J. C. (2010). *Income, Poverty, and Health Insurance Coverage in the United States, 2009*. Current Population Reports, P60–238. Washington, DC: US Census Bureau. http://www.census.gov/prod/2010pubs/p60-238.pdf [accessed 26 July 2012].

DeNavas-Walt, C., Proctor, B. D., and Smith, J. C. (2011). *Income, Poverty, and Health Insurance Coverage in the United States: 2010*. Current Population Reports P60–239. Washington DC: US Census Bureau. http://www.census.gov/prod/2011pubs/p60-239.pdf [accessed 26 July 2012].

Department for Work and Pensions (2011). *Households Below Average Income: An Analysis of the Income Distribution 1994/95–2009/10*. London: DWP.

Deutsche Bundesbank (2011). 'Zeitreihe BJ9959: Verschuldung gem. Maastricht-Vertrag—Deutschland—Gesamtstaat in % des BIP. Stand vom 20.06.2011 12:06 Uhr'. http://www.bundesbank.de/statistik/statistik_zeitreihen.php?lang=de&open=&func=row&tr=BJ9959 [accessed 26 July 2012].

Dipartimento delle Finanze (2010). *Dichiarazioni Fiscali*. Rome: Ministero dell'Economia e delle Finanze. http://www.finanze.gov.it/export/finanze/Per_conoscere_il_fisco/studi_statistiche/dichiarazioni.html [accessed 26 July 2012].

Dolls, M., Fuest, C., and Peichl, A. (2011). 'Automatic Stabilizers, Economic Crisis and Income Distribution in Europe', in H. Immervoll, A. Peichl, and K. Tatsiramos (eds), *Who Loses in the Downturn? Economic Crisis, Employment and Income Distribution* (*Research in Labor Economics*, Vol. 32). Bingley: Emerald Group Publishing Limited, 227–55.

Dolls, M., Fuest, C., and Peichl, A. (2012). 'Automatic Stabilizers and Economic Crisis: US vs. Europe', *Journal of Public Economics*, 96: 279–94.

Dustmann, C., Ludsteck, J., and Schönberg, U. (2009). 'Revisiting the German Wage Structure', *Quarterly Journal of Economics*, 124: 843–81.

Dyrda, S., Kaplan, G., and Rios-Rull, J.-V. (2012). 'Business Cycles and Household Formation: the Macro vs. the Micro Labor Elasticity'. NBER Working Paper 17880. Cambridge MA, National Bureau of Economic Research. http://www.nber.org/papers/w17880 [accessed 26 July 2012].

Esping-Andersen, G. (1990). *The Three Worlds of Welfare Capitalism*. Cambridge: The Polity Press.

Evans, L., Grimes, A., and Wilkinson, B., with Teece, D. (1996). 'Economic Reform in New Zealand 1984–95: The Pursuit of Efficiency', *Journal of Economic Literature*, 34: 1856–902.

Expert Group on Household Income Statistics (The Canberra Group) (2001). *Final Report and Recommendations*. Ottawa: Statistics Canada. http://www.lisproject.org/links/canberra/finalreport.pdf [accessed 26 July 2012].

European Central Bank (ECB) (2012), 'Residential Property Price Indicator', *Statistical Data Warehouse*. http://sdw.ecb.europa.eu/browse.do?node=2120781 [accessed 26 July 2012].

References

Eurostat (2011). 'Income and Living Conditions' (online database). Accessed 18 December 2011. http://epp.eurostat.ec.europa.eu/portal/page/portal/income_social_inclusion_living_conditions/data/database [accessed 26 July 2012].

Farber, H. (2011). 'Job Loss in the Great Recession: Historical Perspective from the Displaced Workers Survey, 1984–2010', NBER Working Paper 17040. Cambridge MA: National Bureau of Economic Research. http://www.nber.org/papers/w17040 [accessed 26 July 2012].

Farré, L. and Vella, F. (2008). 'Macroeconomic Conditions and the Distribution of Income', *Labour*, 22: 383–410.

Federal Statistical Office (2010). 'Knapp 9% aller Arbeitsverträge waren im Jahr 2008 befristet'. Pressemitteilung Nr.103 vom 16.03.2010. Berlin: Federal Statistical Office.

Federal Statistical Office (2011). *Bruttoinlandsprodukt. Statistical Yearbook 2009*. Chapter 24, Volkswirtschaftliche Gesamtrechnungen. Berlin: Federal Statistical Office.

Feenberg, D. and Coutts, E. (1993). 'An Introduction to the TAXSIM Model', *Journal of Policy Analysis and Management*, 12: 189–94.

Ferrera, M. (1996). 'The 'Southern Model' of Welfare in Social Europe', *Journal of European Social Policy*, 6: 17–37.

Figari, F., Salvatori, A., and Sutherland, H. (2011). 'Economic Downturn and Stress Testing European Welfare Systems', in H. Immervoll, A. Peichl, and K. Tatsiramos (eds), *Who Loses in the Downturn? Economic Crisis, Employment and Income Distribution (Research in Labor Economics*, Vol. 32). Bingley: Emerald Group Publishing Limited, 257–86.

Fondeville, N., Özdemir, E., and Ward, T. (2010). 'Over-indebtedness'. Research Note 4/2010. Brussels: Social Situation Observatory—Income Distribution and Living Conditions. http://www.socialsituation.eu/research-notes [accessed 26 July 2012].

Franz, W., and Steiner, V. (2000). 'Wages in the East German Transition Process: Facts and Explanations', *German Economic Review*, 1: 241–69.

Frick, J. R. and Grabka, M. M. (2003). 'Imputed Rent and Income Inequality: A Decomposition Analysis for the UK, West Germany and the USA', *Review of Income and Wealth*, 49: 513–37.

Frick, J. R. and Grabka, M. M. (2009). 'Wealth Inequality on the Rise in Germany', *DIW Berlin Weekly Report*, 10/2009: 62–73.

Frick, J. R. and Grabka, M. M. (2010). 'Old-Age Pension Entitlements Mitigate Inequality—but Concentration of Wealth Remains High', *DIW Berlin Weekly Report*, 8/2010: 55–64.

Frick, J.R. and Krell, K. (2010). 'Measuring Income in Household Panel Surveys in Germany: A Comparison of EU-SILC and SOEP', SOEP Papers on Multidisciplinary Panel Data Research 265. Berlin: DIW. http://www.diw.de/documents/publikatio nen/73/diw_01.c.346496.de/diw_sp0265.pdf [accessed 26 July 2012].

Fuchs-Schündeln, N., Krueger, D., and Sommer, M. (2010). 'Inequality Trends for Germany in the Last Two Decades: A Tale of Two Countries', *Review of Economic Dynamics*, 13: 103–32.

German Bundesbank (2011). Zeitreihe CEB00I: Geldvermögen insgesamt S: Sektoren insgesamt G: Private Haushalte (inkl.Org) vom 17. Mai 2011. http://www.bundesbank.de/statistik/statistik_zeitreihen.php?lang=de&open=wirtschaftsdaten%20&func=row&tr=CEB00I [accessed 26 July 2012].

German Council of Economic Experts (2006). Jahresgutachten 2006/07. Wiederstreitende Interessen—ungenutzte Chancen. Wiesbaden: German Council of Economic Experts. http://www.sachverstaendigenrat-wirtschaft.de/fileadmin/dateiablage/down load/ gutachten/gaob-ges.pdf [accessd 26 July 2012].]

German Council of Economic Experts (2009). 'Die Zukunft nicht aufs Spiel setzen', *Jahresgutachten 2009/10*. Wiesbaden: German Council of Economic Experts. http:// www.sachverstaendigenrat-wirtschaft.de/fileadmin/dateiablage/download/gutach-ten/ga09_ges.pdf [accessed 26 July 2012].

German Council of Economic Experts (2010). 'Chancen für einen stabilen Aufschwung', *Jahresgutachten 2009/11*. Wiesbaden: German Council of Economic Experts. http://www.sachverstaendigenrat-wirtschaft.de/fileadmin/dateiablage/download/ gutachten/ga10_ges.pdf [accessed 26 July 2012].

Gernandt, J. and Pfeiffer, F. (2007). 'Rising Wage Inequality in Germany', *Journal of Economics and Statistics*, 227: 358–80.

Glaeser, E. (2010). 'Children Moving Back Home and the Construction Industry', *New York Times*, 16 February. http://economix.blogs.nytimes.com/2010/02/16/kids-moving-back-home-and-the-construction-industry/ [accessed 26 July 2012].

Goldin, C., and Katz, L. (2008). *The Race between Education and Technology*. Cambridge MA: Harvard University Press.

Goodman, A. and Oldfield, Z. (2004). 'Permanent Differences? Income and Expenditure Inequality in the 1990s and 2000s'. IFS Report 66. London: Institute for Fiscal Studies. http://www.ifs.org.uk/comms/r66.pdf [accessed 26 July 2012].

Gottschalk, P. and Danziger, S. (1985). 'A Framework for Evaluating the Effects of Economic Growth and Transfers on Poverty', *American Economic Review*, 75: 153–61.

Government of Sweden (2011). *Fördelningspolitisk Redogörelse (Distributional Consequences of Government Budget)*. Bilaga 3, vårpropositionen (Appendix to spring budget).

Grabka, M. M. and Frick, J. R. (2010). Weiterhin hohes Armutsrisiko in Deutschland: Kinder und junge Erwachsene sind besonders betroffen, *DIW Wochenbericht*, 7/2010: 2–11.

Grabka, M. M., Schwarze, J., and Wagner, G. G. (1999). 'How Unification and Immigration Affected the German Income Distribution', *European Economic Review*, 43: 867–78.

Greenspan, A. and Kennedy, J. (2007). 'Sources and Uses of Equity Extracted from Homes', Finance and Economics Discussion Series Working Paper 2007–20. Washington, DC: Divisions of Research & Statistics and Monetary Affairs, Federal Reserve Board, Updated data at: http://www.efxtraders.com/market-updates/financial-news/ q1–2011-mortgage-equity-withdrawal-strongly-negative.html.

Greenstone, M. and Looney, A. (2011). 'The Great Recession May Be Over, but American Families Are Working Harder than Ever: Wages, Jobs and the Economy. U.S. Economic Growth, Children & Families', Hamilton Project on-line article. Washington, DC: Brookings Institution. http://www.brookings.edu/opinions/2011/ 0708_jobs_greenstone_looney.aspx [accessed 26 July].

Gregg, P. and Wadsworth, J. (1998). 'It Takes Two. Employment Polarisation in the OECD'. Centre for Economic Performance Discussion Paper 304. London: London School of Economics.

Gregg, P. and Wadsworth, J. (2010), 'Unemployment and Inactivity in the 2008–2009 Recession', *Economic and Labour Market Review*, 4: 44–50.

Gregg, P., Scutella, R., and Wadsworth, J. (2010). 'Reconciling Workless Measures at the Individual and Household Level. Theory and Evidence from the United States, Britain, Germany, Spain and Australia', *Journal of Population Economics*, 23: 139–67.

Grusky, D. B., Western, B., and Wimer, C. (eds) (2011). *The Great Recession*. New York: Russell Sage Foundation.

Guiso, L., Paiella, M., and Visco, I. (2006), 'Do Capital Gains Affect Consumption? Estimates of Wealth Effects from Italian Household's Behavior', in L. R. Klein (ed.), *Long-Run Growth and Short-Run Stabilization: Essays in Memory of Albert Ando*. Cheltenham: Edward Elgar, 46–82.

Gustafsson, B. (2000). 'Poverty in Sweden: Changes 1975–1995, Profile and Dynamics', in B. Gustafsson and P. J. Pedersen (eds), *Poverty and Low Income in the Nordic Countries*. Aldershot: Ashgate, 169–206.

Gustafsson, B. and Pedersen, P. J. (2000). 'Introduction', in B. Gustafsson and P. J. Pedersen (eds), *Poverty and Low Income in the Nordic Countries*. Aldershot: Ashgate, 1–20.

Gustman, A., Steinmeier, T., and Tabatabai, N. (2010). 'What the Stock Market Decline Means for the Financial Security and Retirement Choices of the Near-Retirement Population.' *Journal of Economic Perspectives*, 24: 181–2.

Hauser, R. (2008). 'Problems of the German Contribution to EU-SILC—A Research Perspective, Comparing EU-SILC, Microcensus and SOEP'. SOEP Papers on Multidisciplinary Panel Data Research 86. Berlin: DIW. http://www.diw.de/documents/publikationen/73/diw_01.c.78924.de/diw_sp0086.pdf [accessed 26 July 2012].

Haveman, R. and Smeeding, T. M. (2006). 'The Role of Higher Education in Social Mobility', *Future of Children*, 16: 125–50.

Heathcote, J., Perri, F., and Violante, G. (2010). 'Inequality in Times of Crisis: Lessons from the Past and a First Look at the Current Recession', *VOX*, 2 February. http://www.voxeu.org/index.php?q=node/4548 [accessed 26 July 2012].

Heer, B. (2007). 'On the Modelling of the Income Distribution Business Cycle Dynamics'. Working Paper 1945. CESifo, Munich. http://www.cesifo-group.de [accessed 26 July 2012].

Herzog-Stein, A., Lindner, F., Sturn, S., and van Treeck, T. (2010). 'From a Source of Weakness to a Tower of Strength? The Changing German Labour Market'. Report 56e. Düsseldorf: IMK. www.boeckler.de/pdf/p_imk_wp_6_2011.pdf [accessed 26 July 2012].

Hirschman, A. O. and Rothschild, M. (1973). 'The Changing Tolerance for Income Inequality in the Course of Economic Development: With a Mathematical Appendix', *Quarterly Journal of Economics*, 87: 544–66.

Howell, D. and Azizoglu, B. (2011). 'Unemployment Benefits and Work Incentives: The US Labor Market in the Great Recession', *Oxford Review of Economic Policy*, 27: 221–40.

HM Treasury (2010). *Spending Review 2010*, Cm 7942. http://cdn.hm-treasury.gov.uk/sr2010_completereport.pdf [accessed 26 July 2012].

Iacovou, M. (2010). 'Leaving Home: Independence, Togetherness and Income', *Advances in Life Course Research*, 15: 147–60.

International Monetary Fund (2010). 'Fiscal Exit: from Strategy to Implementation', *Fiscal Monitor*. http://www.imf.org/external/pubs/cat/longres.cfm?sk=24220 [accessed 26 July 2012].

Istat (2011a). *Rapporto annuale. La situazione del paese nel 2010*. Rome: Istat.

Istat (2011b). 'Reddito e condizioni di vita. Anno 2010'. *Statistiche report*. Rome: Istat.

Istat (2011c). 'La povertà in Italia. Anno 2010'. *Statistiche Report*. Rome: Istat.

Istat (2011d). 'La soddisfazione dei cittadini per le condizioni di vita. Anno 2011'. *Statistiche Report*. Rome: Istat.

Jäntti, M. and Danziger, S. (2000). 'Poverty in Advanced Countries', chapter 9 in A. B. Atkinson and F. Bourguignon (eds), *Handbook of Income Distribution, Volume 1*. Amsterdam: Elsevier Science, 309–78.

Jäntti, M. and Jenkins, S. P. (2010). 'Examining the Impact of Macro-Economic Conditions on Income Inequality', *Journal of Economic Inequality*, 8: 221–40.

Jäntti, M. and Ritakallio, V.-M. (2000). 'Income Poverty in Finland: 1971–1995', in B. Gustafsson and P. J. Pedersen (eds), *Poverty and Low Income in the Nordic Countries*. Aldershot: Ashgate, 63–99.

Jäntti, M., Sierminska, E., and Smeeding, T. M. (2008). 'How is Household Wealth Distributed? Evidence from the Luxembourg Wealth Study', chapter 10 in Organisation for Economic Cooperation and Development (ed.), *Growing Unequal? Income Distribution and Poverty in OECD Countries*. Paris: OECD.

Jenkins, S. P. (1995). 'Accounting for Inequality Trends', *Economica*, 62: 29–63.

Jenkins, S. and Van Kerm, P. (2011). 'Trends in Individual Income Growth: Measurement Methods and British Evidence'. Working Paper 2011/06. Colchester: ISER, University of Essex. http://www.iser.essex.ac.uk/pubs/workpaps/pdf/2011–06.pdf [accessed 26 July 2012].

Jin, W., Joyce, R., Phillips, D., and Sibieta, L. (2011). 'Poverty and Inequality in the UK: 2011'. *Commentary 118*. London: Institute for Fiscal Studies. http://www.ifs.org.uk/comms/comm118.pdf [accessed 26 July 2012].

Johnson, D. S., Smeeding, T. M., and Boyle Torrey, B. (2005). 'Economic Inequality through the Prisms of Income and Consumption', *Monthly Labor Review*, 128: 11–24.

Jonsson, J. O., Mood, C., and Bihagen, E. (2010). 'Fattigdomens Förändring, Utbredning och Dynamik'. Chapter 3 in *Social Rapport 2010*. Stockholm: Socialstyrelsen, 90–126. http://www.socialstyrelsen.se/publikationer2010/2010-3-11 [accessed 26 July 2012].

Keeley, B. and Love, P. (2010). *From Crisis to Recovery. The Causes, Course and Consequences of the Great Recession*. Paris: OECD. http://www.oecd-ilibrary.org/finance-and-investment/from-crisis-to-recovery_9789264077072-en [accesed 26 July 2012].

Kelly, E., McGuinness, S., and O'Connell, P. J. (2009a). 'Benchmarking, Social Partnership and Higher Remuneration: Wage Settling Institutions and the Public-Private Sector Wage Gap in Ireland', *Economic and Social Review*, 40: 339–70.

Kelly, E., McGuinness, S., and O'Connell, P. J. (2009b). 'The Public-Private Sector Pay Gap in Ireland: What Lies Beneath?'. Working Paper 321. Dublin: Economic and Social Research Institute.

Kowalski, A. (2011). 'Existing Home Sales in U.S. Slump; Prices Drop to Lowest Since April 2002'. http://www.bloomberg.com/news/2011-03-21/u-s-february-existing-home-sales-fall-to-4-88-million-rate.html [accessed 26 July 2012].

Krueger, D., Perri, F., Pistaferri, L., and Violante, G. L. (2010). 'Cross-Sectional Facts for Macroeconomists', *Review of Economic Dynamics*, 13: 1–15.

Krugman, P. (2009). 'Free to Lose'. *New York Times*, 12 November. http://www.nytimes.com/2009/11/13/opinion/13krugman.html [accessed 26 July 2012].

Kuznets, S. (1955). 'Economic Growth and Economic Inequality', *American Economic Review*, 45: 1–28.

Lane, P. R. and Milesi-Ferretti, G. M. (2011). 'The Cross-Country Incidence of the Global Crisis', *IMF Economic Review*, 59: 77–110.

Lansing, K. (2011). 'Gauging the Impact of the Great Recession,' *FRBSF Economic Letter, 2011–21 July 11*. www.frbsf.org/publications/economics/letter/2011/el2011-21.html [accessed 26 July 2012].

Larrimore, J., Burkhauser, R. V., Feng, S., Zayatz, L. (2008). 'Consistent Cell Means for Topcoded Incomes in the public use March CPS (1976–2007)', *Journal of Economic and Social Measurement*, 33: 89–128.

Layte R., Nolan B., and Whelan C. T. (2004). 'Explaining Poverty Trends during Ireland's Boom', *Irish Banking Review*, Summer: 2–14.
http://www.esri.ie/pdf/Explaining%20Poverty%20Trends%20in%20Ireland%20during%20the%20Boom_Irish%20Banking%20Review.pdf [accessed 26 July 2012].

Leigh, A. (2007). 'How Closely do Top Income Shares Track Other Measures of Inequality?', *Economic Journal*, 117: F619–33.

Leonhardt, D. (2011a). 'Men, Unemployment and Disability', *New York Times*, 8 April.
http://economix.blogs.nytimes.com/2011/04/08/men-unemployment-and-disability/

Leonhardt, D. (2011b). 'We're Spent', *New York Times Review*, 16 July.
http://www.nytimes.com/interactive/2011/07/15/sunday-review/consumer-spending.html?ref=sunday-review [accessed 26 July 2012].

Levy, F. and Temin, P. (2009). 'Institutions and Wages in Post-World War II America', chapter 1 in C. Brown, B. Eichengreen, and M. Reich (eds), *Labor in the Era of Globalization*. Cambridge: Cambridge University Press.

Levy, F. and Kochan, T. (2011). *Addressing the Problem of Stagnant Wages*. Champaign, IL: Employment Policy Research Network.
http://www.employmentpolicy.org/sites/www.employmentpolicy.org/files/field-content-file/pdf/Mike%20Lillich/EPRN%20WagesMay%2020%20-%20FL%20Edits_0.pdf [accessed 26 July 2012].

LIS Inequality and Poverty Key Figures (2011). http://www.lisdatacenter.org [accessed 15 September 2011]. Luxembourg: LIS.

Maliar, L., Maliar, S., and Mora, J. (2005). 'Income and Wealth Distributions along the Business Cycle: Implications from the Neoclassical Growth Model', *The B.E. Journal of Macroeconomics*, 5: article 15.

Marchal, S., Marx, I., and Van Mechelen, N. (2011). 'Do Europe's Minimum Income Schemes Provide Adequate Shelter against the Economic Crisis and How, If at All, Have Governments Responded?'. IZA Discussion Paper 6264. Bonn: IZA. http://ftp.iza.org/dp6264.pdf [accessed 26 July 2012].

Matsaganis, M. and Leventi, C. (2011). 'The Distributional Impact of the Crisis in Greece', DEOS Working Paper 1124. Athens: Athens University of Economics and Business. http://wpa.deos.aueb.gr/docs/The_distributional_impact_of_the_crisis_in_Greece.pdf [accessed 26 July 2012].

McGuinness, S., McGinnity, F., and O'Connell, P. (2008). 'Changing Returns to Education During a Boom? The Case of Ireland'. Working Paper 22. Dublin: Economic and Social Research Institute.

McWatters, C. J. and Beach, C. M. (1990). 'Factors behind the Changes in Canada's Family Income Distribution and the Share of the Middle Class', *Relations Industrielles*, 45: 118–33.

Mendershausen, H. (1946). *Changes in Income Distribution During the Great Depression*. New York: National Bureau of Economic Research. http://ideas.repec.org/b/nbr/nberbk/mend46-1.html [accessed 26 July 2012].

Metcalf, C. E. (1969). 'The Size Distribution of Personal Income During the Business Cycle', *American Economic Review*, 59: 657–68.

Mishel, L., Bernstein, J., and Schmitt, J. (1998). 'Wage Inequality in the 1990s: Measurement and Trends'. Unpublished paper. Washington, DC: Economic Policy Institute.

Mocetti, S., Olivieri, E., and Viviano, E. (2011). 'Le famiglie italiane e il lavoro. Caratteristiche strutturali e effetti della crisi', *Stato e Mercato*, 2: 223–43.

Möller, J. (2010). 'The German Labour Market Response in the World Recession—Demystifying a Miracle', *Zeitschrift für ArbeitsmarktForschung*, 42: 325–36.

Muriel, A. and Sibieta, L. (2009). 'Living Standards During Previous Recessions'. Briefing Note BN85. London: Institute for Fiscal Studies. http://www.ifs.org.uk/bns/bn85.pdf [accessed 26 July 2012].

Mykyta, L. and Macartney, S. (2011). 'The Effects of Recession on Household Composition: 'Doubling Up' and Economic Well-Being'. SEHSD Working Paper Number 2011-4. Washington, DC: US Census Bureau.

Nolan, B. (1988–89). 'Macroeconomic Conditions and the Size Distribution of Income: Evidence from the United Kingdom', *Journal of Post-Keynesian Economics*, 11: 196–221.

Nolan, B. (2007). 'Long-Term Trends in Top Income Shares in Ireland', in A.B. Atkinson and T. Piketty (eds), *Top Incomes over the 20th Century: A Contrast between Continental European and English-Speaking Countries*. Oxford: Oxford University Press, 501–30.

Nolan, B. and Maître, B. (2000). 'A Comparative Perspective of Trends in Income Inequality in Ireland', *Economic and Social Review*, 31: 329–50.

Nolan, B. and Smeeding, T. M. (2005). 'Ireland's Income Distribution in Comparative Perspective', *Review of Income and Wealth*, 54: 537–60.

Nolan, B., Maître, B., O'Neill, D., and Sweetman, O. (2000). *The Distribution of Income in Ireland*. Dublin: Oak Tree Press.

Nolan B., Munzi T., and Smeeding T. M. (2005). 'Two Views of Irish Poverty Trends'. Background note prepared for Human Development Report 2005. Dublin: ESRI.

Nolan, B., Voitchovsky, S., and Maître, B. (2010). 'Earnings Inequality, Institutions and the Macroeconomy—What Can We Learn from Ireland's Boom Years?' Geary Institute Working Paper 10/16. Dublin: University College Dublin.

Office for Budget Responsibility (2011). *Economic and Fiscal Outlook—November 2011*, Cm 8218. http://budgetresponsibility.independent.gov.uk/economic-and-fiscal-outlook-november-2011/ [accessed 26 July 2012].

Ohanian, L. E. (2010). 'The Economic Crisis from a Neoclassical Perspective', *Journal of Economic Perspectives*, 24: 45–66.

Oreopoulos, P., von Wachter, T., and Heisz, A. (2012). 'The Short- and Long-Term Career Effects of Graduating in a Recession', *American Economic Journal: Applied Economics*, 4: 1–29.

References

Organisation for Economic Co-operation and Development (OECD) (1996). *OECD Economic Surveys: Sweden 1997*. Paris: OECD.

Organisation for Economic Co-operation and Development (OECD) (2001). *Employment Outlook*. Paris: OECD.

Organisation for Economic Co-operation and Development (OECD) (2006). *Economic Outlook*, No. 80. Paris: OECD.

Organisation for Economic Co-operation and Development (OECD) (2008). *Growing Unequal? Income Distribution and Poverty in OECD Countries*. Paris: OECD.

Organisation for Economic Co-operation and Development (OECD) (2009). *Employment Outlook*. Paris: OECD.

Organisation for Economic Co-operation and Development (OECD) (2010*a*). *Employment Outlook*. Paris: OECD.

Organisation for Economic Co-operation and Development (OECD) (2010*b*). *Economic Outlook*, Number 87. Paris: OECD.

Organisation for Economic Co-operation and Development (OECD) (2010*c*) *Economic Outlook*, Number 88. Paris: OECD.

Organisation for Economic Co-operation and Development (OECD) (2011*a*) *Economic Outlook*, Number 89. Paris: OECD.

Organisation for Economic Co-operation and Development (OECD) (2011*b*) *Economic Outlook*, Number 90. Paris: OECD.

Organisation for Economic Co-operation and Development (OECD) (2011*c*). *Employment Outlook*. Paris: OECD.

Organisation for Economic Co-operation and Development (OECD) (2011*d*) *Restoring Public Finances*. Special Issue of the *OECD Journal on Budgeting*, Vol. 2011/2. Paris: OECD.

Organisation for Economic Co-operation and Development (OECD) (2011*e*), 'House prices', *Economics: Key Tables from OECD*, No. 17. http://dx.doi.org/10.1787/hsprice-table-2011-1-en [accessed 26 July 2012].

Organisation for Economic Co-operation and Development (OECD) (2011*f*). *Divided We Stand: Why Inequality Keeps Rising*. Paris: OECD.

Organisation for Economic Co-operation and Development (OECD) (2011*g*). *OECD Economic Surveys: Sweden 2011*. Paris: OECD.

Painter, G. (2010). *What Happens to Household Formation in a Recession?* Report prepared for the Research Institute for Housing America. http://www.housingamerica.org/RIHA/RIHA/Publications/72429_9821_Research_RIHA_Household_Report.pdf [accessed 26 July 2012].

Panetta, F. (ed.) (2009). 'L'andamento del mercato immobiliare italiano e i riflessi sul sistema finanziario', *Questioni di economia e finanza* (Occasional Papers) no. 59. Rome: Banca d'Italia.

Parker, S. C. (1998–99). 'Income Inequality and the Business Cycle: A Survey of the Evidence and Some New Results', *Journal of Post-Keynesian Economics*, 21: 201–25.

Parker, S. C. (2000). 'Opening a Can of Worms: The Pitfalls of Time-Series Regression Analyses of Income Inequality', *Applied Economics*, 32: 221–30.

Pedersen, P. J. and Smith, N. (2000). 'Low Incomes in Denmark, 1980–1995', in B. Gustafsson and P. J. Pedersen (eds), *Poverty and Low Income in the Nordic Countries*. Aldershot: Ashgate, 21–62.

Peseran, M. H. and Smith, R. P. (2011). 'Beyond the DSGE Straitjacket', *Manchester School*, 79, supplement S2: 5–16.

Piketty, T. (2001). 'Income Inequality in France, 1901–1998', *Journal of Political Economy*, 111: 1004–42.

Piketty, T. and Saez, E. (2003). 'Income Inequality in the United States, 1913–1998', *Quarterly Journal of Economics*, 118: 1–39.

Piketty, T. and Saez, E. (2006). 'The Evolution of Top Incomes: A Historical and International Perspective', *American Economic Review, Papers and Proceedings*, 96: 200–5.

Piketty, T. and Saez, E. (2007). 'Income Inequality in the United States, 1913–2002,' in A. B. Atkinson and T. Piketty (eds), *Top Incomes over the Twentieth Century: A Contrast Between European and English Speaking Counties*. Oxford: Oxford University Press, 141–225.

Plotnick, R. D., Smolensky, E., Evenhouse, E., and Reilly, S. (1998). 'Inequality, Poverty and the Fisc in Twentieth-Century America', *Journal of Post-Keynesian Economics*, 21: 51–75.

Poterba, J. M. and Summers, L. H. (1986). 'Reporting Errors and Labor Market Dynamics', *Econometrica*, 54: 1319–38.

Quiggin, J. (2010). *Zombie Economics: How Dead Ideas Still Walk Among Us*. Princeton NJ: Princeton University Press.

Reinhart, C. M. and Rogoff, K. S. (2009). *This Time is Different: Eight Centuries of Financial Folly*. Princeton, NJ: Princeton University Press.

Roine, J. and Waldenström, D. (2012). 'On the role of Capital Gains in Swedish Income Inequality', *Review of Income and Wealth*, 58: 569–87.

Roine, J., Vlachos, J., and Waldenström, D. (2009). 'The Long-Run Determinants of Inequality: What Can We Learn from Top Income Data?', *Journal of Public Economics*, 93: 974–88.

Rosemann, M. and Kirchmann, A. (2010). 'Wer sind die Betroffenen der Krise? Parallelen und Unterschiede zur vorangegangenen Krise', *WSI Mitteilungen*, 11: 560–9.

Rosenbaum, D. (2011). 'Ryan Budget Would Slash SNAP Funding by $127 Billion Over Ten Years: Low Income Households in All States Would Feel Sharp Effects', 11 April. Washington, DC: Center on Budget and Policy Priorities. http://www.cbpp.org/cms/index.cfm?fa=view&id=3463

Rosolia, A. (2010). 'L'evoluzione delle retribuzioni in Italia tra il 1986 e il 2004 secondo i dati dell'archivio WHIP', *Politica Economica*, 26: 179–201.

Rosolia, A. and Torrini, R. (2007). 'The Generation Gap'. *Temi di discussione*, no. 639. Rome: Banca d'Italia.

Ruggles, N. D. and Ruggles, R. (1977). 'The Anatomy of Earnings Behavior', in F. T. Juster (ed.), *Distribution of Economic Well-Being*. New York: National Bureau of Economic Research, 115–62.

Ryscavage, P. (1995). 'A Surge in Growing Income Inequality?', *Monthly Labor Review*, 118: 51–61.

Saez, E. (2010). 'Striking it Richer: The Evolution of Top Incomes in the United States' (online database updated July 2010). http://elsa.berkeley.edu/~saez/saez-UStopincomes-2008.pdf [accessed 26 July 2012].

Salverda, W., Nolan, B., and Smeeding, T. M. (eds) (2009). *The Oxford Handbook on Economic Inequality*. Oxford: Oxford University Press.

Schorfheide, F. (2011). 'Estimation and Evaluation of DSGE Models: Progress and Challenges'. NBER Working Paper 16781. Cambridge, MA: National Bureau of Economic Research. http://www.nber.org/papers/w16781 [accessed 26 July 2012].

Schwarze, J. (1996). 'How Income Inequality Changed in Germany Following Reunification: An Empirical Analysis using Decomposable Inequality Measures', *Review of Income and Wealth*, 42: 1–11.

Sherman, A., (2011). 'Despite Deep Recession and High Unemployment, Government Efforts—Including the Recovery Act—Prevented Poverty from Rising in 2009, New Census Data Show', Center on Budget and Policy Priorities, January.
http://www.cbpp.org/cms/index.cfm?fa=view&id=3361 [accessed 26 July 2012].

Shorrocks, A. F. (1982*a*). 'Inequality Decomposition by Factor Components', *Econometrica*, 50: 193–212.

Shorrocks, A. F. (1982*b*). 'The Impact of Income Components on the Distribution of Family Incomes', *Quarterly Journal of Economics*, 98: 311–26.

Smets, F. and Wouters, R. (2003). 'An Estimated Dynamic Stochastic General Equilibrium Model of the Euro Area', *Journal of the European Economic Association*, 1: 1123–75.

Solon, G. (1999). 'Intergenerational Mobility in the Labor Market', in O. Ashenfelter and D. Card (eds), *Handbook of Labor Economics, Volume 3*, New York: Elsevier Science, 1761–800.

Smeeding, T. and Thompson, J. (2011). 'Recent Trends in Income Inequality: Labor, Wealth and More Complete Measures of Income', *Research in Labor Economics*, 32: 1–50.

Smeeding, T., Garfinkel, I., and Mincy, R. (2011). 'Introduction to Young Disadvantaged Men: Fathers, Families, Poverty, and Policy', *Annals of the American Academy of Political and Social Science*, 635: 6–23.

Snyder, T. and Dillow, S. (2011). *Digest of Education Statistics 2010* (NCES 2011–015). Washington, DC: National Center for Education Statistics, Institute of Education Sciences, U.S. Department of Education.

Statistics New Zealand (1999). *Incomes*. Wellington: Statistics New Zealand.
http://www2.stats.govt.nz/domino/external/pasfull/pasfull.nsf/c5828a294cb9951b4c25
67ed00094103/4c2567ef00247c6acc256b03000bdbe0/$FILE/Incomes.pdf

Stiglitz, J. E., Sen, A. K., and Fitoussi, J. P. (2009). *Report by the Commission on the Measurement of Economic Performance and Social Progress*. Paris: Stiglitz-Sen-Fitoussi Commission. http://www.stiglitz-sen-fitoussi.fr/documents/rapport_anglais.pdf [accessed 26 July 2012].

Sum, A., Khatiwada, I., McLaughlin, J., and Palma, S. (2011*a*). 'The 'Jobless and Wageless' Recovery from the Great Recession of 2007–2009: The Magnitude and Sources of Economic Growth Through 2011 and Their Impacts on Workers, Profits, and Stock Values'. Unpublished paper. Boston, MA: Center for Labor Market Studies, Northeastern University.

Sum, A., Khatiwada, I., McLaughlin, J., and Palma, S. (2011*b*). 'The Unemployment Experiences of Workers in the U.S. Who Were Displaced from Their Jobs During the Great Dislocation of 2007–2009', Unpublished paper. Boston, MA: Center for Labor Market Studies, Northeastern University. http://www.employmentpolicy.org/sites/ www.employmentpolicy.org/files/field-content-file/pdf/Andrew%20M.%20Sum/June %202011%20Unemployment%20Dislocated%20Worker%20Paper.pdf [accessed 26 July 2012].

Sum, A., Khatiwada, I., McLaughlin, J., and Palma, S. (2011*c*). 'No Country for Young Men', in T. Smeeding, I. Garfinkel, and R. Mincy (eds), *Young Disadvantaged Men: Fathers, Families, Poverty, and Policy, Annals of the American Academy of Political and Social Science*, 635: 24–55.

Swedish Ministry of Finance (2009). *Arbetsutbudseffekter av Reformer på Inkomstskatteområdet 2007–2009 (Labour Supply Effects of Income Tax Reforms 2007–2009)*. Report. Stockholm: Ekonomiska avdelningen på Finansdepartementet.

Thurow, L. C. (1970). 'Analyzing the American Income Distribution', *American Economic Review (Papers and Proceedings)*, 60: 261–9.

UN Department of Economic and Social Affairs (2011). *The Global Social Crisis. Report on the World Social Situation 2011*. Paper ST/ESA/334. New York: United Nations. http://social.un.org/index/ReportontheWorldSocialSituation/2011.aspx [accessed 26 July 2012].

US Census Bureau (2010). 'Income, Poverty, and Health Insurance Coverage: 2009', September. Washington, DC: US Census Bureau. http://www.census.gov/prod/2011pubs/p60-238.pdf [accessed 26 July 2012].

US Department of Labor. (2011). BLS Statistics of Unemployment and Employment. http://www.bls.gov/bls/unemployment.htm [accessed 26 July 2012].

Vandenbroucke, F. and Vleminckx, K. (2011). 'Disappointing Poverty Trends: Is the Social Investment State to Blame?', *Journal of European Social Policy*, 19: 450–71.

Visco, I. (2011). 'Indagine conoscitiva sul decreto legge recante disposizioni urgenti per la crescita, l'equità e il consolidamento dei conti pubblici', Testimony before Joint Commissions 5th of House of Deputies and 5th of Senate of the Republic, 9 December. Rome: Banca d'Italia.

Vis, B., van Kersbergen, K., and Hylands, T. (2011). 'To What Extent did the Financial Crisis Intensify the Pressure to Reform the Welfare State?', *Social Policy and Administration*, 45: 338–53.

Von Wachter, T. (2010). 'Avoiding a Lost Generation: How to Minimize the Impact of the Great Recession on Young Workers', Testimony before the Joint Economic Committee of the U.S. Congress, 26 May. http://jec.senate.gov/public/?a=Files. Serve&File_id=c868a8d3-3837-4585-9074-48181c5320e6 [accessed 26 July 2012].

Vroman, W. and Brusentsev, V. (2009). 'Short-Time Compensation as a Policy to Stabilize Employment'. Research Report. Washington, DC: The Urban Institute. http://www.urban.org/url.cfm?ID=411983 [accessed 26 July 2012].

Wagner, G. G., Frick, J. R., and Schupp, J. (2007). 'The German Socio-Economic Panel Study (SOEP)—Scope, Evolution and Enhancements', *Schmollers Jahrbuch*, 127: 139–69. http://www.diw.de/documents/publikationen/73/diw_01.c.60184.de/diw_sp0001. pdf [accessed 26 July 2012].

References

Waldenström, D. (2009). 'Inkomstskillnader', chapter 9 in SNS Välfärdsråd (ed.), *SNS Välfärdsrapport 2009*. Stockholm: SNS.

Ward, T., Lelkes, O., Sutherland, H., and Tóth, I. G. (eds) (2009). *European Inequalities: Social Inclusion and Income Distribution in the European Union*. Budapest: Tárki. http://www.tarki.hu/adatbank-h/kutjel/pdf/b251.pdf [accessed 26 July 2012].

Weber, B. and Schmitz, S. W. (2011). 'Varieties of Helping Capitalism: Politico-Economic Determinants of Bank Rescue Packages in the EU during the Recent Crisis', *Socio-Economic Review*, 9: 1–31.

Will, H. (2011). 'Germany's Short Time Compensation Programme: Macroeconom(etr)ic Insight'. IMK Working Paper 1/2011. Düsseldorf: IMK. http://www.boeckler.de/pdf/p_imk_wp_1_2011.pdf [accessed 26 July 2012].

Name Index

Name Index

Subject Index